In Struggle against Jim Crow

NUMBER EIGHTY-ONE:
*The Centennial Series
of the Association of Former Students,
Texas A&M University*

In Struggle against Jim Crow

Lulu B. White and the NAACP, 1900—1957

Merline Pitre

Texas A&M University Press
College Station

The paper used in this book meets the minimum requirements
of the American National Standard for Permanence
of paper for Printed Library Materials, Z39.48-1984.
Binding materials have been chosen for durability.

⊗

Library of Congress Cataloging-in-Publication Data

Pitre, Merline, 1943-
    In struggle against Jim Crow : Lulu B. White and the NAACP,
1900-1957 / Merline Pitre. — 1st ed.
        p.   cm. — (The centennial series of the Association of Former
Students, Texas A&M University ; no. 81)
    Includes bibliographical references and index.
    ISBN 978-1-60344-199-5 (pbk — alk. paper)
        1. White, Lulu B. (Lulu Belle). 2. Afro-American women civil
rights workers—Texas—Biography. 3. Civil rights workers—Texas—
Biography. 4. Afro-Americans—Civil rights—Texas—History—20th
century. 5. National Association for the Advancement of Colored
People—History—20th century. 6. Houston (Tex.)—Biography.
7. Houston (Tex.)—Race relations. I. Title. II. Series.
F391.W575P58 1999   98-42050
323.1'196073'0092—dc21   CIP

For four strong African American women

Florence Pitre
Helen Little
Thelma Cobb
Jewel Prestage

Contents

Illustrations

Preface

Within three decades following the civil rights movement, scholars have amassed a rich body of literature detailing the battle for racial and political equality. Yet, although black women were leaders and activists in crusades against lynching, poll taxes, and Jim Crow statutes, very few studies document the major role played by them in the modern movement for social change. An examination of the literature covering the decades of the 1940s and 1950s bears out this point. While most accounts of this period focus on male leaders and the organizations they led, very little is known about the countless black women who were the backbone of the civil rights struggle in local communities across the country. These women not only were supporters, fulfilling traditional female roles as nurturers and caretakers, but also were major leaders, organizers, and strategists. They led, shaping the direction the movement would take. This was true especially of Lulu Belle Madison White and the civil rights movement in Texas.

Lulu B. White, female activist, executive secretary of the NAACP's Houston branch, and the NAACP's state director of branches, was a significant force in the struggle against Jim Crow during the 1940s and 1950s. She stood at the helm of the local chapter of the NAACP in 1944, when the Supreme Court, in *Smith v. Allwright,* struck down the white Democratic primary statute. Similarly, she led fights to get more blacks elected to public office, to secure economic parity for African Americans, and to integrate the University of Texas. Despite these and other efforts by Lulu White to destroy the legal bases of Jim Crow, to the average person in Texas, she is an obscure figure. Simply put, very little is known of Lulu White's activities because very little has been written about her. Thus, the purposes of this study are, first, to place Lulu B. White in proper perspective in Texas, southern, African American, women's, and American history; second, to call attention to her successes and achievements, as well as to the problems and conflicts she faced in trying to eradicate Jim Crow; and, third, to look at the strategies and techniques that White, in her leadership role, used in responding to Jim Crow.

Using an approach that is descriptive, analytical, and interpretive, I have divided the book into seven chapters. Chapter 1 chronicles Lulu White's early years in East Texas, her college days, and her marriage to Julius White. Further, it places her in the historical context of twentieth-century Houston and the civil rights movement that was gripping the city and state. Chapter 2 looks at the manner in which Lulu White created her space within the NAACP to become a civil rights activist. Chapters 3 and 4 examine Lulu White's role in securing political, social, and economic rights for black Americans. White's efforts to desegregate the University of Texas, while other African Americans wanted the State of Texas to establish a separate black university, are the focus of chapter 5. This chapter is an altered version of my article, "Black Houstonians and the Doctrine of Separate but Equal: Carter W. Wesley Versus Lulu B. White"; it has been adapted and published with permission of the *Houston Review*. White's role in, and services to, the NAACP are analyzed in chapter 6. Chapter 7 examines how Lulu White dealt with the issue of gender in her leadership role in the NAACP. This book ends with an epilogue commenting on Lulu White's life.

For a number of reasons, this work should be useful to academicians and the general public. First, Lulu White's life spanned a broad era in American history. My hope is that this breadth will help professors avoid the "add women and mix" syndrome too frequently seen in the teaching of history. This comprehensive examination of Lulu White's life invites professors to integrate her experiences into courses dealing with women, race, interest group politics, and social reform.

Writing *In Struggle against Jim Crow* was more than an intellectual enterprise for me. Along the way I realized that I could tell the story set forth in this volume only because of Lulu White's effort to destroy the apartheid system in the United States and the sacrifices she made toward that end. Indeed, White's struggles, failures, and successes took on new meanings as I saw them afresh. Writing this book put me back in touch with feelings I had experienced as a child growing up in segregated southern Louisiana. That is, to be black was "to struggle to struggle"—to struggle to salvage the "self," to struggle against racial and gender stereotypes in order to struggle against prejudice, injustice, and hatred. Lulu White's life story is reflective of this collective memory of Jim Crow.

Merline Pitre
Houston, Texas

Acknowledgments

This study of the life experiences of Lulu B. White began ten years ago, longer than I wish to remember. Naturally, in working on this project, I have incurred enormous debts. It is my pleasure now to extend sincere appreciation to my family, friends, and colleagues, and to an entire community of scholars and historical actors. With gratitude I acknowledge the assistance I received from the staff at the Manuscript Division of the Library of Congress, Washington, D.C.; the Center for American History and the Lyndon Baines Johnson Library, University of Texas at Austin; the Houston Metropolitan Research Center at the Houston Public Library; the University of Houston Archives; the Rice University Archives in Houston; the Heartman Collection, Texas Southern University, Houston; the Clayton Library, Center for Genealogical Research in Houston and the Bishop College Archives, Dallas. Two Faculty Research Grants from Texas Southern University allowed me to travel to collections outside Houston. I also received funding from the National Endowment for the Humanities to sponsor a Faculty Seminar on Jim Crow—the period from 1896 to 1964 when blacks were separated and subordinated according to law, custom, and habit. This grant provided an opportunity for me to engage in dialogue on Jim Crow issues with scholars across the country. By doing so, I enhanced my knowledge of this important phenomenon in American history.

Lulu White's family members, friends, and contemporaries have given much assistance and support. Johnnie Jordan, Lulu White's niece, not only gave freely of her time for interviews, but also permitted me to peruse Lulu White's scrapbook, a valuable tool for reconstructing her early college years. Likewise, I am grateful to Thelma Bryant, Ercelle Pinson Hall, Onita Cavitt, Billie Hardin, Edwin Hardin, Luelelia Harrison, Earnestine Moore, Frances Mosely, George Nelson, Alan Nimer, Pearl Suel, Althene Watkins, Grace G. Wetlaw, Martha Whiting, and Lois Woods for granting me interviews that deepened this manuscript greatly. In the same vein, I owe a debt to Bob Lee, guru historian of the Fifth Ward of Houston, Texas.

In various stages of its development, this book has benefited from the encouragement, suggestions, and criticisms of many friends and professional colleagues. I am grateful to Darlene C. Hine for the opportunity to present my first paper on Lulu B. White at the Southern Historical Association's annual meeting. I also owe debts to Richard Blackett, Howard Jones, Jewel Prestage, and Linda Reed for hosting, at their respective universities, my presentations on various aspects of Lulu White's life. My indebtedness to Wilma King, too, is considerable. Not only did she read every draft of this monograph, but also she shared my excitement at new insights and frustration of trying to find words adequate to express what I wanted to say. Along with King, Maude Guildford, Patricia Prather, Mark S. Scheid, Billy Turner, Gwendolyn Mami and Gladys Washington read this manuscript, despite the pressing demands of their teaching, research, and other professional and personal responsibilities. The insights and suggestions of these persons significantly improved both substance and style of this work. Also, many thanks go to Mary Parrish and Sharon Mitchell, who were responsible for word processing the first draft of this manuscript.

I am grateful to my colleagues within and outside the Department of History at Texas Southern University for keeping uppermost in my mind one question—when is the manuscript going to be completed? This question, coupled with the prodding of Howard Jones, Jewel Prestage, and Charles Tatum, was a driving force in helping me to accomplish my goal.

My family members bore the making of this book with good humor, understanding, and patience. I suspect that occasionally they doubted it ever would be finished, but they kept those doubts to themselves and instead offered encouragement and emotional support. To them and everyone else who believed that Lulu White was worth the effort, I am forever grateful.

In Struggle against Jim Crow

CHAPTER I

Coming of Age in Texas

L ulu Belle Madison White, a rebel with a cause and a team player with the National Association for the Advancement of Color People (NAACP), occupied a strategic position for observing the Jim Crow system, fighting against it, and witnessing its dismantling. She came of age in East Texas, a region of the state noted for its segregationist laws and customs. Born in August 1900, young Lulu grew up in a large family where she felt secure and received generous portions of love and attention. Her father, Henry Madison, had been born as a slave in Mississippi in 1857. After emancipation, upon reaching the age of twenty, he married Easter Norwood, three years his junior. Of that union would come twelve children, five boys and seven girls. The first seven siblings—Alzie, Aquilla, Orza, Phillip, Sophie, Hattie, and Harriette—were born in Hattiesburg, Mississippi. After the birth of Harriette in 1891, Henry Madison moved his family to East Texas, where five other children were born: Leola, Millifil, Willie, Lulu, and Sam.[1]

Madison's decision to leave Mississippi no doubt had something to do with the oppressive conditions under which blacks lived at the turn of the century. While Mississippi was not unique in its legally sanctioned oppression of blacks, it had the worst reputation of the former Confederate states. Like every other place in the South, it was segregated by law and custom, and many of its white residents viewed violence and intimidation as tools essential for maintaining the subordinate position of blacks. Blacks also effectively were barred from voting by an outrageously complex literacy test that required them to interpret the Mississippi State Constitution. But perhaps most oppressive of all was the sharecropping system that replaced slavery and kept blacks under the yoke of white landowners for life. As elsewhere in the South, land reform did not accompany the manumission of slaves in Mississippi; consequently, only a small number of blacks managed to acquire land. By 1890, all but a few remained farmers without land. Probably lured to the Lone Star State by advertisements of "good, cheap farming land," Henry Madison settled in Frog, a section of Elmo, Texas.[2]

Elmo, a small, rural, predominantly black community, is located in Kaufman County, six miles from the nearest town of Terrell, thirty-four miles east of Dallas and sixty miles west of Tyler. Kaufman County lies at the heart of the North Texas watershed that drains through giant rivers into the Gulf of Mexico. The Trinity River forms the western boundary, with East Fork on the northwest. The Sabine River meandered along just outside the county limits to the northeast until it was dammed to form Lake Tawakonie. Although part of it sits on an open Texas plain, Kaufman County is ill suited for ranching. It is, however, well suited for farming. Culturally and economically, this East Texas county has far more in common with the southern states to the east than with the rest of Texas.[3]

Aside from Native Americans, the first settlers of Kaufman County were white, slave-owning, southern farmers who arrived before the Civil War. Most came from Mississippi, but some came from as far away as North Carolina. During the Civil War, Kaufman County's white citizens gladly sent their sons to fight for the Confederacy. Later, the town of Terrell and the community of Elmo were built by veterans of the Lost Cause. Established in 1874, Elmo was located at the convergence of two railroads, the Texas Pacific and the International Great Northern. It was a "right of away," a crossroad where agricultural products were transferred from one rail line to another. Otherwise, there was little in the surrounding countryside to put Elmo on the map. Still, outsiders were attracted to it because of its fertile soil and mild climate.[4]

For the reasons cited above, the largest influx of blacks into Elmo and Kaufman County occurred primarily after Reconstruction. Among those who came were the Henry Madison family. The 1900 census reported that Kaufman County had a total population of seventeen thousand; of that number, five thousand were African Americans. Whites outnumbered blacks 65 percent to 35 percent. In Elmo, the number of blacks was even smaller, with black women outnumbering black men. The gap between genders was widest for those between the ages of fifteen and forty-four, suggesting that black men moved away to find jobs, usually on farms or on the railroads, while black women stayed at home to rear children. Most Elmo adults were poorly educated, and few could look forward to opportunities outside agriculture.[5]

Not much was occurring to upset the social order in Elmo on the day that Lulu Belle Madison was born in August 1900. If anything, Elmo seemed to have entered the new century with the old order unchanged. Cotton was the main cash crop, and a drop in prices would send shivers through the black community. The masses of blacks were sharecroppers to whom the franchise did not extend. Not every store in the community or in the neighboring towns was open to business with "colored" people. Although some stores welcomed black clients, any white who happened to come into the store was served first. In short, segregation was the order of the day. At that time, an accident of birth, the color of Lulu Madison's skin, was a fact that mattered more than any other. Of all the events of her life, nothing loomed larger in shaping who she was and what she was about than being born black in segregated East Texas at the turn of the century.

Segregation was not just a system of physical separation of races. It was a social system that denied blacks equal access to everything from health care and jobs to education and justice. However one views or analyzes segregation, its peculiarities in East Texas demand attention. During the era of Jim Crow, in certain sections of this region, black males were expected to tip their hats in the presence of whites, even if they were walking on the opposite side of the street. Well into the 1940s, railroad porters were required to pull down the window shades on the "colored" side of passenger cars as the train passed through Grand Saline, a community twenty miles east of Elmo, to prevent upstanding white citizens from looking at black faces.

By an odd coincidence, the town of Terrell had its name stamped on discriminatory reform election laws throughout the state. Travis County's state representative, Alexander Watkins Terrell, authored and supported the Terrell Election Bills. These bills, in 1902, 1903, and 1905, respectively, provided for a poll tax requirement for voting, a first and second primary, and a voter declaration of party membership. The Terrell Election Bill of 1905, designed to disenfranchise blacks, laid the foundation for the white Democratic primary by giving the party's executive committee the right to determine eligibility for party membership and by making it a misdemeanor to pay poll taxes for blacks.[6]

Blacks in Elmo experienced the racial discrimination common in East Texas. A man who happened to be born "colored" in East Texas at the dawn of the twentieth century was lucky if he learned to read and write, and he probably worked on a farm or a ranch. He endured indignities large and small and was likely to die relatively young, never having seen the inside of a hospital or a voting booth. Black women lived somewhat longer, but they too were poorly educated. At best, they could look forward to the relative luxury of living away from home "in service" with a well-to-do white family.

Despite these adversities, many blacks who lived through segregation, including Lulu Madison, recalled it as a time when families were closely knit, when everyone looked out for each other, and when grandmothers ruled neighborhoods. Work was hard, but there was much to look forward to at the end of the week—visiting and chatting with friends and family, Sunday worship, and other weekend diversions. To judge from the data available, Lulu Madison's earliest memories of segregation reflected these pleasant activities, rather than the harsher realities of the Jim Crow system. Yet little can be understood about the values and methods used by Lulu Madison to fight Jim Crow without an understanding of the real influence of segregation in her youth.[7]

As Lulu Madison grew to maturity, East Texas was a risky place for African Americans to live. By all accounts, the potential for danger never was far from the minds of blacks. Violence was used with alarming frequency. Many whites in East Texas harbored an attitude toward blacks that was extreme even by the white supremacist standards of the rest of Texas. Over time, these individuals developed and enacted a unique glossary of racial hatred. *Whitecapping*, for example, was an East Texas word defined loosely as violent intimidation, short of death, inflicted upon a Negro. Whipping, warning shots, threats, and destruction of property were methods of whitecapping used in East Texas in Lulu Madison's youth.[8]

When whitecapping proved ineffectual, some East Texans resorted to lynching—the most chilling of crimes inflicted by whites on blacks to enforce segregation. At the dawn of the twentieth century, East Texas was notorious for lynching and was considered one of the worst regions in the state, leading the state in 1908 with twenty-four deaths. One of the most gruesome episodes in American history occurred in 1897 in Tyler, forty-five miles east of Elmo. There, a black man, Robert Henson Hillard, was suspected of raping and murdering a white woman. Before he could stand trial, a white mob pulled him from jail and burned him at the stake. Lulu Madison's father and mother vividly remembered when Hillard was tortured and murdered. Three decades later, blacks of that region still could recount with accuracy this tale of terror. They often compared it to the Longview Race Riot of 1919, one of the worst in Texas during the first half of the twentieth century. Such incidents shaped how an entire generation of African Americans in East Texas reared their children and grandchildren.[9]

Over the years, violence in East Texas proved too much for white lawmakers in Austin. After Hillard's lynching, white politicians became afraid that, if such violence continued, it would scare away northern investors. Consequently, at the turn of the century, these politicians pushed the state legislature into passing a series of anti-lynching laws. But this goodwill gesture was only an exercise in futility, because few if any of the sheriffs in East Texas would enforce such measures. Between 1890 and 1920, sheriffs were more powerful than elected mayors and legislators. If anything, many sheriffs considered whitecapping and lynching valuable tools for keeping blacks in "their place." By 1910, Lulu Madison's tenth birthday, more than one hundred blacks had been lynched in the Lone Star State. Most of these atrocities occurred in East Texas, making this small region the third worst in the nation.[10]

If politicians were uncomfortable with the negative image that lynching gave the Lone Star State, so were other white leaders. Like the politicians, these leaders made concerted efforts to help stop the lynching and to improve race relations in the state. They held discussions, formed interracial groups, and had conferences with the governor. In 1920, the governor went to Texarkana to meet with the new Texas Commission on Interracial Cooperation, formed, among other reasons, for the purpose of addressing mob violence. A year later, the white business community called upon the chief executive and the Texas Commission on Interracial Cooperation to take action against the reign of terror. Finally, the state dispatched the National Guard to break up mob violence. Despite these efforts, however, state leaders did nothing to repeal segregationist laws—cornerstones of the Jim Crow system. Consequently, segregation deepened.[11]

Fortunately for Lulu Madison, she was born into a family that managed to circumvent some of the most important obstacles to black progress erected by segregation—in the areas of education and land ownership. Lulu's father, Henry Madison, a hardworking farmer, embodied a hearty spirit of self-reliance and the commitment and sense of responsibility that attended that belief. Determined to prove to himself, and to white Texans, that a black man could survive on his own economically in Jim Crow Texas, Madison rented thirty-five acres of land when he arrived in Elmo in 1891. Within ten years, he had purchased 120 acres of land; these remain in the family today. A forceful man of great dignity and a hot temper, Henry Madison constantly told his children: "Get an education and don't let anyone be your boss."[12] A strong, deeply religious man who could neither read nor write but who believed in the accumulation of wealth and the importance of education, Henry Madison had a presence that commanded respect from those around him, whites and blacks alike. Like most men of his day, he stood as the unchallenged authority figure in his family and ran his household with a conviction that God had ordained his absolute leadership.

By contrast, Lulu's mother, Easter Madison, was a soft-spoken, pious, retiring woman. As a caring, nurturing mother, Easter stressed through precepts and examples the importance of church, school, and discipline. She took her children to Sunday School and church services each week and acquired a rudimentary education a few years after moving to Texas. As the conventions of her time dictated, Easter was deferential to her husband in all things save domestic matters.[13]

Henry and Easter Madison did their best to shield their children from the harshness of the old southern system by refusing to discuss with them the Ku Klux Klan's activities and the humiliation that other blacks had to endure meekly simply to retain their status as sharecroppers. For the older generation of African Americans, the lesson of segregation was simple: survival required maintaining a deferential, subservient posture in relation to whites, at least outwardly.

But a different idea was percolating through the Madison household: "Use your brains to get what you want, even if you have to be competitive." Lulu Madison's family provided her with a set of skills that proved well suited not only for coping with Jim Crow, but also for a future leadership role. Never taught to think or act like a second-class citizen, she was competitive. She would improvise, could think and talk fast on her feet, and was not afraid of anyone. Her family was the center of everything during her upbringing, and she was the center of attention in the family. Lulu Madison somehow never gave up that spotlight. In fact, she grew to expect and even to demand it. Both as a child and as a young adult, she was confident, made friends easily, and could put anyone at ease or cut them down to size in a flash.[14]

No matter how confident Lulu Madison might have felt during her early years, the indelible marks of segregation never were erased completely. Accepting and acknowledging this inevitability, Henry and Easter Madison urged their children to get as much "schooling" as they could, because the two viewed education as the best way out of segregation. But in Elmo, as in many areas throughout Texas, blacks could not very easily obtain an adequate education. Many of Elmo's children earned money in the fall of each year by picking cotton hundreds of miles away in West Texas. If the harvest was late, they missed school; as a result, many children lagged behind two to four grade levels by the time they reached high school. Fortunately for Lulu Madison, such was not the case with her. Her chronological age was appropriate for each grade level of her elementary training in Frog, Texas; therefore, upon graduating from Shady Grove Elementary, she went on to Old Terrell Colored High School. This school was not much, but it was all blacks had in Terrell and the surrounding area. It was a school where teachers taught multiple grades in a small number of rooms. There was no gymnasium, cafeteria, or running water. Children relieved themselves in outhouses constructed behind the school. Separate was anything but equal in Terrell. Whites went to vastly better schools. The only library in Terrell was the one at the white high school. Desks, books, and other supplies for blacks were handed down from white schools. Despite these obstacles, Henry Madison was persistent in his demand that Lulu "get a good education."[15]

When Lulu Madison finished Old Terrell Colored High School, her dreams and ambitions were big but unfocused. She wanted to become "somebody," but exactly who, she was not sure. One thing she knew was that her dreams could not be fulfilled in Elmo. At the end of the summer in 1917, in search of a good job and a better life, she decided to move to Fort Worth to live with her brother. Her stay in that city was short, and her experiences with Jim Crow in the workplace soon made her accept the advice of her father, which was to get a good, sound education.[16]

Throughout her formative years, Lulu Madison recognized some of the debilitating effects of racism; but, both as a child and as a young adult, she resigned herself to the Jim Crow laws and practices imposed on African Americans in East Texas. The acculturation process designed to keep blacks in their places ultimately would fail, however; and in her adult years, Lulu's resentment of the system would overcome her forced youthful acceptance of it.

College Years

Lulu Madison's journey toward her eventual civil rights mission, then, began in 1923, when she left Fort Worth and enrolled at Butler College in Tyler. Although Tyler was noted for lynching and whitecapping, to its credit, it also had a black college. Butler College, a black coeducational institution formally known as Texas Baptist Academy, had been established in 1905 by black ministers of the East Texas Baptist Association. After the death of its president, C. M. Butler, in 1924, the name and status of the institution changed to Butler Junior College. Its mission, like that of most church-related institutions, was to provide a Christian education for African Americans. Located in the northwestern section of Tyler, small Butler College provided foundation courses for students who wished to pursue higher education. With the segregated city of Tyler offering few distractions, Butler proved a good environment for its students, especially the females.[17]

When Lulu Madison stepped onto the Butler College campus on September 1, 1923, she was virtually indistinguishable from the few hundred other students at the college. She dreamed of becoming a teacher, and if she lacked any self-confidence, no one perceived it. At bottom, her enrollment at Butler was a sign of maturity. Away from the watchful eyes of her relatives, collegiate life forced Madison to fend for herself and to chart her own course. Her first year was rewarding and refreshing. Not only did she meet new friends and set new goals for herself, but she made the dean's list. Because Madison excelled in her studies, one might infer that she found a measure of happiness in her life at Butler. At the end of her first year, however, for reasons that are open to conjecture, Madison decided to leave Butler and transfer to Prairie View College. Her grades were sufficiently high, and the foundation courses that she took were adequate to enable her to pursue a career in teaching. Perhaps Madison left because she wanted to go to a four-year institution, and Butler was only a junior college. Perhaps she needed financial assistance that her family could no longer provide. During 1923, too, she had met a prominent Houston businessman whom she later would marry, and this may have had some influence on her decision. Whatever the reasons, in May 1924 Madison left Butler College, with no intention of returning.[18]

In September, Lulu Madison became a member of Prairie View College's freshman class of 1924. Although only a five-hour trip by automobile from Butler College, Prairie View was a world away from the life that young Lulu had known in Tyler. Located in northwestern Waller County, on a sheltered site formerly occupied by a slave plantation, Prairie View was off the beaten path. It was situated sixty miles from Houston and six miles from the nearest town. On the southern and western sides were a few scattered farmhouses inhabited by blacks, and on the northern and eastern sides were white communities. Prairie View College was a self-contained institution that housed faculty, students, staff, and administrators. It had less than two thousand students, most of whom were African Americans from all walks of life. Expected to become race leaders, these students came from all over the United States and Canada, with the majority being from Texas and the South. Some were poor and worked to pay school fees; others received some type of financial assistance from the college; still others were sons and daughters of well-to-do African American ministers, teachers, doctors, lawyers, and businessmen and paid their own way.[19]

When Lulu Madison arrived on the campus, Prairie View was in the midst of a building program, physically and academically. This was an era of modernization and readjustment for the college; telephones, steam heat, and electricity were installed in most, if not all, of the buildings on campus by 1925. By 1926, Prairie View had evolved from being mainly a normal school for teachers into a full-fledged college with a new principal (president), Willette R. Banks. In keeping with these changes, Banks stressed the need to expand the curriculum to include service areas and to provide training for a black leadership cadre. Directing much of his energy toward securing money from foundations and federally sponsored programs for land-grant colleges, Banks was able to procure enough funds to continue the building program that had begun a year prior to his arrival. This program included a female dormitory, a hospital, nursing quarters, and a trades building for males.[20]

Meanwhile, during her first year at Prairie View, Lulu Madison resided in the Home Economics Cottage with other female boarding students. In general, the rules of the cottage and the dormitories resembled those of a well-regulated household, in which everyone was treated fairly but firmly in matters affecting all personal habits—working, bathing, eating, studying, and sleeping. Students were to observe all regulations concerning conduct, attendance, and study, and were disciplined for any activity deemed immoral or unworthy, whether on or off campus. They were given a list of practices strictly forbidden—cursing, gambling, playing cards, drinking, and smoking. These rules of conduct were enforced by Principal Banks, who placed a great deal of emphasis on discipline, religion, and character building. Because Prairie View competed for students with church-related colleges, Banks wanted parents to know that he would look out for their children; therefore, he regulated all aspects of a student's life, from males wearing shirttails out of trousers to dress lengths for females. Banks also stressed, as did most presidents of historically black colleges, attendance at Sunday and midweek vespers. Inasmuch as Lulu Madison formerly had attended a Baptist college, she was not unfamiliar with the religious emphasis so basic to life on black college campuses. Yet, for the extroverted Lulu, now twenty-four years old, the highly structured, protective environment of Prairie View might have been unbearable, had it not been for her interest in her studies and in the extracurricular activities of campus.[21]

Like other students in the Teacher Preparation Program, Lulu undertook four years of rigorous study. Her classes lasted fifty minutes, and she usually took five to six classes per semester. Class attendance was mandatory, with three unexcused absences meriting a failing grade. Madison met this challenge by majoring in English and maintaining a B average. The rigors of college life left the average student little time for anything other than class attendance, preparation, and study. The brilliant, restive Lulu, however, became a dormitory leader; a member of the Aristo Club, the Literary and Dramatic (L&D) Society, and the YWCA; and vice president of her senior class. The administration also encouraged her to become involved in extracurricular activities as a means of fostering recreation and creative leadership.[22]

At Prairie View, the basic forms of recreation outside the athletic area focused on current events and literary group discussions, classical music, essays, orations, and rhetoric. Students and faculty alike valued the intellectual rigor, skill, discipline, and competition provided by these activities. These qualities were viewed as keys to leadership and success. The faculty and dormitory staff allotted special time during the day for tutorial assistance and rehearsals for these activities. Contests were held regularly to sharpen talents in these areas. More specifically, the L&D Society, the Excelsior Literary Society, and the Aristo Club were geared toward debate, the mastery of the written and spoken word, and the study of literature. Lulu Madison's participation in the L&D Society and the Aristo Club enhanced her debating skills and helped perfect her talents as an extemporaneous speaker—talents that later would help her sway audiences. More often than not, Madison applied such skills in groups sessions held periodically in the dormitory to discuss specific issues or current events. These discussion groups broadened her knowledge of the humanities, enhanced her love of reading, and whetted her appetite for books. Upon her graduation, Professor A. Wendell Burks, faculty advisor of the Aristo Club, asked Madison to "use [her] influence for furtherance of the campaign to [recruit new members]. We feel your influence will be of much avail," wrote Burks.[23]

Despite Madison's love for and involvement in extracurricular activities, the Spartan, rigid nature of communal existence at Prairie View kindled her need for flexibility, aggressive leadership, and a more inclusive society. The dormitory experience allowed Madison the opportunity to demonstrate her ability to take charge. Strict observance of the rules of conduct often put the students at odds with the administration. "Whenever we wanted a change in the rules or customs in the dorm, it was to Lulu that we turned," said Frances Mosely, Madison's classmate. Similarly, the intimate contact and competition with male and female students in classes, in the dormitories, and in extracurricular activities helped to shape Madison's attitudes about segregation and about the need for a more inclusive society. In Madison's opinion, students needed to experiment with the new discoveries and hypotheses discussed in the classroom, and they needed to examine new ideas with people of varied backgrounds. Congruent with that position, in her senior year, Madison expressed a desire to become part of Houston's Interracial Committee, an organization espousing the idea that, if the "better class of people of both races would come together, they could find solutions to the race problem." Although she never became a member of that group, Madison was determined that in time she would play a major role in helping to solve the race problem.

During her enrollment at Prairie View, L. M. Tobin, professor of social sciences, recognized Madison's leadership ability, mentored her, and exposed her to books and articles dealing with race issues. Further, he demanded hard work from her, and she responded. When she graduated, he wrote to her, "Your determination and studious application to your work will make a way for you in the world." This statement was prophetic. The Prairie View experience not only provided Madison a great opportunity for personal growth, but also made it possible for her to become a professional, a leader, and later a social reformer.[24]

In 1924, when Lulu Madison decided to pursue a degree in the Teacher Education Program, few other opportunities for professional careers existed for women of color. The 1920 census shows that 54 percent of employed African American females worked in agriculture, 36 percent in domestic and personal services, and 4 percent in professional services, including teaching. The percentage of females pursuing degrees in teaching declined each year, as many got married and became pregnant and had to quit their jobs, as required by law. In a word, Madison was aware that, upon completion of her degree, she would join a relatively elite caste of African American women—all of whom, by virtue of their preparation, were destined to become leaders, administrators, superintendents, supervisors, and teachers in their chosen profession. At the very least, they could anticipate becoming servants of humanity, whether in remote villages of the state or in urban centers.

Lulu Madison's desire to reach her career goal was stimulated by observing outstanding Prairie View alumni and their commitment to the motto, "Lifting as We Climb." This list included such notables as M. V. Mabry, one of the organizers of the Texas Federation of Colored Women; Nellie Bly Robinson, a teacher who was responsible for the Brazoria Colored Elementary School's receiving its first accreditation; Hobart Taylor, insurance man and taxicab company owner; Owen Pullman DeWalt, businessman and theater owner; and Thornton M. Fairchild, teacher, businessman, and philanthropist.[25]

On June 6, 1928, Lulu Belle Madison joined this elite group by graduating *magna cum laude* from Prairie View College. While she may have interpreted her success in completing her training as a teacher as a signal honor for herself and her family, she could not and did not escape the broader reality that, although teaching liberated her from financial dependence, it did so within rigidly fixed racial parameters. Prairie View was a racially defined school, and her attendance there not only affirmed her racial identity but also consigned her to race- and gender-specific employment.[26]

Marriage and Teaching

After Lulu's graduation, she married Julius White, a businessman, nightclub owner, promoter of public entertainment, and policy runner. A stout black man standing five feet, seven inches tall, Julius was considered a power in Houston's black community. With only a third-grade education, he had come to Houston in 1900 from Victoria, Texas, at the age of sixteen. By 1925, he had amassed considerable wealth, including a nightclub, a ranch, several houses, and a great deal of liquid capital. Thus, Julius often hobnobbed with members of the black and white elites. In the black community, he "put his money where his mouth was," giving generously to the Negro Chamber of Commerce and the Odd Fellows Temple, and financing most of the lawsuits brought against the white Democratic primary. According to Carter Wesley, editor of the *Houston Informer,* "He was a man who had a wealth of common sense which matured into wisdom [and] which made him stand head and shoulders above many who began life with greater opportunity and whose training and experience gave them greater advantages." A man with a forceful personality, Julius White would fight at the drop of a hat and was regarded as one of the meanest black men in town. He carried a gun on his person and never backed away from a fight, whether physical or political. So, when Julius met Lulu, it did not take much for him to sweep her off her feet.[27]

Lulu probably met Julius in the spring or summer of 1924, for, according to oral sources, he helped finance her education at Prairie View. Like Butler College, Prairie View did not allow married or engaged female students and even looked askance at serious courtship. Perhaps because of such rules, Lulu and Julius did not marry until June 28, 1928, one month after her graduation. It appears that Julius was attracted to Lulu from their first encounter. A veritable man on the make, Julius seemed untroubled by his choice of a marital partner. His wife was intelligent, attractive, and educated. That she lacked standing among prominent black Houstonians seemed not to bother him. What was important was the fact that he found in this woman, sixteen years his junior, a compatible spirit.

Julius, for his part, appealed to Lulu's desire for social prominence and economic security. Described as a father figure, Julius was an engaging man with an Old World charm. He was very attentive to his wife's material and psychological needs and admired her fashionable attire, urbane worldliness, and determination to become self-sufficient. In turn, Lulu found in Julius a protective mentor and affectionate partner who was unconventional enough to allow for her own individuality.

To be sure, Lulu considered her marriage a move upward on the social ladder, Julius's rudimentary education notwithstanding. His wealth, standing as a power broker, and connections with "important" people of Houston's downtown establishment were enviable attributes. His generous giving to social, charitable, and civil rights causes placed him on a first-name basis with most, if not all, members of Houston's black elite. Even in terms of church affiliation, Julius and Lulu belonged to the upper class. They were members of Antioch Baptist Church, the city's church with the largest number of middle- and upper-class blacks.

Lulu's marriage took her to Julius's residence at 2620 Tuam Street in the Third Ward. The property that she would call home was a two-story brick building occupying a corner lot. Situated in the Third Ward near Emancipation Park, the Whites' home was located approximately two miles from downtown, near the black commercial district on Dowling Street, and was accessible to public transportation. In fact, the only streetcar which ran through the Third Ward in the early 1920s was the LaBranch Street Car, which came from downtown and made its way up to Jackson and Tuam streets. The community in which Lulu White lived was a neighborhood comprised largely of upwardly mobile individuals with good jobs. Its residents included the families of such men as J. T. Lindsay, physician; John W. Davis, dentist; Thornton M. Fairchild, philanthropist and undertaker; James H. Jemison, owner of Franklin Beauty School; Truesse Brown, a railway clerk; W. L. D. Johnson, teacher at Old Washington Colored High; Charles Johnson, physician; Benny Smith, pharmacist; Ira Bryant, teacher and principal; Richard Randolph Grovey, barber; L. H. Spivey, printshop and theater owner; and Theodore Hogrobrooks, businessman. Not very far from where Lulu and Julius resided was the home of B. J. Covington, physician, whose house was used as a hotel when black celebrities came to town. Within this physical and social environment, Lulu White felt at ease. Now, after more than a decade on her own, she had a home and suitable companions.[28]

During the first summer of their marriage, Lulu White applied her skills in homemaking to her household. She took pride in decorating, cooking, and entertaining. The couple frequented musical and theatrical productions. Julius was especially pleased with Lulu's interest in civil rights and in books written by and about African Americans. Since Lulu had shown a propensity for joining many social clubs, Julius found nothing odd in her reading or attending a club meeting all day. It is safe to say that, after a brief honeymoon, Lulu spent the entire summer of 1928 housekeeping, reading, socializing, and looking for a job.

While Lulu luxuriated in her new position as Julius's wife, wearing expensive frocks and driving a black Cadillac, she never aspired to be an idle Cinderella. She wanted her own limelight and sought to develop her personal talents and abilities. When unable to get a teaching position in the Houston Independent School District, due in part to her husband's involvement in civil rights activities, Lulu accepted a teaching post in Lufkin, Texas, a small town about 120 miles north of Houston. Although larger in population, Lufkin, in size, appearance, and resources, was very similar to Elmo. It was a small agricultural town that consisted basically of two ethnic groups—blacks and whites. Most of the African American population lived much as it had in the nineteenth century, without the benefit of improved educational facilities, health services, indoor plumbing, or adequate wages. Yet Lulu White arrived in Lufkin looking forward to her job. She taught English and physical education and coached the girls' basketball team. Her students described her as "efficient, friendly, and demanding." On a salary of forty dollars a month, she stayed in Lufkin during the week and commuted to Houston on weekends.[29]

In several ways, Lulu White was out of place in Lufkin. This self-contained community lacked the fluidity of the civil rights movement and the scope of activities characteristic of urban Houston. Here White lacked the space to develop her full potential. The social and racial environment of the "Bayou City," coupled with the presence of her husband, drew Lulu back toward Houston. Therefore, in 1935, when she secured a job at Highland Heights Elementary, she moved home. She remained at that school for only two years before she resigned her post. To be sure, she loved teaching and the service it provided to the black community, but her interest in political activism proved more compelling.

As Julius's wife, Lulu soon developed a characteristic that would mark her middle adult years: ambition. Her ambition mirrored that of her husband—to be a power broker and community activist. Postwar Houston offered African Americans new opportunities and career directions. The period also provided black men and black women new potential for growth and development. Simultaneously, Houston saw an expanding economy and rising black expectations. It witnessed the beginning of Black Houstonians' twenty-three-year struggle to gain citizenship rights via retrieval of the ballot. Given the racial, economic, and political climate in Houston and the social milieu of established and emerging African American political activists among whom she now circulated, Lulu White was determined to become something more than a teacher. Precisely what she might become remained vague, but involvement in work dealing with race relations clearly was a career option. While still a student at Prairie View, she had expressed a desire to help solve the problems of Jim Crow. Now Houston would provide her with a good laboratory for exploring, investigating, testing and analyzing race relations.

Race Relations in Houston

In terms of race relations, the city that Lulu White now called home was not very different from the place of her birth. Segregation was the barometer by which black life was measured—politically, economically, and socially. Politically, blacks in Houston lacked the franchise. Economically, blacks were mostly marginalized and denied opportunities to improve their circumstances. Socially, the Jim Crow system required that blacks be submissive and deferential on the job, as well as in casual contacts with whites in public. Generally speaking, the "historic structure of southern race relations that [had] stressed systematic inequality" in Elmo was merely modified and continued in Houston. Yet, while segregation dominated black life and defined black-white relations, it was not a monolithic force that affected all blacks equally. Nor were blacks merely passive victims. Among the African Americans who lived in or migrated to Houston during World War I and the immediate postwar years, many were in no mood to settle for the same subservient roles they had hoped to leave behind.

The nature and impact of segregation on the lives of blacks varied at different times and in different places. Arguably, black Houstonians experienced some of the most devastating effects of Jim Crow between 1917 and 1930. During that period, race relations were affected by World War I, the great migration of newcomers to the city, and the discovery of oil in the region surrounding Houston. The Great Migration and the oil industry transformed Houston almost overnight. In response to burgeoning economic opportunities, the city's total population almost tripled, while its black population doubled. Houston expanded in geographical extent, population, and economic activity. Not only was it the first boom town in the Southwest, but also it would continue to grow in years to come.

While Houston possessed the population and economy to qualify as a full-fledged city, the transition from town to city was not easy for everyone. The rapid change was exciting, but some Houstonians found it frightening. Many white residents did not, could not, and would not adjust to the inevitability of change. For the most part, these whites came to Houston from small, rural communities in Louisiana and Texas. They came to enjoy the comforts and conveniences of city life. Soon, however, they found themselves lost and alienated amid the hustle and bustle of the large city, with its wealthy white elite, omnipresent black men and women, and growing black middle class. At an almost subliminal level, whites' fear and discomfort with the presence of blacks influenced race relations in the Bayou City before and immediately after World War I. An example of such influence was seen in the race riot that occurred in Houston on August 23, 1917.[30]

The Houston riot had its roots in a clash between white citizens and black soldiers. When the Twenty-Fourth Infantry arrived in Houston on July 17, 1914, the city had not before been visited by black soldiers. Upon hearing of the U.S. Army's decision to send such troops to the Bayou City, white Houstonians immediately started writing letters to the governor and other governmental representatives, imploring them to use their influence to prevent such a move. These efforts notwithstanding, black military troops were sent to Houston, against the wishes of most whites.

Not long after their arrival, the black soldiers began to resent the indignities inflicted on blacks by local whites, especially the way in which the police enforced segregation. This simmering unease reached a boiling point on August 23, 1917, when a white passenger assaulted a black woman on a bus in the presence of black soldiers. Feeling that police officers had not done, and would not do, anything to resolve this situation, the soldiers wasted no time in becoming involved. As a result, approximately one hundred black soldiers marched on the city, killing sixteen whites and wounding at least a dozen. These soldiers were accused of inciting the riot, and the climate of white public opinion at that time demanded revenge. So, following one of the largest courts-martial in this country's history, thirteen black soldiers were executed at Fort Sam Houston on December 11, 1917, and forty-one were sentenced to life in prison.[31]

Apparently dissatisfied with the court's findings in the first case, the army tried an additional fifty-five soldiers in two courts-martial. Subsequently, sixteen were sentenced to hang on August 22, 1918, and twelve received life in prison. President Woodrow Wilson spared the lives of ten of the sixteen and commuted their sentences to life in prison.[32] While blacks across the country were shocked at the mockery of justice, this outbreak of violence in Houston spurred fear to new heights and increased demands by whites for mechanisms to control blacks and keep them in "their place." This control was accomplished via an expanded system of segregation, one notable for terrorism. The period following the riot witnessed the rebirth of the Ku Klux Klan, an increase in the number of police brutality cases, and exclusion of blacks from county and state Democratic primaries.

The Ku Klux Klan in the 1920s was a viable force in Houston and throughout the state. In Texas, this vigilante group occupied a position of power and influence unequaled in any other state, giving Texas the designation of Star Klan State. Houston was dubbed as the Star Klan City. With anti-immigrant, anti-Catholic, anti-Jew, and anti-black sentiments on the rise, the 1920s saw a rebirth of the Klan. The group's main objective, however, remained what it always had been: to instill fear in the targeted groups and so ensure that "white supremacy must obtain." Houston did its best to live up to this credo. For example, in 1921, Houston Klansmen, led by Deputy Sheriff George E. Kimbro, attacked and castrated a black dentist and beat a white lawyer who represented him. Several years later, the Klan tarred and feathered a black physician. In 1928, a Houston mob dragged a black man, accused of killing a white police officer, from his bed in a local hospital and hanged him from a bridge—a murder for which no one was ever convicted. Additionally, a Klan newspaper, *Colonel Mayfield's Weekly,* circulated throughout the city.[33]

Klan terrorism in the 1920s paralleled the expanded system of racial segregation and found support in the Jim Crow laws passed during that decade. In 1920, backed by a city ordinance, the American Legion excluded blacks from the annual Armistice Day parade. Blacks also were prohibited from voting in the municipal elections of February 1921. In 1923 and 1924, respectively, blacks were banned from standing in the same lines as whites to purchase stamps at the post office and to pay property taxes at the Harris County Courthouse. In 1925, the Electric Company excluded blacks from riding its buses, while in 1926, the Majestic Theater refused to admit blacks on weekends.[34]

By the 1930s, Houston probably was the most segregated city in the Southwest. The city had instituted new Jim Crow laws and had reinforced white supremacy by excluding blacks from some public places, barring them from political participation, and denying them due process. Despite the Terrell Election Law of 1905, which was designed to deny blacks the franchise, African Americans in Houston, El Paso, San Antonio, Galveston, Dallas, and Fort Worth continued to vote in nonpartisan municipal elections. In 1921, the executive committee of Houston's Democratic party decided to end this limited participation, passing a resolution allowing only whites to vote in the upcoming Democratic primary. Two years later, the Texas Legislature followed suit, passing a law stating that "only white Democrats and none other" could vote in primary elections. Under no circumstances were blacks eligible to vote in Democratic primaries, and election judges were ordered to discard the ballot of any black who attempted to vote.[35]

The full impact of the latter statute cannot be grasped unless it is understood that Texas—like the entire South—was a one-party state, and winning in the Democratic primary was tantamount to winning in the general election. To be excluded from the Democratic primary was, in effect, to be disfranchised. According to Darlene C. Hine, "The white man's primary was like an iron curtain, for even if blacks became literate, acquired property, and paid poll taxes, they could not conceal or change the color of their skin." Thus, as long as the whites-only primary existed, blacks could not become active participants in Texas' electoral process. The white primary, then, symbolized blacks' powerlessness, their second-class citizenship, and their castelike position in society. In the minds of most black Texans, lack of access to the ballot exacerbated their vulnerability to the capriciousness of whites. This assault on the ballot not only resulted in the mobilization of blacks, but also created black solidarity and fueled the modern civil rights movement in Texas. During the 1920s, blacks organized pressure groups to develop strategies, to agitate, and to fight to retrieve access to the ballot. It was those pressure groups and their strategies, methods, and philosophies that catapulted Lulu White to the center of the civil rights struggle in Texas.[36]

Black Response to the White Primary

Psychologically, Black Houstonians were predisposed to counter the white primary challenge for several reasons. First, Houston was an urban enclave with a larger number of blacks living in close proximity than occurred anywhere else in Texas. Second, Houston had a large black middle class which was not dependent on white landlords for employment. As early as 1902, Houston had a black professional and entrepreneurial class. The Bureau of the Census reported nine lawyers, four dentists, sixteen medical doctors, ten real estate agents, five newspapers, thirty restaurants, and forty stores. In most cases, those figures doubled by the 1920s. No other city in the South could boast of such a conglomerate of middle-class blacks. Although locked out of participation in the Democratic primaries, black Houstonians were politically active. Black newspapers reported political developments, while black leaders—religious, economic, and political— urged payment of poll taxes and participation in the general election. Furthermore, World War I produced a new "black man and woman"—individuals (many of them veterans) who would rather die "nobly" than submit to Jim Crow.[37]

For these reasons, in 1921, only four days after the executive committee of the Houston Democratic party adopted its white primary resolution, the black leadership of the city responded in kind. C. N. Love; W. L. Davis; William Nickerson, Jr.; Newman Dudley, Jr.; and Perry Mack filed an injunction seeking to restrain G. W. Griffin, chairman of the Houston Democratic executive committee from executing the disfranchisement resolution. *Love v. Griffin* (1927), after being denied in the district court of Harris County and in the Court of Appeals for the First Judicial District of Texas, finally reached the Supreme Court in 1927, where it met with defeat. The Supreme Court ruled that the case was moot, since the election for which the injunction was sought had already taken place.[38]

By the time the case reached the Supreme Court, Lulu White was thoroughly familiar with the white primary statute and blacks' efforts to dismantle it. In fact she personally felt the impact of the struggle when she graduated from Prairie View in 1928 and the Houston Independent School District refused to hire her because of what many described as "her husband's role" in *Love v. Griffin*.[39]

Although the court decision in *Love v. Griffin* was adverse, all was not lost for blacks who were appalled by the blatant discrimination inherent in the white primary statute. This case generated support from people throughout the city, state, and nation, prompting the NAACP to become involved in cases dealing with the white primary. Because of its discriminatory nature and dubious constitutionality, the Texas white primary statute deepened the NAACP's involvement in voting rights litigation. Upon hearing of the *Love* decision, W. E. B. DuBois, the noted black historian, wrote, "There is a chance to bring this matter of the white primary directly before the Supreme Court, when a proper case can be framed." It was not long before DuBois's prophecy would come true.[40]

The first serious challenge to the white primary came with the NAACP as counselor on July 26, 1924, in El Paso. On that date, L. A. Nixon, a black physician and a member of the Democratic party who had paid his poll taxes, attempted to vote by requesting a ballot and was refused. He asked the judge if he would sign a statement declaring that his denial was based on race. The judge did so, and Nixon took his case to court in *Nixon v. Herndon* (1927). The lower court upheld the election officials in their refusal to allow Nixon to vote, whereupon the plaintiff appealed his case all the way to the Supreme Court. When the Court rendered its decision in 1927, it voided the Texas statute as a denial of the equal protection clause of the Fourteenth Amendment, awarding Nixon damages. For black Texans, this victory was hollow, because the white primary was not overturned. More interesting, during the trial, the Court allowed the State of Texas the opportunity to correct a legal error—allowing the state rather than the Democratic party to deny blacks the right to vote. Because of the Court's ruling, the Texas Legislature in 1928 passed a modified version of the 1923 statute, stating that "the executive committee of political parties should have the power to prescribe the qualifications of its [*sic*] members and to determine who should be eligible to vote."[41]

To counter the state's action, the NAACP decided to file another lawsuit. Soon, however, friction arose between the group and black leaders in Houston. At the time that the NAACP filed the second Nixon lawsuit as *Nixon v. Condon* (1932), black Houstonians, who had become disgruntled about the way the NAACP had handled the first Nixon case, decided to take matters into their own hands and filed their own suit. Arguing that the constitutionality of the white primary had not been addressed in the previous cases, in 1928 J. B. Grigsby, president of the American Mutual Insurance Company, and O. P. DeWalt, president of the Houston NAACP, asked for an injunction against the Harris County Democratic party's executive committee. The national office of the NAACP refused to help these individuals because of a perceived conflict between the two cases.[42]

While the national office persuaded DeWalt and Grigsby to drop their effort, it failed to pacify other blacks, such as J. Alston Atkins, James Nabrit, Carter Wesley, and Julius White. These men were not hesitant in challenging the status quo and were determined to have their say about how to eliminate the white primary. Fearless in their stance, they became the mouthpieces, brains, and strategists of the movement. In November 1930, before *Nixon v. Condon* reached the Supreme Court, Carter Wesley of the *Houston Informer* announced that, at his own expense, he had employed the firm of Nabrit, Atkins, and Wesley to aid black Houstonians in their quest for the ballot. In the first case handled by the firm, attorney James Nabrit sought to force the court to enjoin Harris County's Democratic executive committee from pursuing discriminatory acts against blacks in the upcoming election on January 23, 1931. Since the Supreme Court's decision in *Love v. Griffin* had rendered the issue of discrimination moot because the suit was filed after the election, the plaintiffs now filed an action prior to the election. Despite the merits of the case, however, Judge J. C. Hutcheson of the federal district court denied the injunction.[43]

Undaunted by this denial, the group of black Houstonians established a permanent organization, the Harris County Negro Democratic Club, to coordinate their attack on the white primary. In January 1932, the Texas Secretary of State granted a charter to this club, with officers listed as Julius White, president; James Nabrit, chairman of the board; C. A. Gilmore, secretary; Carter Wesley, treasurer; and J. Alston Atkins, general counsel. Julius White not only was a plaintiff in most cases filed by the club, but he also helped to finance all of them. Once organized, the club pledged to use every legitimate means necessary to expose this "prejudiced group" of Democratic party managers. "We plan to use reason with the public press and the courts to let the world see Texas

Democracy as it really is," wrote Richard Randolph Grovey, labor activist and president of the Third Ward Civic Club.[44]

Next the club members turned their attention to the *Nixon v. Condon* case, which was scheduled for argument before the Supreme Court in March 1932. Differing with the NAACP's national officers on how to handle primary cases and feeling that, by virtue of living in Texas, its members were closer to the situation, the Negro Democratic Club, via its general counsel, filed an *amicus curiae* brief in *Nixon v. Condon*. This brief discussed the history of the white primary cases which Atkins, Love, Nabrit, Wesley, and White had fought in Houston. They also asserted that the law which enabled the state Democratic executive committee to establish qualifications for voting and membership in the Democratic party was unconstitutional. Therein lay the difference between their approach and that of the NAACP. The NAACP did not focus on the constitutionality of the white primary, but rather on the fact that Nixon's right to vote had been abridged because of the state's enforcement of a restrictive covenant. In its final decision, the Supreme Court sided with the NAACP, ruling that the Texas statute had violated the equal protection clause of the Fourteenth Amendment in denying Nixon the ballot. The decision stopped short of declaring the white primary unconstitutional.[45]

Consequently, these club members found themselves protesting one thing after the other. In an attempt to preserve the white Democratic primary, the chair of the Harris County Democratic Executive Committee proposed a new disfranchisement plan at the 1932 state Democratic convention. Named for its author, W. O. Huggins, the Huggins Plan called for repeal of the resolution by the state Democratic executive committee and making the state Democratic convention a new device for restricting participation in the political process. The underlying rationale was that the Supreme Court would not rule that the convention was an agency of the state, and therefore any resolutions to prevent blacks from voting would not be viewed as violations of law. When members of the Negro Democratic Club heard of this plan, they tried to appear before the resolution committee to register a complaint but were rebuffed. Incensed by what they regarded as total disregard for the findings of the Supreme Court in the two Nixon Cases, the club went to court again, with Julius White as plaintiff, requesting an injunction against the Harris County Democratic Executive Committee. Again relief was not forthcoming from the court.[46]

By 1932, Lulu White, who was still teaching in Lufkin, wanted to have her say on the issue of retrieving the ballot, but her situation did not allow her to achieve this desire. The distance from Houston, the limited time she could spend there, her occupation, and her gender all militated against her becoming a public reform activist in the Negro Democratic Club, a role for which she was temperamentally suited. Barred from joining the all-male Democratic Club, White contented herself with working in the background with her husband and other club members to map out strategies to attack the white primary.

Meanwhile, leaders of the Negro Democratic Club felt certain that they possessed the expertise and financial resources needed to succeed in attacking the white primary. Equally, they believed that the white Democratic primary statute of 1923 and its 1928 modification did not apply, and were not enforceable, at the municipal level. Thus, after much discussion, J. Alston Atkins, James Nabrit, Carter Wesley, and Julius White ignored the advice of national NAACP leaders and, with Richard Randolph Grovey as plaintiff, took their case to court in *Grovey v. Townsend* (1935).[47]

Richard Grovey, known as the militant leader of the Third Ward Civic Club, had been born in Brazoria County in 1889. He graduated from Waco Colored High School in 1910 and from Tillotson College in Austin in 1916. Following graduation, he served as principal of a rural high school near Waco, before moving to Houston in 1917. There he opened a barbershop on Dowling Street and became a community organizer and later a labor union leader. Fearless in controversial issues, Grovey's guiding principle was: "I intend to fight to my dying day in order that the Negroes' right to be a man shall not be curtailed."

On April 11, 1934, Grovey requested an absentee ballot from County Clerk Albert Townsend for the coming Democratic primary election. Anticipating the negative response that he received, Grovey and his lawyer moved quickly to take advantage of a state law stating that, when an individual filed a lawsuit for damages of less than ten thousand dollars and lost, the plaintiff could bypass the court of appeals and go directly to the Supreme Court.[48]

The struggle to eliminate the white primary gained momentum with the Grovey case. After all, Grovey was a local resident, and his long record on civil rights made it easier for black Houstonians to put their trust in him and the cause for which he was fighting. The charismatic, articulate barber, then, became both an opponent of the white primary statute and a symbol of hope in the face of political and economic oppression. The Grovey case unified Houston's black community along class, gender, educational, and economic lines. Support came from everywhere—labor leaders, ministers, women, the church, and the press, to name a few, as a plethora of groups worked toward a common goal. Carter Wesley used his black newspaper, the *Houston Informer*, to emphasize the need for close cooperation by the total black population. Lulu White galvanized women's organizations around the Grovey case—the YWCA, Metropolitan Council of Negro Women, the Eastern Star, and the Grand Court of Calanthe. These women knocked on doors, raised money, attended mass meetings, and participated in demonstrations. The Grovey case allowed Lulu White a window of opportunity to express her views on suffrage and racial oppression, as well as on strategies for eliminating the white primary.[49]

Despite the organizational efforts of black Houstonians, Grovey lost his case. On April 1, 1935, in a unanimous decision, the Supreme Court rejected Grovey's plea on the grounds that political parties were not "creatures" of the State of Texas, but were private voluntary associations possessing the right to limit their membership. The Supreme Court's adverse decision stunned blacks in Houston and across the country. Carter Wesley called it "Political Slavery." William J. Thompkins, in the Recorder of Deeds office in Washington, D.C., declared, "This decision is worse than *Dred Scott* (1857)." In his autobiography, Walter White, executive secretary of the NAACP, noted, "It should not be difficult to imagine the gloom that we all felt."

The Grovey decision left local, state, and national black leaders in a state of confusion. For the first time, local attorneys J. Atkins and Carter Wesley openly discussed the problems that blacks had with the NAACP, citing (1) the need for a black legal counsel to be retained at the national level; (2) the NAACP's failure to develop a white primary case around local black leaders who had initiated the case; and (3) the NAACP's failure to use African American attorneys in local trials. After pondering these criticisms for a number of weeks, the NAACP reached a compromise with black leaders of Houston. Charles H. Houston, who had been vice dean of Howard University since 1929, would become special counsel to the NAACP; and black lawyers of Houston would play a major role in litigating future cases concerning the white primary. In retrospect, it can be said that the chilling effect that the Grovey decision had on black Texans, as well as on the NAACP's national office, led to a reconciliation of the two groups.[50]

This *rapprochement* also allowed Lulu White an opportunity to become actively involved in the Texas civil rights movement. Although she and a number of women had played important roles in the Grovey case as organizers, fundraisers, and errand runners, the record does not reflect any attempt or desire on part of the Negro Democratic Club to place women in leadership roles. Thus, when reconciliation between local blacks and the national NAACP occurred, Lulu White cast her lot with the latter, working to create her own place within the NAACP.

CHAPTER 2

Carving a Niche in the NAACP

By the mid-1930s, Lulu White more than ever was determined to carve a niche for herself in the civil rights movement that was gripping her city and state. As a self-made woman seeking her own public identity, White was one of the best-known African American women in Houston. Her marriage to Julius had served as a form of social empowerment. Although marriage may be viewed as synonymous with reduction and denial of power for many females, for an African American woman from a working-class background, an advantageous marriage can provide ready-made respectability, conferring a status long denied her during slavery and segregation. During the era of Jim Crow, the married African American woman assumed an enhanced place not only in the larger society, but also in her own self-perception. She was free to pursue her own interests without encountering challenges to her morals or good name. Marriage to Julius, then, improved Lulu's social standing and removed some obstacles to her personal advancement. As wife of an activist, she found it easier to create her space within the local branch of the NAACP and gain access to important people who would help to implement changes in the black community.

At least two reasons underlay White's decision to become affiliated with the NAACP. First, it was a nationally based civil rights organization with great resources and legal expertise. Second, it was one of a few civil rights organizations that had placed women in leadership positions. White's desire to become involved in the NAACP seemed natural, as she represented a younger, impatient, militant group who wanted to steer the organization in another direction. Lulu White was fairly certain that, if she became part of this civil rights organization, her maturity and confidence would quickly mark her as a potential star in the small-group setting of this local chapter.

Before examining the role that Lulu White played in the organization, it is necessary to look briefly at the history of the NAACP in Houston. Although interest had been expressed locally as early as 1915, the Houston Riot of 1917 served as a catalyst for the establishment of the Houston chapter of the NAACP.

Investigating the 1917 riot, NAACP field worker Martha Gruening found the time ripe for organizing a Houston chapter. Considering the state of race relations in Houston, and aware of the large middle class and the politically active black population of the city, Gruening wrote to NAACP Executive Secretary James Weldon Johnson that she had "never seen a situation more promising." Shortly after Gruening's trip to Houston, M. B. Patten, a postal worker, wrote to Assistant Executive Secretary Walter White, requesting advice about organizing a local chapter. Upon receiving a positive reply from Walter White, Patten elicited the support of the Civic Betterment League, a black civil rights organization formed immediately after the riot. When that organization showed no interest in Patten's idea, he called a meeting of the city's leading black professionals, clergymen, and business people and presented his case. Subsequently the Houston chapter of the NAACP was established on May 31, 1918.[1]

Members of the Civic Betterment League, who had intended to become the founders of the chapter, quickly screamed foul and accused Patten of stealing their thunder. A rift opened between the two groups, and official recognition of the chapter was held up for two months. After intervention by the national office, the Civic Betterment League finally cleared the way for Patten's group to carry out its function as a civil rights organization. The duly constituted branch, then, elected an executive committee, consisting of Horace F. Edwards, Henry Mims, M. B. Patten, and Clifford F. Richardson. Once established, the branch, through its officers, proceeded to litigate against individuals and groups who violated the civil rights of blacks.

By the end of 1918, membership in the Houston branch had reached 414, and there was hope that it would increase even more. But this proved to be wishful thinking. In part because of misappropriation of local funds by some members and competition from other black organizations, the NAACP ceased to function in 1919 and appears to have been inactive in 1920 and 1921. In the 1920s, Houston blacks established two major political groups—the Progressive Voters League and the Independent Voters League—in reaction to the increased hostility of Lily White Republicans, a group who wanted to oust blacks from the Republican party in Texas. Additionally, they organized the Negro Chamber of Commerce to support economic advancement and the Texas Interracial Committee for those who wanted to work with sympathetic whites. During the early twenties, then, many blacks found themselves pulled by dual loyalties—to the NAACP and to some other race-based organizations formed locally.[2]

From 1922 to 1937, the Houston NAACP branch experienced many obstacles in its quest for money, membership, and survival. In 1922, John Adkins, secretary of the local branch, complained that the wealthiest blacks in the city had contributed little or nothing to the organization. In his opinion, the situation in 1923 would be no different. But this level of pessimism about the organization's future was not shared universally. When other officers drew up a plan to increase the membership in 1923, Adkins eventually embraced this idea, saying, "If we could line up colored preachers, we could take Houston." He also asked Robert Bagnall, the NAACP's national director of branches, to solicit contributions from leading black clergymen and wealthy business people. To complement this effort and reinvigorate the organization, a new president, Owen Pullman DeWalt, a local theater owner, was elected in 1924. Despite these efforts, however, the membership campaign fell short, largely because of the existence of competing organizations.[3]

The difficulty that the branch encountered did not prevent it from fulfilling its mission. Despite its small war chest and limited membership, the local organization did well in taking on and resolving issues of concern to blacks in the early 1920s. For example, the local branch achieved the exoneration of a black man, Luther Collins, who had been accused of raping a white woman. Without assistance from the national headquarters, the group conducted a campaign to free Collins, selected attorneys, and collected two thousand dollars to finance the legal battle. Similarly, the Houston chapter initiated an injunction against the Harris County Democratic Executive Committee in 1928, but was persuaded by the national office to drop it because the requested injunction appeared to conflict with that in *Nixon v. Herndon*. The efforts of some members notwithstanding, the local association again faded from public view in 1927. DeWalt's charisma, money, and influence kept the organization afloat until 1931, when he met an untimely death at the hands of one of his employees at the Lincoln Theater. With his demise, efforts to reinvigorate the branch also died.[4]

For the next seven years, 1931–37, the Houston branch lay dormant. Whatever Lulu White's aspirations may have been during these years, circumstances prevented her from pursuing them. The Great Depression diminished hope of even meager financial contributions, much less of increasing the organization's war chest. According to John Adkins, "Geting [*sic*] money was like plowing cotton with a blind mule." To a certain extent, Adkins was right. Many local branch members also belonged to the Negro Democratic Club. This meant that their time and efforts were split between the two organizations, with most of their money going to the club. This was true especially in 1934, when black Houstonians pooled their energies and resources to help the Negro Democratic Club take *Grovey v. Townsend* all the way to the Supreme Court. It is not surprising, then, that, for the ordinary citizen, a plea for money fell on deaf ears.[5]

With a membership of less than one hundred in 1934, the NAACP made another move to reorganize its branch. Despite significant help from the national office, the only visible outcome was the election of G. Duke Crawford as president. Without a doubt, in 1935 the Houston branch of the NAACP was at a crossroad. It had fallen behind other self-help and civil rights organizations in popularity, financial support, and members. An added concern was that the national office did not always agree with its branches, including Houston, on specific issues. The oligarchic structure of the national office left little room for input from the branches. Given these problems, if the Houston branch were to survive, it needed new approaches, new strategies, and new blood. Young, talented, ambitious, local black leaders would have to be drawn into the association and become integral parts of its operation.[6]

In 1937, a new movement developed to raise the local NAACP chapter to a prominent role within the black community of Houston. Interestingly, the impetus for this change came from students at a historically black college—Houston College for Negroes. To expand the membership list of the senior branch, students at Houston College for Negroes, under the leadership of Roy Lee Hopkins, reorganized their chapter. Simultaneously, Sanders A. Mason, advertising manager of the *Houston Informer*, wrote an editorial expressing his interest in unifying thirty thousand young blacks under the NAACP banner. These efforts coincided with a plan by the national headquarters to initiate a youth program among blacks in the country. This plan envisioned two divisions, a college group and a non-college group. Encouraged by this wave of interest in the Bayou City's NAACP, the national office sent Juanita E. Jackson, special assistant to the executive secretary, to Houston in the summer of 1937. She had a threefold mission: to establish a youth council, to revive the senior branch, and to examine the work of the chapter at Houston College for Negroes. When Jackson returned from her visit to Houston, she reported that her objectives had been met. The Houston College for Negroes chapter was doing well, in both programs and recruitment. Cliff Richardson was responsible for the reorganization of the senior branch, while Lulu B. White initiated a youth council.[7]

After being asked by Juanita Jackson to serve as director of the local Youth Council, Lulu White resigned her teaching post and devoted herself full-time to the NAACP. She was pleased with this career change, because she had long had aspirations of becoming a "race woman." Her objective was a career as a social activist, raising racial and political consciousness. Inspired by the interest of Houston's young people in the NAACP, White soon began to envision her role as a youth director: she would travel across the city and state, garnering support for the organization and working with the leadership of the local senior branch, the state branch, and the national office. Although the post of youth director conferred status, it did not pay a salary. The satisfaction Lulu derived from her work compensated for the loss of her teacher's pay. This job gave her access to the hierarchy in the NAACP and allowed her an opportunity to create her own space within the organization. Equally, it served as a mechanism by which White could help revive and strengthen the senior branch. Also, it provided a platform for her to sponsor popular programs on civil rights, literary topics, and current events. Very often, Lulu White's ideas for such programs came from the literary and social clubs of which she was a member. Each year, these clubs sought out new books and public figures who were authorities on the race issue and presented them to the public. Lulu White capitalized on the activities of these clubs by inviting their guests to teas she hosted regularly on Sunday afternoons. Thus she recruited new members for the NAACP and advanced the organization's agenda. These Sunday socials became so regular that people knew they could drop by during certain hours and expect to meet interesting people who were discussing civil rights issues. Lulu White was at ease in this setting, and she communicated effectively across generational lines to market her product—the NAACP.[8]

Despite Lulu's efforts to build a strong NAACP in Houston, the local chapter, like many other branches, excluded females from decision-making positions in the organization. With the exception of Ora Lee Terry, who served as assistant secretary, women usually worked as committee members, field workers, or volunteers.[9] Lulu White's position as director of the Youth Council was a token one. While this post was higher than that held by most women in the organization, it was below that of most male officers. To change this situation, White decided to use her position as director of the Youth Council to become part of the "inner circle." As such, she did not envy the achievements of her male superiors, nor was she estranged from them. Rather, she became increasingly close to them, relating to them as colleagues, role models, and mentors. No longer dependent solely upon her husband for social contacts, Lulu White now was in a position to interact independently with the upper echelon. From 1937 to 1940, she cemented her relationship with future branch presidents Clifford Richardson and Albert A. Lucas; with A. Maceo Smith, executive secretary of the Texas Conference of Branches; Thurgood Marshall, NAACP counsel; Daisy Lampkin, national field worker; Walter White, executive director; and Roy Wilkins, assistant executive director.

Meanwhile, reorganization of the senior branch led to the selection of Clifford Richardson as president. He had left the local branch in 1922 under of a cloud of controversy and had been a critic of the branch's inactivity in recent years. His past experience had given Richardson unique insight in his attempt to rejuvenate the branch, and many of his peers eagerly awaited his actions. Almost immediately, he went about the business of recruiting new members. Richardson's election signaled the return of many Negro Democratic Club members to the local chapter of the NAACP. Consequently, by April 1937, the Houston branch claimed one hundred members and had initiated a campaign to gain five thousand more. This recruitment effort was made easier through the assistance of Lulu White. So, with Clifford Richardson, Lulu White, former members of the Negro Democratic Club, and a number of youthful neophytes all "on the same page," pursuing a common objective, it is not surprising that a local black physician would write to Walter White in 1937 that "'a very militant' branch of the NAACP has been formed in Houston."[10]

At about the same time that the Houston chapter was regrouping, local branches throughout Texas agreed to coordinate their efforts with the national office by creating the Texas Conference of Branches. At the first meeting of the Conference, held in June 1937 and attended by Lulu White, delegates from Houston, Marshall, Waco, San Antonio, and Dallas resolved to achieve full political rights, to lobby for equal public funds in education, to support labor union movements, to investigate possible cases of racial discrimination in state offices of the Work Projects Administration, and to encourage the organization of new branches and youth councils in cities throughout the state. Approximately one year after the establishment of the Texas Conference of Branches, Clifford Richardson became its first president. Through their close contact with him, Lulu White and other Houston branch officials were brought into frequent and direct contact with the national office.[11]

Even as they worked to establish rapport with the national office, members of the Houston chapter were dissatisfied with the slow pace of the NAACP in retrieving the ballot. When an acute shortage of funds prevented the NAACP from developing another case before the 1938 elections, the Houston branch took matters into its own hands. Clifford Richardson, Julius White, and William Marcellus Drake in 1938 sued the Houston Democratic party. These men were quite familiar with the ruling in the Grovey case, which designated state party conventions as the only entities able to decide the qualifications of party members. The trio's concern, however, was whether the court's ruling was applicable within the city of Houston, since the city's charter declared that "all qualified voters of the city shall vote in all primary elections." Upon the court's denial of a request for an injunction, Richardson forwarded copies of the petition, as well as the court's decision, to the national headquarters of the NAACP, inquiring whether it was interested in using this material to challenge the decision in the Grovey case. While the response from the national office was noncommittal, the Richardson case generated some support in Houston. Unfortunately, however, infighting and allegations of fiscal improprieties in the local branch drew attention away from the case.[12]

Internecine fighting was not new to Houston's NAACP, but the 1939 fight came at a time when the branch was undergoing many changes. The period between 1939 and 1943 was a formative period for the NAACP, for Lulu White, and for the civil rights movement in Texas. It was a time when the mantle of leadership passed from an older to a younger generation and when the national office and the local branch seemed unified. At this time, too, Lulu White became centrally involved in the organization that would propel her into national prominence. By 1939, as the local branch increased its membership and even attracted some white members, the organization found itself mired in controversy and dirty politics. These threatened its very existence.

The first major fight within the organization came in 1939, when Clifford Richardson chose the NAACP's national convention in Richmond, Virginia, as a place to distribute leaflets supporting John Nance Garner's candidacy for vice president of the United States. Richardson may have felt some special loyalty to Vice President Garner, who was a former congressman from Uvalde, Texas. Yet Richardson's action embarrassed officials of the national office, as well as those in Houston, because First Lady Eleanor Roosevelt had been invited to the convention to present the Spingarn Medal of Honor to Marian Anderson, a world-renowned black contralto. When chided, Richardson took full responsibility for his action, but members of the Houston chapter felt that he had tarnished their organization's image, making the branch a political football and clearly violating its rules. As a means of achieving damage control, the executive committee of the Houston branch sent a resolution to the national office disavowing Richardson's behavior. Additionally, Carter Wesley, in an editorial, called for his ouster as president of the branch. Less than two weeks after the national convention adjourned, Richardson died of nephritis. Lulu White became acting president.[13]

But the Richardson controversy was only one of the troubles that plagued the Houston branch. Accusations of misconduct and malfeasance, leveled against several leading officers, could not be ignored. While attending one of the sessions of the NAACP convention in Richmond, Virginia, Lulu White had an opportunity to talk alone with Walter White. Upon returning to Houston, she reminded him, in a letter, of their conversation. "Some existing conditions in our branch are quite out of line with the aims and purpose of the Association. A visit from you," said Lulu White, "would mean saving of our branch." Rather than making the trip to Houston himself, White asked Daisy Elizabeth Lampkin, national field workers' chair, to examine the Houston branch's problems in conjunction with her October membership drive in the Bayou City.[14]

Daisy Elizabeth Adams Lampkin was an interesting NAACP figure. Born in the District of Columbia on March 8, 1884, she completed high school in Reading, Pennsylvania, and moved to Pittsburgh in 1909. There she met and married William Lampkin and began a lifelong association with the *Pittsburgh Courier,* a national Negro newspaper. Her relationship with the *Courier* began in 1913, when she won a cash award for selling the most subscriptions to the newspaper. She subsequently traded in this award for stocks in the publishing company. Because of her continuous investment, Lampkin soon became vice president of the *Courier,* a post she held for thirty-six years.[15]

Due to her community activism, Lampkin held several prominent positions during her public career, including president of the National Women Franchise League in 1915, several posts in the women's division of the Republican party, and national organizer and chair of the executive board of the National Association of Colored Women. Lampkin was the only woman among twelve blacks invited to the White House by President Calvin Coolidge in 1924 to discuss the 1917 Houston Riot. Named national field secretary of the NAACP in 1935, she embarked upon an astonishing fundraising and membership drive schedule, often reporting more than forty meetings in one month. Equally remarkable was her ability to garner nearly all of her expenses from the branches' monies, thus keeping costs to the national office to a minimum. Although Lampkin had few rivals in fundraising, she made other contributions to the organization as well. When she resigned as field secretary in 1947, she accepted, at the urging of Walter White, Roy Wilkins, and Thurgood Marshall, a post on the national board of directors of the NAACP.[16]

Over the years, Lampkin used the NAACP and the *Courier* as effective weapons to help blacks secure their rights. She wrote many articles on race and gender for the *Courier.* Reading those articles, one gets the impression that Lampkin not only heightened African American political consciousness, but also gave her reading audience a keen feminist understanding of the conditions of women. Such sensitivity particularly endeared her to Lulu White, who was embarking on a new career. Lampkin's background, credentials, achievements, and style impressed White, who regarded her as an extremely accomplished woman. Following their first meeting, Lulu White and Daisy Lampkin became very close friends. In subsequent years, each time Lampkin came to Houston, she stayed at the Whites' home.[17]

Shortly after starting her examination of the Houston branch, Lampkin, in a letter to her friend Richetta Randolph, described the situation as "one grand mess." After sifting through the evidence, she wrote to Walter White: "You talk about a hornet's nest. This is the worst that I have ever seen. Charges and countercharges of dishonesty, much of which is true." Lampkin explained further that the most serious issue was the alleged misappropriation of funds by the deceased Clifford Richardson and by Edwin L. Snyder, the branch's promotional secretary. Reportedly, they collected money to fund delegates' expenses to the Richmond convention, and "a portion of the fund was never adequately accounted for, and this irregularity created distrust for the branch officers." Lampkin also confirmed reports that the Houston branch was being used as a political football by unscrupulous men. These allegations notwithstanding, she added that not everyone in the branch was unethical. She described William Marcellus Drake, branch treasurer, as an "honest man" who was above question and referred to Lulu White as "honest and upright." Without being specific, Lampkin informed Walter White that "the branch and the Chamber of Commerce (Negro) have the same men as officers and there has been so much stealing and so many irregularities that each man is forced to support the other. There have been even threats of murder from one another." According to Lampkin's findings, the alleged mishandling of funds had a direct effect upon the small amount of money sent by this branch to the national office. In Lampkin's words, "Many who have money are gingerly giving one dollar as they want to have the right to vote, but do not trust the handling of their money to the present administration."[18]

Disgusted with her findings, Lampkin wrote Walter White once more. This time she recommended "revocation of the branch's charter unless we can get honorable men elected." Agreeing with Lampkin, Walter White exclaimed, "It is utterly contemptible that grafters and crooks like these, should prostitute the good name of the Association and jeopardize it." Walter White, however, stopped short of asking for immediate revocation and told Lampkin to "keep a stiff lip and straighten the situation out." He suggested that "a more effective step than immediate cancellation could be to recommend to the Board that any office to which Snyder is elected to be declared vacant, and the same thing be done with anybody else who is guilty of practices such as he had been pulling."[19]

Somewhat reluctantly, Lampkin accepted the advice of her superior and remained in Houston to reorganize the branch, conduct a membership drive, and hold an election of new officers. By mid-November 1939, a slate of officers was presented to the branch. That slate did not include Lulu White's name; she refused to run, even at the urging of her peers. Why she did not seek office is open to conjecture. Perhaps she felt that her old job as director of the Youth Council would be less stressful. It is also possible that she wanted more experience at the lower level before moving up. For whatever reason, she decided to continue in her former capacity as salesperson (field worker) for the organization.[20]

Elected to head the organization was Rev. Albert A. Lucas, a minister of one of Houston's largest black Baptist churches—Good Hope Missionary Baptist Church. Lucas was a native of Burleson County and had completed his theological training at Conroe College in Conroe, Texas. He then became an ordained minister and pastored several churches throughout the state before coming to Good Hope in 1934. Within two years, he raised enough money to pay off an $8,000 church debt and purchase two additional buildings. Lucas was viewed as a person with superior organizational and fundraising skills—talents sorely needed in the struggle against the white primary. So, at the end of the 1939 election, Daisy Lampkin left the city confident that the Houston NAACP was in good hands.[21]

Lulu White was pleased with the selection of Reverend Lucas. She looked upon him as a mentor, one from whom she could gain some knowledge of potential strategies. True to form, Lucas moved quickly to unify Houston's blacks behind an all-out attack on the white primary. Within a very short time, observers noted a substantial increase in the membership rolls. In fact, Lucas's well-coordinated campaign attracted 1,484 new members to the Houston branch. By February 1940, new leaders of other organizations and long-standing members of the NAACP were coming together again. Such groups as Phi Beta Sigma fraternity, the Interdenominational Ministerial Alliance, and the Progressive Voters League resolved to work closely with the local chapter in various fundraising drives. Among those advising and supporting Lucas financially and intellectually were Carter Wesley, the newspaper editor; James Nabrit, attorney; Mack H. Hannah, Jr., businessman; Hobart Taylor, taxicab company owner; and Julius and Lulu White.[22]

Seizing the enthusiasm of the moment, in March 1940, Lucas called a citywide mass meeting to formulate plans to eliminate the white Democratic primary and to secure full political rights for blacks. Out of this gathering came the idea of a statewide meeting to discuss a common strategy. Thus, Lucas issued a call for blacks across the state to attend the annual conference of the state branches of the NAACP, scheduled for Corpus Christi in May 1940. National officers, too, were invited.

At the Corpus Christi meeting, members of the NAACP's various Texas branches met with Thurgood Marshall, NAACP legal counsel, who assisted them in developing a ten-year program of action. The chief goal of this group was to eliminate the white primary statute. Other objectives included the achievement of complete educational equality and an all-out attack on segregationist laws. The conference decided on a three-pronged strategy to reach its goal. First, the NAACP would select a local attorney to coordinate the fight against the white primary. Second, the delegates would appeal to all blacks to contribute more money and would appoint a director for fundraising. Third, the state body would start a search for a plaintiff for the next lawsuit against the white primary. Referring to this conference as "the greatest in the history of our State Conference," A. Maceo Smith, executive director of state branches, reported to Walter White, "We laid plans that will realize for the Negroes of Texas a new era in the fight for civil rights." Elated over the success of the conference, Thurgood Marshall acknowledged that "this Texas group will really go down in history and they are not afraid to fight for their rights."[23]

When the conference adjourned, black Houstonians left with even stronger resolve to increase local membership and to gain the necessary financial resources and expertise to eliminate the white primary. Shortly after that, fundraising activities and the search for a plaintiff began in earnest. The projected expense for the upcoming case was eight thousand dollars. Most black organizations contributed toward this goal, but when they failed to reach the mark, Carter Wesley made up the difference. As the primary election approached, three possible plaintiffs were identified: Clifford Richardson, Jr., son of Clifford Richardson; Lonnie B. Smith, a dentist; and Sidney Hasgett, a mail carrier. In the end, Thurgood Marshall, along with the local branch and the national office, decided to use Sidney Hasgett as plaintiff. Accordingly, on August 24, 1940, Hasgett, accompanied by Carter Wesley and Julius White, attempted to vote in the Houston Democratic primary. With poll tax receipt in hand, he was turned away. He then sued in federal district court; on April 1941, the court again handed Hasgett a defeat. The NAACP then appealed the case.[24]

While Hasgett was waiting for a hearing on the appeal, scheduled for November 1941, the Supreme Court, in *United States v. Classic* (1941), reversed its previous stance concerning primary elections. The Court ruled that primary elections had become so much a part of the electoral process that they no longer could be considered merely private activities. Upon hearing of this decision, Thurgood Marshall decided to abandon *Hasgett v. Werner* (1941) in favor of a new case based on the latest ruling of the Court. This action frightened and angered some Texas leaders who were involved in the white primary struggle. After all, they had worked very hard to reach the appeal level in the Hasgett case and were drained psychologically, energetically, and financially. For many, this was not the time to "change horses in the middle of the stream." The harshest criticism of Marshall's action came from leaders of the Houston branch. In very obscene terms, Julius White warned Marshall that he had better win the next case or not return to Texas.[25]

Marshall's strategy for the new case was to use Lonnie B. Smith as the plaintiff. Smith had gone through the same steps as Hasgett had. Both had gone to the county clerk's office in July 1940, had requested an absentee ballot, and had been turned away. After presenting the above argument to the local, state, and national offices of the NAACP, Marshall conferred with Smith, spoke to a number of witnesses to confirm Smith's story, drafted a complaint, and then filed a lawsuit that became as known *Smith v. Allwright* (1944).[26]

As black Texans, especially those in Houston, began to prepare for what they hoped would be the final assault on the white primary, they soon realized that more money, members, and workers were needed badly. Consequently, in the fall of 1942, the executive board of the Houston chapter voted to set a goal of five thousand members for the upcoming drive. Initially, many members, including Carter Wesley, thought this goal was unrealistic; but they quickly changed their minds as they witnessed the enthusiasm generated by *Smith v. Allwright*.[27]

When Daisy Lampkin returned to Houston in 1943 to direct the fundraising campaign, she found, much to her delight, a black community much changed from the one she had left in 1939. Donald Jones, assistant field secretary, who accompanied Lampkin on this trip, stated, "The cohesion here among Negroes is remarkable despite the usual factionalism." After a few more days in Houston, Jones reaffirmed his earlier comment: "There is not the slightest doubt in my mind that the Houston branch is going to carry through and be the wonder of the nation in another year. It has the leadership and the followership, which is [*sic*] equally important."[28]

The leadership of the Houston chapter soon realized that, if the organization were going to fulfill its objectives, it needed an executive secretary to handle the day-to-day operations of the branch and free the president from some responsibilities. The decision to employ an executive secretary came at a most opportune time for the branch. Factionalism had declined, and other black organizations were willing to work with the NAACP to overturn the white Democratic primary. Hence, amid increased political awareness and membership, Lulu Belle White was selected as the first full-time salaried secretary of the Houston branch, making her the only woman in the South to hold such a post. In contrast to 1939, when she declined the offer to serve as president of the local branch, Lulu White readily accepted the executive secretary position. Her work as director of the Youth Council had proven good training for the more service-oriented career position of executive secretary. Over the years, White had become skilled in public relations and propaganda, in public speaking and letter writing. Furthermore, she had met and worked with black leaders on the highest local, state, and national levels.

With this experience behind her, Lulu White was armed for the challenge of being executive secretary. Upon hearing the news that she had been selected for the position, she could barely control her emotions. In a letter to Walter White, she exclaimed, "Give me five years, and I'll be darned if I do not give you 5,000 members in Houston. I won't be a bit surprised if you won't [*sic*] move your headquarters here."[29] True to her word, in six years Lulu White took the organization from the brink of ruin to the pinnacle of success in terms of racial advancement. She moved the organization from 2,000 to 12,000 members, transforming a fledgling organization into one that was second in size only to the Detroit branch. In that period, too, the civil rights organization that had dealt primarily with legal issues also came to employ direct action.

CHAPTER 3

Raising Her Voice
Gadfly or Crusader?

I n the spring of 1943, Lulu White began the most remarkable period of her public life. She was embarking upon her work as executive secretary of the Houston chapter of the NAACP at a time when the organization's fate was bound up with the white primary struggle. Moreover, White was assuming leadership of the organization approximately sixteen months after the United States entered World War II. Gunnar Myrdal, a Swedish scholar, correctly predicted that "there was bound to be a redefinition of the black man's status in America as a result of the war."[1] Wartime exigencies prompted legislation aimed at reducing and eliminating racial discrimination.

While the war affected the civil rights movement positively in many ways, it exacerbated racism and racial discrimination in Texas and throughout the South. Within this racial and wartime environment, Lulu White seemed determined to make a name for herself among civil rights activists. These latter were mostly males, who heretofore had viewed her as little more than an average foot soldier in the movement. Confident and enthusiastic, however, Lulu White came to her job with the blessing of the national headquarters. She felt that she was equal to the task.

The First Year

In size and appearance, Lulu White in 1943 was a likely candidate to challenge the State of Texas. Standing five feet, six inches tall and weighing over two hundred and fifty pounds, she was bold, brave, and loud, but also amiable, dignified, and respected by friends and foes alike. An acid-tongued individual who was not afraid to speak her mind to powerful whites and to differing black factions, Lulu White combined political radicalism with the administrative skill needed to effect change. When milder techniques did not work, she became openly defiant. To many, she seemed exactly what the doctor ordered for the civil rights movement in Houston and in Texas during the 1940s and 1950s.

At the end of World War II, Houston stood on the threshold of a transformation, growing from a small city into a metropolis. World War II stimulated growth in the city's petroleum production and in chemical, metal, and construction industries. As a result, one observer in Houston wrote, "[People] came *en masse* [to the city] during the war and most remained." A close look at the census data supports this impression. From 1940 to 1950, the total population of Houston grew from 384,514 to 596,163, while the black population increased from 86,302 to 125,400 during the same period. Although Houston had grown rapidly between 1900 and 1940, it remained small enough to be controlled politically and economically by a few wealthy businessmen. With the creation of a cosmopolitan city, however, the situation would become more complex.[2]

The changes in Houston's economy and culture and the increasingly cosmopolitan character of its population would dictate alterations in laws, government policies, and customs. To many whites who had lived in Houston in the prewar era, World War II would leave behind not confidence, but uncertainty, confusion, and fear; they would fear strangers in the land, black folks and their growing militancy, and job competition. To black Houstonians such as Lulu White, this was a time for blacks to achieve first-class citizenship, to attack Jim Crow directly, to move away from "separate but equal" and toward a more inclusive society.

Lulu White's political sensibility was informed by a belief in racial equality and in federally protected citizenship rights. Guided by this philosophy, she was not hesitant about raising her voice on any issue pertaining to the civil rights of blacks. She publicly advocated the right of blacks to vote and to participate at all levels of government. She pushed for equal access to jobs and education. She defended the political and civil rights of blacks and complained loudly whenever anyone trampled upon them. In her capacity as executive secretary of the Houston chapter of the NAACP, White increasingly adopted an outspoken, almost deliberately provocative style. Both her natural speaking talent and her defense of the right of free expression reinforced her candor. The NAACP's legal success in breaking down racial barriers in the 1940s, the growth of its branches, an increase in the number of black civic organizations and liberal labor unions—all these broadened the parameters of Lulu White's activism. Needless to say, White thrived on the activities of her office, as the city of Houston and the state of Texas offered new opportunities and challenges to those working to move the South beyond the politics of racial difference.

One of the first challenges facing Lulu White as NAACP executive secretary was discrimination in defense industries in the Houston shipyard. During the war, the federal government identified the South as the nation's major economic problem area, a region plagued by huge labor surpluses and chronically low wages. As a result, the government targeted the South for special treatment with respect to military training centers and contracts for shipyards and aircraft plants. Consequently, southern plants, dormant during economic depression, sprang alive with the infusion of federal money. Naval and private shipyards in Norfolk, Houston, Charleston, Pensacola, Mobile, and Pascagoula issued calls and more calls for workers. The explosion of job opportunities in defense-related industries of the North and South absorbed the surplus labor bottled up in southern agriculture. Yet, because of discrimination in hiring and firing practices, blacks found themselves continually shut out of the employment lines in these industries. When A. Philip Randolph, founder of the Sleeping Car Porters Union, threatened a march on Washington, President Franklin D. Roosevelt issued Executive Order 8802 and created a temporary Fair Employment Practices Commission (FEPC). Executive Order 8802 encouraged full participation in defense programs by all citizens, regardless of race, color, or creed, while the FEPC investigated violations of Executive Order 8802, reviewed complaints, and made recommendations to the Defense Department.[3]

When Lulu White received complaints of discrimination in the Houston shipyard, she arranged to visit the plant. After talking to workers of color and listening intensely to their stories, she wasted no time in writing a letter in which she lodged complaints with the War Manpower Commission. Apparently White's letter impressed the commission, because within a few weeks the shipyard moved several supervisors and changed some of its discriminatory practices. By war's end, both the number of black shipyard workers and the levels at which they were employed had risen.[4]

Feeling confident that other industries, too, would yield if the NAACP adequately exposed discrimination and pressed for it to be rectified, White challenged the discriminatory practices at the Atlas Dress Manufacturing Industry. She protested such practices as relegating most black females to the night shift and placing a partition between white and black workers during the day. Before Atlas Dress Industry could respond to the above allegations, however, the national office requested that White go to Beaumont, Texas, to investigate a race riot started by shipyard workers on June 15, 1943.[5]

The Beaumont riot erupted when a rumor spread that a black day laborer had raped a white woman. The underlying cause of the riot, however, was the fear held by white shipyard workers that the government was going to take away their jobs and give them to blacks. Already upset over reports of impending black employment at the shipyard, two thousand white workers marched on City Hall to protest the alleged crime. When they arrived, the sheriff told them that the alleged perpetrator had not been taken into custody. Frustrated, these workers joined other Beaumont whites and rampaged through the black section of the city, burning, pillaging, and terrorizing everyone in their path. One eyewitness reported that he was notified by a policeman to lock up his place of business and turn out the lights because of an approaching mob. "I immediately obeyed," said L. P. Riddeaux, "and about ten minutes later, there was a crowd of about three hundred around my place. They started . . . by breaking the window glasses and breaking down the door. But this wasn't all," continued Riddeaux. "They threw gasoline through the door and lighted a match, putting the whole place in flames." Because of this riot, war production in Beaumont stopped, businesses closed, and property valued at thousands of dollars was damaged. Two individuals died (one white and one black), and more than seventy-five persons were injured. It took martial law, the Texas Rangers, and volunteers to quell this riot.[6]

The riot left Beaumont's black leadership in total disarray. The local NAACP branch was essentially inactive and in search of leadership. Other black leaders were divided about whether they should sue in order to bring the rioters to justice and to cover damages sustained by black businesses, or accept donations from wealthy whites of the city. This confusing situation begged for outside assistance, if the black community of Beaumont were to return to normalcy. Only a dispassionate onslaught of facts and figures, Lulu White believed, could ease the tension surrounding the riot. So, in keeping with her directives from the national headquarters, Lulu White sent a special investigator, David J. Butler, to gather at first hand information on the causes, results, and damages of the riot. She also sent a resolution to the state legislature asking for a statute on rioting, requiring compensation for the destruction of property that resulted from such acts.[7]

While the riot damaged a large number of black businesses on Forsyth and Gladys streets, many black professionals, particularly those associated with the Beaumont school board, opposed going to court. For many reasons, they thought that it was in the best interest of the black community not to "rock the boat." Instead, they decided to accept goodwill gestures by whites. R. T. Tatum, principal of Charlton Pollard High School, wrote to Lulu White: "A finance committee composed of several prominent white businessmen put up money to the amount of probably Three Thousand Dollars or more for the purpose of refunding in whole or in part the loss sustained by Negro businessmen in the recent riot here." Tatum was of the opinion that "all of the Negroes [had] been well paid and no cash was needed to refund any business establishment." According to Beulah Johnson, whose husband died in the riot, Albert. L. Price, principal of Adams Elementary School, gave her a check for one hundred dollars and "informed [her] that his check was an expression of good will from a group of whites, whom he represented."[8]

In trying to comprehend the African Americans' response to the riot, David Manual, a letter carrier who had lived in Beaumont for twenty-five years, informed White that "the NAACP was working at disadvantages caused by the so-called leaders of the Negro population." To Manual's way of thinking, black leaders were more concerned with appeasing whites than with finding the real culprits in the riot. His sense was that the police officers were not blameless in this incident: "It is common knowledge that the police department was negligent in its duty, the source of all the trouble." According to Manual, during the same year as the riot, police officers assaulted a YMCA secretary for walking down the street late at night and shot a black soldier for no apparent reason. For these and other reasons, David Manual could not understand why blacks like Rev. Charles Graham would start an Interracial Goodwill Council.[9]

Confused after reading Manual's letter, Lulu White wrote to Walter White, executive secretary of the national NAACP, indicating that several blacks who suffered actual damage to property were told by a group of black leaders not to name the alleged perpetrators. "We are trying to find out," said Lulu, "whether these leading people are playing this sort of role because of 'pressure' or whether they are being paid to do this job." It is logical to assume that black school principals wished to curry white favor, inasmuch as they were employed by white school administrators. A lack of evidence prevents one from knowing if Lulu White ever discovered the real cause of the actions taken by the leaders of Beaumont's black community. What is known is that she did encounter a great deal of resistance from the Interracial Goodwill Council. This opposition aside, Lulu White would not be swayed from her main goal—to bring the perpetrators to justice. In this instance, she was instrumental in persuading Frank Hadnott, a victim of the riot who worked at Magnolia Ice Company, to seek redress in the courts. That more Beaumont blacks did not aid White in bringing the perpetrators to justice may be attributed to the divided leadership and the inactivity of the local NAACP branch.[10]

Although Beaumont's riot did not match in intensity the racial violence that took place elsewhere during the bloody summer of 1943, it nevertheless profoundly affected social attitudes and working conditions among African Americans. It also heightened the race consciousness of blacks and signaled the need to revitalize the Beaumont NAACP chapter, a branch that, with Lulu's help, became active again in 1950. The Beaumont riot did something else, too: nationally and locally, it put the NAACP on notice that it needed to change its business operations and methods of recruitment.

During her first year in office, White in many ways made good on her promise that she would not fit the conventional mold of executive secretary. Many of her followers, who had been members of the NAACP for decades and who looked upon the organization as an elite club, soon found White overturning tradition. Some changes she initiated; others were instigated by the national office. For example, to become a member of the NAACP, one no longer had to reach a certain level of education or income. The qualifications for membership were reduced to signing an application and paying a one-dollar fee. White concentrated a great deal of her effort on recruiting new members and on starting new chapters in cities, as well as in the "hinterland." She defied tradition by going to both churches and nightclubs to get new members. While she continued the legalistic strategy used by the NAACP in the past to secure civil rights for blacks, she also employed a more direct form of protest by boycotting, picketing, demonstrating, and simply "raising hell" in order to achieve her objectives. For example, in 1943, an NAACP boycott against Winegarten Store led to the dismissal of one of the store's security guards, who had struck a black customer. Another protest led to the establishment of Reserve Officer Training Corps Units in some of the city's black high schools. Similarly, an NAACP-led demonstration made it possible for blacks to attend a production of *Porgy and Bess* at the Houston Music Hall and be seated on the same floor levels as whites.[11]

Along with utilizing the method of direct action during her initial year in office, White concentrated on making the NAACP's views and activities known to the public via her use of the press. Not only did White welcome interviews by the media, but she also initiated press conferences. Most of her press coverage, however, was in the *Houston Informer,* owned by Carter Wesley, a personal friend of the Whites. At times, however, Lulu White raised her voice so loudly that she received notice in the white media. Although such publicity, more often than not, was negative, it had the positive effect of keeping White and the NAACP in the spotlight and thus inadvertently aided the civil rights cause.

Lulu White's first year as an NAACP executive broadened her horizons and left her more determined than ever to make a difference in the lives of African Americans. An ardent advocate of "lifting as [we] climb," she often made special contributions to economically disadvantaged persons at holidays or assisted them in other ways. Although such acts of generosity were not the function of the NAACP, Lulu White believed that "one should be his brother's keeper." It was not long, however, before she came to realize that individual acts of generosity—whether from the branch or on her own—could not begin to solve the problems of blacks in "Jim Crow" Texas. There would have to be changes in the political and economic structure of the state. And if the NAACP were going to help bring about this change, it would have to develop a plan for achieving this goal. Fortunately for her, the white primary struggle was a first step in that direction.

The Struggle for Political Rights

In taking the helm of the NAACP in 1943, Lulu White placed herself squarely in the forefront of the movement for political equality, beginning with the elimination of Texas' white Democratic primary. Since White already was familiar with that phase of the civil rights struggle, she needed no briefing on this issue. She was in daily contact with the national headquarters and served as liaison among the national office, the local chapter, and the black press. Additionally, she sent communications to black churches; lodges; fraternal orders; and civic, social, and professional organizations, informing them all of the status of the white primary struggle. In anticipation of a favorable court decision, White mounted a "pay your poll tax" campaign two months prior to the Supreme Court's decision in *Smith v. Allwright* (1944).

Lulu White went to Washington to meet with other NAACP officials on the day that the Supreme Court rendered its decision in *Smith v. Allwright*. When the verdict was read, she joined those blacks in jubilant celebration and looked forward to the day when African Americans would realize the full impact of that decision. When asked by a reporter about the ruling, White hailed it as a "Second Emancipation" but quickly added that she was particularly happy about the timing of it, because she was engaged in a vigorous drive to make Houston the largest NAACP chapter in the South.[12]

Dumbfounded at finding a black woman in a leadership position in the civil rights movement, many white Houstonians refused to acknowledge either the legitimacy or the influence of Lulu White. However much they tried to ignore her leadership, though, White won the respect of both whites and blacks when she recruited over five thousand new members into the Houston chapter in 1944—each determined to win the right to vote and to break down racial barriers. Congratulating White on a magnificent job, national field workers' chair Daisy Lampkin wrote, "Every day I marvel and am moved at your efficiency and the amount of work you are able to accomplish."[13]

It should be noted that Lulu White was not solely responsible for the phenomenal increase in membership. Rev. A. A. Lucas and a network of ministers played important roles, too. They had captive audiences in their churches and encouraged their members to join the NAACP. White herself, of course, was a member of one of the most progressive black churches in the city, and her influence was not lost on her fellow congregants. Moreover, people who frequented productions sponsored by her husband, Julius, met Lulu White when they came to see, hear, or speak with such celebrities as Duke Ellington and Joe Louis. In most cases, White used these occasions to recruit NAACP members.[14]

While Lulu White was thrilled over her membership drive, one of her greatest concerns from 1944 and 1948 was how to get blacks into the political system that opened as a result of *Smith v. Allwright*. The success of the NAACP in overturning the white primary law launched a new era in both black politics and Democratic party elections. Even with the Supreme Court's ruling, however, the number of black voters did not rise precipitously. Many factors still worked against black activists as they sought to increase minority participation. For example, the poll tax remained in place in Texas and effectively excluded many poor blacks from voting. Economic coercion on the part of employers and intimidation by party officials also served as barriers to black enfranchisement.

To overcome these obstacles, White collaborated with several black organizations in developing strategies to get more black Texans to the polls and to elect individuals who were sensitive to blacks' needs and interests. Eventually they designated three general types of activities. First was encouraging poll tax payment. Second was collective endorsement of certain candidates. While the official NAACP policy was not publicly to support any candidate, the organization surreptitiously lent effective support to its favorites. The third strategy was bloc voting, designed to generate organized support for an endorsed candidate. Because the Texas ballot was somewhat complicated, many organizations conducted clinics on how to mark ballots and how to use voting machines. Marking a Texas ballot required drawing a line through the names of all candidates except the one preferred by the voter. Because Texas law prohibited the use of any kind of aid in the polling place, black organizations never endorsed more than a half-dozen names in any election. In this way, the black bloc vote could be more effective.[15]

Probably more than any other black Texan of her time, Lulu White argued that a strong black vote was needed to shape governmental policies at local and state levels in the 1940s and 1950s. To ensure black participation in the movement for social change, she urged blacks to assume greater roles in the political lives of their communities, to learn about political techniques and organizations, and to prepare for future leadership positions. She argued convincingly that those who understood the movement for social and political change must identify with it fully and must interpret it to others. Not only did White urge blacks to vote and seek office, but also she conducted voter registration seminars, helped to select candidates, aided in drafting platforms, and used black churches to address public issues—all without actually campaigning for specific candidates.

Lulu White and the Education Committee of the NAACP also held citizenship classes. The purpose of these classes was to teach individuals about voting rights, civil rights, economic rights, and black history. These classes empowered black people to take control of their destinies, encouraged them to work toward common goals, challenged them to become active and effective in addressing injustices in their lives, and helped them to learn about the power of the vote. With the prospect of many changes emanating from the *Smith v. Allwright* decision, White felt that blacks could not remain passive; they had to respond actively to take advantage of the new opportunities. To translate this idea into practice, White engaged in the politics of reform. Everywhere she went, she "took" the vote with her. Whether she was speaking before Franklin Beauty School graduates, a civic club, or people on the street, her message was the same: "Pay your poll tax and go out to vote."[16]

Lulu White's first test at turning out the vote came in July 1944. Working with a network of Baptist ministers, local organizations, the black press, and members of the NAACP, she was successful in getting many blacks to the polls. On that day she monitored the actions of precinct judges, intending to report irregularities to the NAACP. Remarkably, the election took place without incident. An estimated 2,750 out of 25,000 blacks voted in the primary. This number represented only 11 percent of registered black voters, compared to 47 percent of the white voters who turned out on election day. For White and the other black leaders, this election suggested that a great challenge lay ahead in educating blacks about political strategies and tactics.[17]

Politically, for black Houstonians the period from 1944 to 1946 was one of reflection and preparation. Having flexed their muscles in the municipal election of 1944, they now could assess their strengths and weaknesses. They could decide upon their entry and (via their delegates) input into the Harris County Democratic Convention. In addition, they now could screen candidates, decide who to endorse, and fashion plans to get voters out on election day. The major problem facing them was how and when their "ideas" would be translated into "practice." The answer would come soon enough, with mayoral, city council, and gubernatorial elections in 1946 and elections for the U.S. Senate in 1948.

Mayoral Election of 1946

Houston mayoral elections always have been of great interest to blacks. The election of 1946 was even more interesting than usual, for at least two reasons. First, more blacks would utilize the franchise in this election than at any other time since the Supreme Court overturned the white primary. Second, blacks would have input in determining which type of city government—a strong mayor or a city manager—would best address community needs. In 1942, Houston had adopted a city manager form of government. From its inception, there were arguments pro and con concerning the appropriateness of this form of government for the Houston situation. In theory, a city manager form of government is modeled on the corporation, with its board of directors and chief executive officer. Periodically, a group of experienced individuals would come together to discuss the affairs of the city and set policies for it. The city manager then would be responsible for enforcing and executing these policies. Theoretically, then, much of that manager's responsibility involves applying engineering, accounting, and business methods. In conducting the city's business, he or she also needs to have experience in municipal laws and the principles of government.

The rationale for adopting this system was that Houston's population and cosmopolitan makeup had transformed it from a small city to a metropolis, with many complicated features that had to be managed scientifically by experts. Those pushing the city manager form of government argued for an efficient, business-oriented type of government, so that all people, including average people, would receive their fair share of benefits. Others claimed that someone with experience in municipal law and government probably could do a better job than an ordinary citizen who merely wanted to be mayor. But support for this system was not unanimous. Among the dissenters was Lulu White, who opposed the city manager form of government based on what she perceived to be its inherent insensitivity to minority needs. Like other opponents, she felt that minority groups would have no real hope of using persuasion or civic appeal to influence the manager. Thus, their needs likely would go unattended.

The mayoral election of 1946 offered Lulu White and other interest groups an opportunity to keep, modify, or change the city manager system. Three candidates came forward: John Mann, Holger Jeppeson, and Oscar Holcombe. As far as the issue of city manger government was concerned, Mann was lukewarm, Jeppeson opposed it, and Holcombe straddled the fence. Mann, a former city commissioner, ran on an independent ticket and was given no real chance of winning. Jeppeson, the Citizen Charter Committee's candidate, was a vice president of the Gulf Atlantic Warehouse and a nine-year veteran of the school board.

The People's Party choice, Oscar Holcombe, was the former mayor, who had earned the title "Old Grey Fox." During his tenure in office, Holcombe had flirted with many unpopular causes, ranging from his affiliation with the Ku Klux Klan to red-baiting and witch-hunting Communist sympathizers. His support of the civil rights movement had been lukewarm. Seizing upon the emotions of disgruntled labor supporters and friendships that he had established with black leaders such as the Reverend Lee Hamilton (L. H.) Simpson and Julius and Lulu White and with other disenchanted groups, Holcombe proposed a city charter amendment that would allow citizens to decide whether they wanted to modify the existing form of government.[18]

Although the central focus of the mayoral contest was on the city manager form of government, blacks were concerned with the candidates' stances on other issues, too—police brutality and the civil and voting rights of blacks. Holcombe was no stranger to the black community. He had both name recognition and influence. Though hardly an integrationist, still he could point to some accomplishments in the black community during his tenure in office. Prominent among those was the building of Jefferson Davis and Riverside hospitals.

Holger Jeppeson, too, was well known among African Americans. Having sat on the school board for nine years, he had had direct contact with a large number of middle-class blacks, particularly teachers. He, like Holcombe, urged blacks to protect their God-given right to vote. Apparently some blacks had confidence in Jeppeson. Not only had they voted for him in bipartisan school board elections over the years, but also many (the majority) felt an obligation to continue to support him in his mayoral bid.

Disturbed because so many blacks were supporting Jeppeson's candidacy, Lulu White complained to national executive secretary Walter White: "It is funny how they could vote for this guy because they can't point to anything he has done. The Negro schools are still having to use secondhand books from white schools. They get everything that the white schools do not need or refuse to use." In her opinion, Jeppeson had not fought a single fight to bring about parity in education for blacks. White's opposition to Jeppeson stemmed from allegations that this candidate was a member of the Texas Regulars, a group that had a bill before the legislature to repeal *Smith v. Allwright,* and that Jeppeson's supporters had tried to keep Rev. L. H. Simpson's name off the ballot for city council. Writing to Walter White, she lashed out against Jeppeson: "I am trying to let blacks see what harm they are doing by endorsing Jeppeson because none of the candidates running on Jeppeson's ticket are worth a 'you know what.' . . . They are all against black progress."[19]

Looking at the attitudes many blacks took toward Jeppeson, Lulu White argued that blacks were victims of racism and racial stereotypes. To her way of thinking, in response to the attitudes and practices of whites, black people had created racial myths of their own, reflected not only in their views but also in their political strategies and tactics. So strongly did Lulu White hold to this opinion that Walter White's assistant, Roy Wilkins, had to remind her that only in the narrowest sense could black voters be comprehended as a monolithic minority. He made it clear that the African American population was subject to the same divisive influences as every other group in this nation. As Lulu White continued to lament the situation, Wilkins explained further: "People are people, and they vote according to superstition, rumors, prejudice, religion, jobs, gambling, concessions, handouts, good government, whiskey and promises, etc." A persistent and determined individual, Lulu White wrote directly to Wilkins when she did not get the expected response from Walter White regarding Jeppeson's candidacy. Asking Wilkins to send her a telegram on how to foil Jeppeson's election, White said, "I have talked against this Jeppeson platform, which says that it will not listen to minority groups, until I am almost speechless. (Please send a reply.)"[20]

Earlier in the month, Lulu White had responded to a phrase in Jeppeson's platform, a phrase directed toward a white audience: "Have the courage to resist minority pressure groups." Soon thereafter, White found herself responding to a Citizen Charter Executive Committee's political advertisement that made the same assertion. A crusader with a mission and an opportunity, White responded in a two-page memorandum, asking the respective parties which minority groups they planned to resist. "You will readily appreciate," said White, "that as voters and taxpayers of Houston, we expect to have a say in the affairs of our city." Blacks did have a say in the election; Jeppeson went down to defeat, but not because most black people were swayed by White's opposition to his candidacy. In fact, Jeppeson received more black votes than Oscar Holcombe. Interestingly, the largest percentage of Jeppeson votes came from middle-class black teachers who were familiar with his record on the school board and who resided in the Third and Fifth wards. While she had not delivered the majority vote, Lulu White would have an even greater "say" in the election of city council members.[21]

City Council Election of 1946

In the city council election of 1946, Lulu White tried desperately to bring victory to the Reverend Lee H. Simpson. Simpson was one of eight candidates vying for three at-large seats in 1946. But neither Lulu White's influence nor her support was enough to get Simpson elected that year. Simpson ran not as member of Jeppeson's Citizen's Charter Committee nor as a representative of Holcombe's People's Party, but rather as an independent. Simpson was the pastor of Pleasant Hill Baptist Church, one of the largest black churches in the city. He established this church and organized the Baptist Ministerial Alliance of Houston in 1920. At the same time, he became a member of the NAACP and simultaneously established close ties with Oscar Holcombe. Simpson's affiliation with labor and civil rights organizations probably accounts for the fact that Holcombe gave lip service to Simpson's candidacy, allowing him to use his truck and microphone for campaigning, even though he was not on the Holcombe ticket. By virtue of the potential number of votes that Simpson could deliver via his church and his affiliated Baptist Association, politically he was a power to be reckoned with. This fact, plus the existence of twenty-five thousand potential black voters in Houston with no representative on the city council, caused Lulu White to urge Simpson to seek the council post.[22]

Contrary to the opinions of many blacks who argued that Simpson's candidacy was premature, White believed that a coalition of labor (especially the International Longshoremen's Association and five locals that included white members), the Baptist Ministerial Alliance, and black bloc voting could enable Simpson to emerge victorious. The election results revealed that White was naïve. For one thing, the Democratic party had not yet welcomed blacks into its ranks. Blacks could attend the convention, but until 1948 they had to accept segregated seating. Second, Carter Wesley and many other blacks opposed Simpson's running as an independent candidate, in light of the fact that blacks had waged a twenty-three-year struggle to become part of the Democratic party. Still others felt that Simpson would be a "Lone Ranger" on the council and that what blacks needed most was not a token representative but allies. Obviously, Lulu White felt differently. She thought that symbolism was a necessary ingredient of the movement—the act of running for office made a public statement that blacks were not merely objects of politics, but actors as well.[23]

Lulu White berated those who said that the time was not ripe or that blacks should wait until they understood their roles as voters before seeking elective office. In her mind, these were jealous individuals who themselves did not have the courage to run. She strongly believed that, in order for blacks to benefit from *Smith v. Allwright*, they had to be proactive. They must refuse to be stifled by silence, evasion, or quiet pressure; black leaders should not acquiesce when white men call them in, close the door, and lay upon them the heavy responsibility of averting race trouble. In her own words, "We cannot sit idly by and expect things to come to us. We must go out and get them."[24]

In her attempt to "go out and get them," to have Simpson elected, White decided to exercise the marking of the ballot in the same manner as whites had done in the past. She wrote to Roy Wilkins: "Notice . . . we have scratched all the candidates in the Council-at-Large list but Simpson, which means that we are giving him first choice, which counts as three votes. The Uncle Toms are telling the people that if they vote as such, their vote will be thrown out. This is not true."[25] The outcome of that election, however, did not support White's prediction. Yet, while the campaign was taking place, she gave it all she had.

Acutely mindful that, as an official of the NAACP, she was not supposed to give public support to any candidate, Lulu White described to Walter White her course of action in the Houston city council election: "In all this, the NAACP is not endorsing candidates, only issues. Yet, Walter, I am working like hell to get Simpson elected and to defeat those people running who are not friends of blacks." Lulu White spoke publicly against the platforms of Simpson's opponents. She held debates with black leaders on why blacks should support Simpson. She twisted the arms of several labor leaders to join the Simpson camp.

She even made a special effort to get the voters out on election day. Heeding her advice, blacks went to the polls in massive numbers in November 1946. According to one observer, White arrived at her precinct early on election day and, in her usual bold manner, spoke to a waiting crowd about the platforms of various candidates. White's action offended the precinct judge, who asked her to leave the polling place; when she refused, the guard threatened to take her to jail. She left, but not before exchanging insults and chastising some blacks for being indecisive about candidates who were lukewarm on civil rights.[26]

For all White's efforts, Simpson went down to defeat, although most of his votes came from the black community. In fact, Simpson received the smallest number of votes out of a field of eight candidates, fulfilling the prophecy of those who claimed that the time was not yet ripe for a black to run in a citywide election. To many, though, it seemed worthwhile for blacks to flex their political muscles first and then try to force concessions, as, to a small degree, they did in the race for sheriff.

Sheriff Election and Law Enforcement

Because of the history of police brutality in Houston, newly enfranchised blacks took a special interest in the race for sheriff. Vying for this law enforcement post in 1946 were four candidates: W. P. (Bell) Haley, M. L. (Foy) Woolley, J. P. Davidson, and Neal Polk. Haley was a twelve-year veteran of the police force, a specialist in traffic control, juvenile delinquency, and crime prevention; he had served as patrol officer, sergeant, lieutenant, and captain. Woolley was a constable who had made a prior run for sheriff. Davidson, a former police chief, was a police captain who presided over the Division on Morals. Polk was the incumbent sheriff.[27]

Woolley's platform was appealing to Lulu and Julius White. He promised to appoint black deputies, to confer with civic leaders on law enforcement, and to work to curb black-on-black crime. Again, in defiance of the NAACP rules, Lulu White was quite visible in this election, so much so that supporters of other candidates felt uncomfortable in her presence. White openly expressed the opinion that Woolley's campaign was the best that blacks could hope for, while her husband contributed fifteen hundred dollars to Woolley's coffer. In this campaign, White took a forceful and uncompromising stance, especially since Polk's platform and record were equally appealing to blacks. Despite White's enthusiastic support of Woolley, Polk had no difficulty in getting black votes in the primary election.[28]

While Polk garnered the largest number of votes, he did not secure a majority; therefore, a runoff was necessary between Polk and the second highest vote-getter, Woolley. As soon as the election was over, Davidson, the second runner-up, went to court, charging that irregularities at black precincts 24 and 48 had barred him from the runoff. Many blacks, who were not fond of Davidson initially, became very upset when the court agreed with him. Thus, when the campaign for the runoff between Polk and Davidson began, Davidson made frantic appeals to black voters by pledging that he would recommend a Negro deputy to the Commissioners Court; but blacks ignored his plea. Moreover, there were allegations to the effect that Davidson had mistreated blacks when he was a member of the police force. In the end, Polk, whose record on police brutality was much better than that of his opponent, emerged victorious.[29]

Despite the efforts of blacks to vote the "best" man into office, police brutality continued throughout the city, prompting Lulu White to go before the city council several times to protest such behavior. Without a doubt, there were times when the clashes between white police officers and blacks were provoked by blacks who resisted arrest; however, many white policemen typically acted as if it were their duty to keep black folks in "their place" and make them stand in fear. One might speculate that such views probably precipitated what happened on April 10, 1948, when a deputy sheriff allegedly killed an elderly black man for no apparent reason. After the accused deputy denied any knowledge of the slaying, the police department closed the case, amid cries of protest from the black community and an investigation by the interdenominational ministerial alliance.[30]

A similar incident occurred on July 6, 1948, when a police officer whipped B. B. Watson, a black businessman. The beating was so severe that it caused an outcry in the black community. Wesley Roger, a black minister, questioned the police officer about his action, whereon Roger also was beaten. After this incident, which occasioned press coverage and editorials for four days, Lulu White decided to act. In a resolution of protest to the city council, she pointed out that police brutality damaged Houston's reputation as a "progressive" city and prevented it from realizing the high ideals of "democratic justice" for all its citizens. Perhaps more important, she asked the mayor and city council to give blacks assurance that, in the case of official substantiation of the mistreatment and abuse of citizens by police officers, the responsible party would be punished.[31]

In part because of the power of the black vote and the pressure applied by Lulu White and the NAACP, the number of blacks on the Houston police force increased from six to thirteen by 1948. It should be noted that Houston had had blacks on its police force since Reconstruction. Although its number was small—three, to be exact—Houston maintained a special "colored police brigade." The blacks who served in that brigade could not arrest whites, could not wear uniforms, and were not considered real policemen by their white counterparts. They worked exclusively in Houston's black neighborhoods, and blacks regarded them as symbols of pride and authority. Although the black community welcomed them as law enforcement figures who understood black culture, members of the brigade did not increase in number until 1929. Then the number rose from three to six. In 1948, the brigade increased again, from six to thirteen. By and large, however, black police officers remained powerless, and this increase in numbers did not diminish the tally of police brutality cases.[32]

Lulu White, perturbed by the brutality, informed the national NAACP of the ratio and status of black police officers in 1948. "Houston has a force of 503 police, of which only 15 are African American," she wrote. "Even worst [sic] than sad was the fact that the fifteen were told that they must not arrest anyone except Negroes regardless of what law is broken." One young officer resigned to protest those instructions. According to White, "He gave a ticket to a white man for speeding and was read the riot act." The second-class status of Houston's black policemen reflected the experiences of African Americans throughout the city. The separatist policies legitimized by this system would affect African American police officers for years to come.[33]

White's vocal protests against law enforcement practices in Houston should not be read as indicators of a generally anti-police attitude. Rather, she was persistent in her protests and in developing new tactics to test the commitment of the city's government to protecting all citizens. This test of commitment extended from the local level to the national one, from police brutality to the gubernatorial election of 1946 and the senatorial election of 1948.

Gubernatorial Election of 1946 and Senatorial Election of 1948

At both the state and national levels in 1946, the Texas gubernatorial election was among the most closely watched races. In Texas, observers speculated on whether or not the black vote would make a difference. Nationally, this race was seen as a referendum on the New Deal. In a bitterly contested twelve-man race, Homer Rainey and Beauford Jester emerged as the leading candidates. Labor and liberals rallied behind the candidacy of Rainey, the popular former president of the University of Texas who had been forced from office by the UT Board of Regents in 1944 after a dispute over academic freedom. Rainey held conventional New Deal views and ran on a platform of progressive taxation, increased state spending for public education, and support for welfare programs. Beauford Jester, on the other hand, was a candidate of the Texas Regulars, a group that opposed both the *Smith v. Allwright* decision and a fourth term for Franklin D. Roosevelt. This group espoused limited government and no tax increase.[34]

Initially, Lulu White stood with labor in support of Rainey's candidacy, but when Rainey issued a statement advocating separate polling places for black and white voters, her support began to wane. Partly because of her alliance with labor, White did not go so far as Carter Wesley, who urged "blacks to go fishing on the election day." Rather than support any of the candidates for governor, White remained silent; but to many of her followers, silence meant disapproval. In the end, Beauford Jester emerged victorious. For whatever reasons, the black vote did not carry as much weight in this election as it would in the elections of 1948.

Black voters of Texas did not become numerically significant until 1948. The black voting-age population in Texas tripled, from 30,000 in 1946 to 100,000 in 1948. Moreover, 1948 was the first year when blacks were not banned from participating in Democratic conventions. The 1948 election was the first senatorial primary election in which blacks legally could cast a ballot, and both Republicans and Democrats showed an interest in the black vote. Consequently, the black vote was to play a crucial role in one of the most controversial senatorial races in the history of the United States.

The candidates in this race were U.S. Representative Lyndon Baines Johnson, who had voted against nearly every civil rights bill that crossed his desk, and former governor Coke Stevenson, who never had lost an election. Despite Johnson's voting record on minority issues, he received the support of most blacks in Houston and throughout the state. Why? First, he was a devoted supporter of FDR and the New Deal. Second, his actions as state director of the National Youth Administration (NYA) during the 1930s were remembered favorably. Third, Johnson sought black support even before blacks could vote in primary elections. Finally, Coke Stevenson had a poor record in race relations and hence did not offer a better choice.[35]

Many blacks in Houston and the surrounding area pointed to Johnson's willingness, as state director of the NYA, to enlist blacks in the program. According to black economist Robert Weaver, a member of Roosevelt's kitchen cabinet, Johnson's actions as state director of the NYA infuriated congressmen, because "Johnson was giving a hell of a lot of money to the Mexican-Americans and Negroes." Although Johnson failed to appoint blacks to supervisory positions in the jobs program, he made extensive efforts to enlist young blacks in its ranks. He shuffled project funds from white schools to black schools and sought additional appropriations for black colleges, such as Lulu White's alma mater, Prairie View A&M College. Johnson also made an extra effort to help blacks who were living in poverty, including those living in "Heavenly Houston." Because of these activities, Johnson began to attract attention from black leaders at both local and state levels. Of Johnson's senatorial candidacy, Thurgood Marshall said, "All of our people of the NAACP in that area were enthusiastically behind him."[36]

Black leaders supported Johnson not only because of his connection with

FDR, but also because Johnson and his campaign workers actively sought out such leaders as Carter Wesley, owner of the largest chain of black newspapers in the state; Hobart Taylor, Sr., entrepreneur; and Mack Hannah, Jr., businessman. Johnson also consulted blacks of the Greater Houston Area—Third Ward, Fourth Ward, Fifth Ward, and the Heights. Likewise, he canvassed the Progressive Voters Leagues of Houston and the Colored Voter Leagues of Dallas and San Antonio. Moreover, Johnson's campaign actually sought out both urban and rural black voters and welcomed them to the Democratic party. On the day of the election, Wesley published a sample ballot in his *Informer*, listing all candidates for office. For United States senator, every candidate was crossed out except the name of Lyndon B. Johnson.[37]

The black majority supported Johnson's candidacy in the statewide election. He received 494,191 votes, and Stevenson got 484,104. Johnson won a black majority in Harris County, 2,974 votes to 2,877. He carried Precinct 24, 397 to 369, and won Precinct 47 by a wider margin of black votes, 497 to 297. Stevenson carried one predominately black precinct in Harris County, Precinct 48, by a vote of 493 to 438; but Stevenson returns from this precinct did not equal the combined number of votes for Johnson cast in other black precincts in the county.[38]

For Lulu White and those blacks fighting for civil rights, the choice between Johnson and Stevenson had been easy. While serving as governor, Stevenson did nothing to curb the violence being meted out to blacks. He took no action when a black man was dragged from his hospital bed and lynched in a cotton gin in East Texas. If anything, some of his remarks might have encouraged such crime. For example, in a letter to U.S. Attorney Francis Biddle, Stevenson wrote, "Certain members of the Negro race from time to time furnish the setting for mob violence by outrageous crimes they commit." When the 1943 race riot erupted in Beaumont, Stevenson, who was on his way out of town, did not delay his trip. Instead, he referred the matter to a subordinate. Inasmuch as the civil rights issue was not part of the 1948 campaign, both candidates naturally made a concerted effort to downplay it. When asked during the campaign about his anti–civil rights stance, Johnson argued that, while he opposed civil rights on legal and states rights grounds, he had never attacked blacks in his speeches or campaign literature, as had another candidate. Carter Wesley summed up black support of the two candidates best, when he wrote of Johnson, "He is no angel [but] he is about as good as we have seen in the race." So it was not surprising that black Texans should go to the polls on election day and cast over 90 percent of their votes for Johnson, aiding the congressman in his controversial eighty-seven-vote win over Stevenson.[39]

Gadfly that she was, Lulu White, after the election, constantly reminded

Johnson of the impact that blacks had had on the 1948 election and of the need to support anti–poll-tax legislation. When an anti–poll-tax bill died on the floor of the Senate because of lack of support from Johnson, no one in Texas was more critical of him than Lulu White. Shortly after Johnson gave his blessing to filibustering, White sent him a telegram that read: "The Negroes who sent you to Congress are ashamed to know that you stood on the floor against them today. Do not forget that you went to Washington by a small majority vote and that was because of the Negro vote. There will be another election and we will be remembering what you had to say today." Johnson took note of the concerns of blacks in his district but still did nothing to alter his voting pattern on civil rights, much less on the anti–poll-tax bill. Rather, Johnson's reply was that White had misunderstood his stance on filibustering and that in time he would support blacks. This answer was unacceptable to White. She continued to hold anti–poll-tax rallies at state and local levels and to trumpet the political rights of blacks.[40]

White supported so many causes, traveled so widely organizing branches to fight Jim Crow, and raised her voice so consistently for black political rights that many people came to think of her as a person who could solve any problem. Her advice was sought on fundraising, organizing social clubs, improving black communities, lodging complaints protesting inadequate facilities in black high schools, and solving problems for juvenile delinquents, families of prisoners, and hospital workers who wanted a promotion. Among the many letters that she received weekly were those asking for financial assistance. While officially she could not grant such a request, for a young person seeking a scholarship to college, a young man trying to get a job, a black candidate running for office, Lulu White's support was invaluable. Brave, unafraid to speak out, and almost certain that she would be heard, Lulu White from 1943 through 1957 was an omnipresent gadfly and crusader for the civil and political rights of blacks.[41]

Taking a Fearless Stand
The Fight for Economic Parity

L ulu White's vision of economic reform in the 1940s was positive, practical, and, to some, even revolutionary. Just as she viewed the vote as a necessary ingredient in full citizenship, she believed that, if blacks were to enter the mainstream of American life, it was necessary to expand the general basis of equality through equal economic opportunities. Her awareness of systematic economic injustices had been galvanized while she was a student at Prairie View. Her economics professor assigned her to survey practices concerning wage differentials between black and white employees in Houston industries. Somewhat surprisingly, many industries answered affirmatively when she asked the question, "Is there any discrimination in regards to wages and work pertaining to racial groups?"[1] The candid replies to that question would trouble Lulu White for the rest of her life. By the time she became executive secretary of the Houston branch of the NAACP, her concern for eradicating economic injustices had crystallized into a vision of integrating blacks into America's economic system. Such integration not only would facilitate their entry into the growing industrial society, but also would improve the climate of race relations in this country. Consequently, she pressured white businesses to employ blacks, campaigned for authorization of a permanent FEPC, and established a coalition with labor unions to achieve the desired results.

Equal Work, Equal Pay, and Equal Opportunities

In discussing the future of African Americans, Lulu White often emphasized the importance of expanded economic, educational, and political opportunities. She believed that such opportunities were citizenship rights which a democratic government should provide for all its citizens. Because Lulu White believed that racial prejudice and discrimination often made it difficult for blacks to enjoy these rights, she had difficulty seeing how these rights could be realized without challenging the racial laws, customs, and values that rendered such opportunities unreachable. Based upon this premise, White became intimately involved in the Houston Area Teachers Equalization Salary Case in the early 1940s.

Although Houston provided one of the better school systems for blacks in the South during the 1930s and 1940s, the working conditions for African Americans in that system never were equal to those of whites. Similarly, female jobs differed from those of males. Women mostly were teachers, while men were both principals and teachers. In all cases, despite the positions held, the salaries of whites were higher than those of their black counterparts. Lulu White was in a unique position to work with salary equalization cases, because she herself had been subject to a wage differential. No longer connected with a school system, however, she did not have to worry about economic reprisals. According to oral sources, even before White resigned her teaching position, she held informal discussions with black teachers about salary inequities and about the need to make these conditions known to the public. At that time, white teachers were making 60 percent more than black teachers, and black principals were earning $2,220 while white principals made $3,000. Yet the urging of Lulu White, Carter Wesley, and the Negro Chamber of Commerce was insufficient to move the Houston teachers to action during the 1930s.[2]

Lulu White and Carter Wesley would not let the issue of salary equalization die. They kept it before the public as they interfaced with the NAACP national headquarters, where a strategy was being designed to attack the problem of salary inequities throughout the South. The State of Maryland presented the first test case for the NAACP; in 1937, the Supreme Court ruled the salary differentials unconstitutional. Both Lulu White and Carter Wesley were elated over the outcome of this case, as it was certain to spawn many more lawsuits. Three years later, following a national trend, Dallas area teachers filed the first pay equalization case in Texas.[3]

The Dallas lawsuit prompted dialogue between the Houston school board and area teachers, but neither side took immediate action. The first encouraging sign that the Houston school board was going to yield to the trend of equalizing teachers salaries came on January 25, 1943, when the board decided to increase the salaries of all employees who earned less than two thousand dollars per year. Although some 840 teachers (most of whom were black) received this salary increase, Carter Wesley noted that the board made no comments regarding equalization of pay based on experience and qualifications.[4]

The ruling from the Dallas case did not come until March 1943, at which time Federal Judge William Atwell decreed that 235 black teachers in the Dallas school system would receive the same pay as their white colleagues.[5] While black teachers were jubilant about the success of the Dallas case, it was Carter Wesley's editorials and secret meetings that Lulu White held with leaders of the black Houston teachers that jolted them into action. Never one to mince words, Carter Wesley wrote, "All leaders in the state agree that Negro teachers' salaries should be equalized. But the Houston teachers seem to be waiting for somebody to do the job for them." One week after this editorial, Wesley made a proposal to the teachers—he would underwrite the salary of any teacher who had the courage to step forward and become the plaintiff in a lawsuit. The following week, black elementary school teachers organized and began drafting plans for a lawsuit.[6]

While all this was transpiring in March 1943, White was preparing to become executive secretary of the local NAACP chapter. On April 3, 1943, about the same time that Lulu White received official notification that she was to preside over the Houston chapter, this group of teachers collected five thousand dollars to fund their court battle, prompting Carter Wesley to note that, once Houston's black teachers came alive, they "came alive with a vengeance." Now in an official capacity to work for equalization of salaries, White helped the teachers develop a three-pronged strategy. First, they had to organize and raise money. Second, they were to secure the services of Francis Scott Key Whittaker as attorney and spokesperson. Finally, they were to present a formal petition to the school board requesting pay equalization. If an affirmative response were not forthcoming, the teachers would pursue a lawsuit in the federal district court.

On April 6, 1943, when Whittaker and eleven representatives of the Negro Committee of the Houston Teachers Association presented the school board with a petition for pay equalization, Lulu White and Carter Wesley accompanied them and served as consultants. From the beginning, Whittaker made it clear to the school board that the Supreme Court's ruling in several cases decreed that paying black teachers less than white teachers was unconstitutional. Following a dialogue with the lawyers, the board proposed that the teachers file a "friendly" suit in federal district court. A verdict from the court would make pay equalization legal and binding on both parties and a matter of legal record as well. Then, on April 13, 1943, rather than take a chance on a potentially troublesome lawsuit, the Houston school board agreed to make the salaries of black teachers and principals equal those of their white counterparts who possessed the same credentials and performed the same duties. After the verdict was rendered, Lulu White used every possible means of communication—newspapers, pamphlets, lectures, rallies—to inform the teachers of the role that the NAACP had played in that decision.[7]

By 1943, Lulu White likely viewed the importance of her job in terms of its potential for helping to improve the social status and life circumstances of African Americans. While many black Houstonians boasted that they were better off economically than most blacks in the South, Lulu White had cause for concern. During the first three decades of the twentieth century, black Houstonians found themselves excluded from the mainstream of political and economic life in the city. Many African Americans responded to these conditions by availing themselves of opportunities within their own neighborhoods. They formed an entrepreneurial elite providing goods and services to black consumers. While many argued that the emergence of a separate black economy strengthened the entire black community, the chief beneficiaries were barbers, beauticians, blacksmiths, physicians, dentists, pharmacists, lawyers, and owners of restaurants, grocery stores, and nightclubs. Despite the existence of this elite professional class, most blacks in the city (89.6 percent of them) worked in jobs classified in the lowest-paying categories: service, domestic, semiskilled, and unskilled. Except for the domestic workers, these individuals held jobs that were hot, onerous, and hazardous. Traditionally assigned to the most menial jobs and until the 1930s excluded from major unions, the masses of black Houstonians had become separated from the economic mainstream of American life. An even worse realization for Lulu White was that segregation undermined whatever chances these blacks had for ever obtaining the skills required to maintain employment in the increasingly industrialized city after World War II.[8]

Economically speaking, World War II brought important changes to Houston. According to a *Houston Post* columnist, "No period in the city's history approached the importance of World War II and the decade immediately following." By the end of the war, Houston was leading the United States in value of industrial construction. Ten years later, the annual value of its industrial plants had increased by 600 percent and its consumption of natural gas by 400 percent. The Association of State Planning and Development, citing building permits and telephone, electricity, water, and gas connections in 1948, reported that Houston was the fastest growing industrial area in America.[9]

The economic and industrial transformation of Houston spawned more, as well as new, labor unions; and it encouraged black workers, who still were suffering the effects of the Great Depression, to push for what appeared to them as new economic opportunities. This transformation also reinforced Lulu White's resolve to eradicate discrimination in the workplace. Consequently, a few months into her first year as executive secretary, White conducted a survey of job classifications in Houston, in order to determine the number of blacks who had been hired in civil service jobs. Much to her chagrin, the survey revealed that the only civil service positions held by blacks were in the post office. While she agreed that industrialization called for new skills and methods to facilitate one's advancement up the economic ladder, White argued that a lack of equal opportunities was at the core of black underrepresentation in civil service categories. She urged the city to change its discriminatory policies.[10]

Some of Lulu White's friends, both white and black, believed that it was necessary to expand the general basis of equality with more "separate and equal" jobs to ensure African Americans' ultimate participation in the workforce. She, however, emphasized, as the first necessity, the winning of equal opportunities. Influenced and convinced by New Deal liberalism, White believed strongly that the NAACP's direct action approach could force concessions from white businesses. Not only did she encourage her allies to seek employment at white establishments, but she supported their efforts personally. Her energetic pursuit of equal opportunities took her, more often than not, down a stormy path. Some white managers refused to see her, others slammed doors in her face, and still others were evasive. But the persistent Lulu White refused to accept "no" as an answer.

Notable was her encounter with the manager of Southwestern Bell Telephone Company. After trying unsuccessfully to convince Southwestern Bell to employ blacks, White challenged the telephone company to honor its advertisement: "Wanted to Train and Employ Operators." The manager's response was that the company did not hire blacks, to which White replied, "I understand that you train and hire operators and that's what I am interested in." When Southwestern Bell made no firm commitment to hire blacks, she kept the pressure on. Writing to A. Maceo Smith about this incident, White made it clear that, if the management "does not hire or train Negroes, they will have to take the advertisement out of the paper."[11]

Lack of evidence prevents one from knowing when and if Southwestern Bell yielded to the pressure from the NAACP executive secretary. What is known is that White was persistent in her efforts to get white businesses to employ blacks. In 1948, she wrote to Thurgood Marshall with more pleasant news: "Scott Bakery decided to employ a black female at a handsome salary to work in its public relations office."[12]

Despite the obstacles and setbacks Lulu White encountered in breaking down race-based economic barriers, she was steadfast in her belief that parity should take place within the context of an integrated society. Unlike some blacks, who willingly or unwillingly accepted or engaged in Jim Crow compromises in order to reap economic benefits, pragmatic acceptance of segregation in return for equal economic benefit was not part of Lulu White's *modus operandi*. This was evident in her fight to prevent the federal Office of Price Administration (OPA) from setting up a separate Jim Crow branch within the Negro Chamber of Commerce in 1945.

The OPA was a wartime agency established in August 1941 by President Franklin D. Roosevelt to control inflation by placing ceilings on prices and by conserving food and other essential commodities. Price control was one of the toughest problems for the administration. Every economic interest group wanted rigid policing of the other fellow's prices but tended to regard attempts to police its own prices as antithetical to the free enterprise system. For all of its unpopularity among businessmen and politicians, the OPA was one of the war's brilliant successes, especially for blacks who were employed as attorneys, price analysts, and economists. Blacks also worked in regional and state offices as information specialists, and as clerks and members of the ration board in the local offices of some communities.

Inasmuch as there seemed to be more general satisfaction among African Americans with the administration of the OPA, and especially with its general policy of employing persons regardless of race, a number of black Houstonians requested that the national headquarters of the OPA establish a separate affiliate in the Negro Chamber of Commerce. Organized in the mid-1930s, the Negro Chamber of Commerce worked to promote black businesses by raising consumer consciousness and by encouraging African Americans to "buy black." Because of its philosophy, many blacks felt that the chamber would be a good place to house a separate OPA affiliate.[13]

When Lulu White heard of this request for a separate OPA, she became very perturbed. She called the responsible individuals on the carpet, explaining that a separate OPA violated the philosophy and policy of the NAACP. The only positive response she received came from Rev. A. A. Lucas, who reluctantly removed his name from the list of those making the request. Being unable to convince the other men of her local organization, White wrote to Thurgood Marshall for assistance: "Tell the NAACP people that they must know what they are doing before they run up to these people and ask for segregation. . . . They are sponsoring Jim Crow, discrimination, segregation and every darn thing else by [asking for a black branch]. I told them, we fight discrimination in every form. . . . [Write them] right now before I burst wide open." Marshall responded with wisdom, telling White to take into consideration the customs and culture of segregation and their impact upon black and white citizens alike. While not acquiescing to the forces of segregation, Marshall reminded White that the fight to end Jim Crow practices would be an uphill battle. "You are completely right in opposing Jim Crow," wrote Marshall. "I know you are disgusted . . . but we must keep on until we win." As White continued her crusade against a separate OPA, she remained confident that the combined forces of reform and new technology would bring about an end to segregation; she believed that, regardless of whether blacks wished it or not, they could not remain separated from the rest of society. In a word, there could never be an exclusively Negro economy. Apparently the pressure from White worked. A separate OPA branch did not come into being.[14]

It is well to note that White did not want to maintain the status quo; neither did she want to change America's economic order. She simply wanted to see racial barriers eliminated to allow blacks free entry into an integrated workforce. It was White's hope that the establishment of a permanent Fair Employment Practices Commission (FEPC) would help to achieve this goal. The FEPC, established in 1941 under FDR's Executive Order 8802, encouraged full participation in defense industries, without regard to race, color, or creed. Although it lacked enforcement powers, the FEPC handled many complaints, uncovered many instances of prejudice in hiring, and called to public attention many discriminatory acts by white employers. In May 1943, the FEPC became an independent agency of the executive branch. By the end of 1944, the FEPC seemed destined to die a natural death. Beginning in 1945, all its funding would come from Congress, where southerners were certain to put up a strong fight against it. When Harry S. Truman became president in 1945, he did little to pressure southern senators and representatives concerning the FEPC. No doubt reaching southerners in Congress was an uphill battle, because they wanted to know how the FEPC defined discrimination. They insisted upon a distinction between segregation and discrimination. Some felt that the FEPC legitimately might act against discrimination in employment, but any interference with segregation was considered taboo. Such interference would be construed as an attack upon the customs and traditions of the South—an attempt, by legal fiat, to impose social equality on people who did not want it.[15]

To help overcome the opposition of southern congressmen, Lulu White mounted a campaign in Texas to improve the chances of the FEPC's becoming a permanent entity. In 1945, she called upon Texas Senator Willie Lee O'Daniel to support FEPC, only to be told that "[the FEPC] was damaging to race relations, that it stirs up strife between people of the same race and class." As White pushed forward with her support of the FEPC, one can imagine why Senator O'Daniel would say that FEPC was damaging to race relations. Efforts to build on the fragile victories gained by blacks during World War II required changes in the status and thinking of white Texans. Not only did O'Daniel oppose such changes, but he was quick to blame job competition and violence on the FEPC and the NAACP. On the other hand, one could understand Lulu White's position. The postwar economy brought to the city many black veterans and other newcomers who were seeking jobs and encountering contrived obstacles. Naturally, they turned to Lulu White for help.[16]

Lulu White pushed for a permanent FEPC perhaps because, more than any government agency during the first half of the 1940s, this agency generated hope and indirectly engendered aggressive litigation concerning job discrimination in Texas. It is no wonder, then, that, between 1943 and 1945, Lulu White called rallies periodically to discuss with the black community the importance of FEPC. Less than one year after Truman became president, she joined the chorus of blacks around the country calling for him to act on this issue. White sent a telegram to the White House, asking President Truman "to use [his] influence to see to it that FEPC was made part of our government." Addressing the Senate, Truman read from that telegram: "Please vote cloture as often as is required. End Senate filibuster. Stop Senate fascism. Our sons were in Okinawa when Japan surrendered, where Americans fought and died together. Please give them a fighting chance to live when they return by voting for FEPC." In addition to the communication sent on behalf of the local NAACP chapter, White and her husband, Julius, also sent a telegram of protest.

Moreover, Lulu White joined labor unions in an unsuccessful attempt to send a delegate to the FEPC hearing held in Washington. The Southern Pacific Railroad Company refused to accept reservations for blacks and thus prevented the delegate from making the trip. Despite Lulu White's herculean efforts, the FEPC—hindered by inadequate funds, harassed by segregationist congressmen, and deserted by a president whose hands were tied—expired in 1946.[17]

To Lulu White, however, the FEPC was only one way to eradicate Jim Crow in the workplace. There were other methods. In what can be considered the most controversial stance of her career, White aligned herself with labor to achieve the desired result.

Lulu White and Labor

As head of the NAACP, Lulu White acquired first-hand knowledge of how deeply racial prejudice was embedded in the American economic and political system. She knew that for two decades the NAACP had struggled to garner support for an anti-lynching bill, to no avail. Although the white primary had been overturned, impediments to the black franchise, such as poll taxes, still existed. Given such facts, Lulu White reasoned that, if blacks were to overcome key obstacles, they would need help. They would need to join forces with other groups having shared political and economic interests.

After experimenting with different groups, strategies, and tactics, Lulu White embraced labor, the leftist proclivities of the Congress of Industrial Organizations (CIO) notwithstanding. As she put it, "You take your friends where you find them." White's idea of collaborating with labor was not a novel one. Blacks and labor faced many common problems in the South during the first half of the twentieth century. The South was a stronghold of anti-union, anti-black, and anti-female sentiments. Its powerful elected officials, from the local to the national level, defied the winds of political change that threatened to undermine the region's established order and way of life. Confronting this reality, the national office of the NAACP and organized labor in 1941 entered an alliance. This alliance was a marriage of convenience; blacks and labor faced some of the same enemies. In city halls, state legislatures, and Congress, southern Democrats, western Republicans, conservative northerners, and others viewed the two groups as posing threats to their jobs and to the status quo.[18]

With few exceptions, efforts to organize workers—white or black—remained extremely weak in Texas. This was true in Houston until 1930, when both the American Federation of Labor (AFL), a craft-oriented union, and the Congress of Industrial Organizations (CIO) a semiskilled union, initiated a general campaign in Dixie. Prior to 1935, the International Longshoreman's Association, a separate affiliate of the AFL, conducted most union activities in the city involving blacks. After 1935, it was the CIO that would be most visible in union activities among blacks. Between 1935 and 1945, the CIO was responsible for organizing blacks in several industries, including sugar refineries, oil, fruit, and tobacco. CIO field workers proved especially effective in organizing black steel workers at Hughes Tool Company, Sheffield Steel Company, and the Dedman Foundry. Through these industries, by 1945 almost two thousand blacks had joined the United Steel Workers of America's local union.

While the CIO's campaign in attracting formerly unorganized black workers would prove beneficial in the early 1940s, labor unions still posed problems for blacks, whites, and the NAACP. Sometimes black workers joined enthusiastically; in other cases, they were skeptical and distrustful, as the bitter experience of discrimination had taught them to be. The CIO's interest in and activities with black workers impressed the NAACP, but the latter was constrained from totally embracing the union because of the latter's alleged Communist ties. Likewise, many whites opposed the union movement in general, and the CIO in particular, because of its interracial character and Communist affiliations. To white southern conservatives, the push for civil rights by the CIO and the NAACP was part of a Communist conspiracy. In their minds, both the NAACP and the CIO were led, inspired, and dominated by Communists.[19]

Because of the recurrent labeling of the CIO as Communist, by 1945 the NAACP leadership began to pull away from the CIO. This was not the case for Lulu White. She retained her relationship with labor and used the Communist threat to her advantage. While White was willing and eager to say that she did not embrace Communism, she used the threat posed by Communism to press the NAACP agenda against racism and discrimination in the workplace. In a word, she became more visible and more vocal in her alliance with labor.

Through association with a number of friends who were members, supporters, and organizers of union activities, Lulu White had acquired some knowledge of the labor movement in Houston and in Texas. It was not until she be-came NAACP executive secretary, though, that she acquired first-hand knowl-edge of the activities of the major unions, especially the CIO. White was im-pressed with the CIO's educational program, which increased blacks' desire to struggle for racial equality and made them less willing to tolerate gradualism. Administering this program was a CIO Political Action Committee (PAC) formed in the summer of 1943. The purpose of the PAC was to build a political machine rooted in a national network of local unions and city and state indus-trial councils embracing liberal, progressive, and civil rights activities. This PAC divided the nation into fourteen regional centers and organized branches in states, cities, and wards. Operating under the premise that organized, informed, and active voters were essential for meeting anti-union conservatives at the polls, the PAC made voter education and registration core activities.[20]

The aforementioned PAC activities went hand in hand with the civil rights movement in Texas. Especially encouraging to Lulu White, the CIO's campaign for voting rights was creative and wide-ranging, combining such activities as education, organizing, and publicity. Partially due to the PAC's campaign efforts in 1943, three powerful southern congressmen lost their house seats. Two lost their bid for reelection; and Representative Martin Dies of Texas, chair of the House Un-American Activities Committee (HUAC), withdrew from the race once he learned that the CIO PAC was campaigning against him. Recognizing their effectiveness, White utilized PAC members as teachers for the many citi-zenship classes that the local NAACP chapter sponsored before and after *Smith v. Allwright* (1944).[21] Also, the PAC aided union members in paying poll taxes and in sponsoring rallies to get out the vote in elections held after 1944.

Because Lulu White established a special bond with labor early in her career, it did not take much prodding for her to support the CIO-led United Steel Work-ers Strike of 1946. On January 21, 1946, the national officers of the United Steel Workers of America ordered 750,000 steel workers to cease work and to picket the steel industries of America for a wage increase to 25 cents an hour. When it became apparent that closing down the steel industries would paralyze the na-tional economy, the president of the United States recommended what he con-sidered an equitable solution: raising workers' salaries to 18.5 cents per hour. After some negotiating, many industries accepted the national wage formula, signed contracts, and sent their workers back to the production line.[22]

Unions in the South, particularly those in Houston, did not accept the pro-posed contract because they faced different problems. Having enjoyed wage rate differentials peculiar to the South and having imposed substandard cost-of-living increases on the workers, many industries in this region refused to accept the national wage increase and would not sign a contract with an anti-discrimination clause. So, when these industries—namely, Hughes Tool; Mosher; Reed Roller Bit; Texas Electric Casing; American Can; Continental Can; Tennessee Coal and Iron; American Chain and Cable; Dedman Foundry; Reheem Manufacturing; and Sheffield Steel—attempted to set a wage rate of less than 18.5 cents per hour, five thousand black workers and nine thousand white workers decided to strike. This strike had repercussions in almost every industry in the Houston area. A prolonged steel walkout would halt Houston's construction and reconversion program for at least a year; loss of big weekly payrolls would be felt immediately by the city's retailers. During this strike, black workers refused to work as scabs, despite promises of higher-paying, permanent jobs. The unity of these black workers was due largely to the organizational strategy and leadership of Richard Randolph Grovey and his cohorts: F. T. Henry, Grovey's aide; R. L. Phelps, president of Local 2457; Reed Roller Bit Company's team of Jones and Moore; Alphonse Certenburd, chief shop steward at Sheffield Steel; J. L. Robs of Sheffield Steel; Oscar Lewis at Texas Electric Company; A. C. Ball and James Williams of Tennessee Coal and Iron; and Rev. Lewis Harris of Hughes Tool. Additionally, Grovey had the support of Lulu White and the NAACP. White served as a link between Grovey's group and the labor wing of the national NAACP. Additionally, she and Julius White gave moral and financial support to the striking workers.[23]

After several meetings with management, and after a few acts of scattered violence, many industries began to yield. On the twenty-ninth day of a seventy-day strike, Sheffield Steel signed a contract with CIO workers. Shortly after that, other industries followed suit. Most Texans seemed happy that the strike was about to end and were jubilant about agreeing to a wage increase of 18.5 cents. By the sixtieth day of the strike, all companies except thirteen had agreed with the striking workers.

In its discriminatory policies, Hughes Tool probably was the most blatant among the Houston companies; it also was the most intransigent in its refusal to meet striking workers' demands. Hughes's situation was complicated by the existence of the Independent Metal Workers Union. From the beginning of this strike, Grovey knew that labor would have a vicious fight with management at this company, which employed 1,500 blacks. Therefore, he tried to impress upon management the need for social and economic justice. He emphasized the point that his group was only asking for justice and an equal break. In making his case, Grovey argued that the company's custom had been to hire whites at 60 cents an hour and blacks at 50 cents an hour, although they were performing the same tasks. He further pointed out that it had been the plant's custom to grant white workers 5 cents an hour increase each thirty days until they had reached 75 cents an hour and to grant blacks 2 cents an hour every six months, if the supervisor requested it. Therefore a white worker in one year could raise his pay to 87.5 cents per hour, while the black worker had to wait one to sixteen years before he could reach the rate of 68.5 cents per hour.[24]

When Grovey reported Hughes's practices to Lulu White and the NAACP, they worked with him in developing a strategy to attack the Jim Crow practices at the plant and encouraged him to continue his fight. Grovey then informed his men that the strike would continue and that "the entire CIO was committed to fight to the finish against those companies that were holding out against signing proper and acceptable contracts."

On April 19, 1946, nine out of thirteen plants signed acceptable contracts, with Dedman, Mosher, Reed Roller Bit, and Hughes Tool still refusing. On April 27, the former three signed an agreement; and on April 30, 1946, the strike ended when Hughes Tool acceded to workers' demands. The strikers received a wage increase of 17 cents an hour and contracts that barred wage differentials and discriminatory practices. More important, the majority of these workers returned to their jobs. Needless to say, Lulu and Julius joined Grovey and other workers in a day-long gala (which included a banquet) to savor their labor victory.[25]

Despite the historic CIO victory in helping to eradicate discrimination in the workplace and in securing wage increases for black workers, some blacks, particularly those of the Negro Independent Union, tried to launch a campaign against the CIO at Hughes Tool. C. W. Rice, president of the Texas Negro Business and Laboring Men's Association and self-proclaimed spokesperson for the independent union movement among black locals, was the leading critic of both AFL and CIO in Houston. Rice's argument was that white men dominated these powerful unions and thus limited blacks' participation in decision making. Therefore, blacks should organize their own union over which they would have control. In other words, blacks should be about self-help and racial solidarity. It is worth noting that Rice's assertions were perceived by some as deceptive, in that he was operating an all-black union through which he curried favor with white employers.[26]

Perhaps to downplay the underhanded dealings that allegedly he made to feather his own nest, Rice worked assiduously, with every means at his disposal, to drive the major labor unions out of Houston. To convince the public, Rice appealed to racial consciousness in newspaper propaganda. Failing in this endeavor, he then misused the NAACP's name. Because of Rice's action, Lulu White asked Walter White to expel him from the association, writing, "Here are some clippings which I want you to look at and send down an ultimatum on Rice." White's sense was that Rice was "anti every thing. . . . that [meant] progress for [black] people." Writing a weekly column for the *Christian American,* Rice often gave his bias opinion on a number of subjects, such as "Do you want your daughter to marry a nigger? The FEPC is a menace to white America. The CIO and AFL should be outlawed." Rice's syndicated column did not pose a problem per se, since an editorial is an uncensored form of publication. The problem, however, came when Rice told his readers that the advice he was giving came "from the Fact Finding Committee of the Association for the Advancement of Colored People." Rice refrained from using the term "Association for the Advancement of Colored People" after several discussions with Lulu White, in which she told him in no uncertain terms to cease the practice.[27]

Apparently, C. W. Rice did not really reflect the sentiments or actions of most black laboring men. Not only did they continue to join the CIO, but also they engaged in a number of AFL strikes, the most notable of which was the Houston Municipal Strike of 1946. On February 20, 1946, the *Houston Chronicle* notified its readers that 700 to 900 of the city's 3,800 employees had voted to go on strike. This strike came in response to a rising cost of living, coupled with a decrease in wages. Workers were demanding a 25-percent wage hike. Lulu White played the same role in this strike as she had in the United Steel Workers strike. She provided moral and financial support and conveyed advice on strategy from the labor wing of the NAACP.[28]

Largely responsible for this strike were the city-county employee unions, Local 1317 and the International Hod Carriers Building and Common Laborers Union of America. Prior to 1945, unionized workers of Houston never had threatened or carried out either strikes or militant activities. However, 1946 was different. By the end of World War II, major changes had taken place in the American and the Houston labor markets. The number of workers increased—black and white, male and female. Also, those employed as skilled craftspeople and semiskilled operators doubled between 1940 and 1946. As the economy expanded and brought more jobs to Houston, the workers began to demand higher wages. Since 1942, the workers of these two unions had held talks with the city government concerning working conditions. These meetings continued until 1946 without any significant changes in the workers' situation. Energized somewhat by the United Steel Workers Strike of January 1946, these unions demanded a 25-percent wage hike. When the city refused this request and offered 17 percent instead, the leaders called a municipal strike on February 19, 1946, almost paralyzing the city for a week.[29]

The city leaders responded quickly. Their first reaction was to replace the striking workers, on the grounds that the strike was illegal. City Manager James V. Nagle authorized the Civil Service Commission to seek replacements for the striking workers in essential services—replacements whom he likely assumed would be black. When Nagle issued this order, he did not take into consideration the roles played by Lulu White and the NAACP in the labor movement.

He probably was unaware that White served as a network activator for the labor movement, that she had daily contact with Moses Leroy of the AFL and Richard Randolph Grovey of the CIO, and that she helped to politicize black workers and instruct them concerning their rights, while Moses Leroy and Richard Grovey helped to galvanize the workers and potential scabs around the strike. Therefore, if Nagle thought that a throng of potential strikebreakers existed within the black community, he was wrong. Five days into the strike, the Civil Service Commission had made only 140 to 150 referrals, and local papers reported that no blacks had voted to break the picket line. When the U.S. Employment Service refused to intervene, based on its policy of noninvolvement in local disputes, city services, garbage collection, and street maintenance came to a virtual halt. Negotiations among city officials, unions, the city council, and the mayor then began in earnest.[30]

At first a labor committee, formed to negotiate with the mayor and city council, met a great deal of resistance. This recalcitrance was based on the city's refusal to recognize two of the chief spokespeople on the committee, D. W. Maxwell and A. J. Bannon. Reacting to an impasse with the city, Maxwell called for a "labor holiday." He requested that all AFL members in nonessential industries take a holiday and march on City Hall to protest the "arrogance for the welfare of city employees." Apparently the march was successful, in that more than five thousand AFL members converged on City Hall. The chief of police then escorted Maxwell, along with three other union representatives, to meet with the mayor and city council. In the brief meeting that ensued, the two parties reached a compromise. Workers would get their wage hike. City Hall would not formally recognize union representatives but instead would refer to them as a citizen's committee. Despite the manner of referring to union representatives, the average laborer considered the strike a success, because he or she returned to work with a wage increase and without being fired. To black laborers engaged in this and other strikes throughout the city, the Houston Municipal Strike of 1946 reinforced the belief that, without widespread association with organized labor, black workers possessed very little bargaining power in disputes with employers.[31]

To Lulu White it seemed that, to the extent that labor unions protected all workers from discrimination by employers and raised the wages of workers who were paid less than their white counterparts, they advanced the interests of their black workers and furthered the NAACP's goal of eradicating economic injustice. By 1946, White had come to view the labor movement as a liberalizing force in the civil rights struggle, a force that could help bring the country nearer to actual democracy. Because she viewed the movement as a voice of domestic liberalism, White helped to organize a Houston Area Labor Conference on September 28, 1946. She was the only female on the program when the conference adopted resolutions calling for unity of labor and the abolition of Jim Crow schools, poll taxes, lynching, and HUAC. The conference also adopted a controversial resolution calling "For World Peace—For the Freedom of Oppressed Peoples." This resolution raised the eyebrows of Gloster Current, the NAACP's national director of branches, who sent a memorandum to Walter White noting that the "Houston NAACP Labor Committee saw fit to take a position on foreign policy which paralleled that of Moscow. This is friendship and collaboration of [the] USSR." Current commented further that the political orientation of several of these unions was obvious.[32]

While the above resolutions expressed the philosophy of Lulu White, they do not shed much light on her role in the labor movement. The labor movement among blacks in Houston included public spokespersons and network activators, not simply articulate leaders and a mass of followers. To be sure, White's effectiveness was closely connected to the work of such labor movement advance men as Richard Grovey, Sid Hilliard, Sidney Hasgett, Heman Marion Sweatt, and Moses Leroy. These men worked publicly organizing black workers and privately negotiating with white employers for better wages and working conditions. They risked their reputations and their livelihoods by accepting leadership roles in the fledgling labor movement, by informing Lulu White of the discrimination heaped upon black workers, and by developing with her strategies for securing economic parity. Lulu White's sharp tongue and bold speeches made her widely popular with the labor movement. Yet in essence she was a network activator and gadfly for the movement. For example, in the elections of 1946, she posed the following questions to many candidates: "Are you in favor of equal opportunity? Do you support organized labor? Will you support or oppose legislation planned to curb organized labor in our state?" Depending on the response given, White generated support for, or opposition to, the candidate.[33]

Lulu White's pro-labor stance was magnified during the summer of 1946, when the death of a black man gave rise to the largest mass protest demonstration that the city of Houston ever had witnessed. White and the NAACP not only converted the funeral for Berry Branch, killed by a white bus driver, into a rally, but used this occasion to denounce discrimination and to call for a coalition with labor. All labor unions in the city were represented at the funeral, and CIO and AFL officials participated on the program and served as pallbearers. Blacks of all classes, as well as socialists, labor leaders, and white radicals were there. Houston's two white newspapers both carried stories about the event, and both branded Lulu White an agent of the "Red" movement.[34]

At this point, the Communist label seems not to have bothered Lulu White, for she continued to stand up for labor. In response to strikes throughout the city and state, the Texas Legislature in 1947 passed a Right to Work Act, designed to curtail and restrict labor unions' activities. More specifically, this law denied public employees the right to bargain collectively. Adding insult to injury, the State of Texas embraced the Taft-Hartley Bill, which outlawed the closed shop but allowed a measure of union security. This bill called for a contract requiring workers to join the union after signing a contract, as opposed to joining before employment. It also codified the right to work, according to which states could forbid the requirement of union membership as a condition of employment. Additionally, the bill provided for a "cooling off" period for both sides before employees resorted to strike.[35]

Labor leaders throughout the country denounced the law. Lulu White joined the chorus and made several speeches across the state, trying to garner support for its repeal. When she appeared in Galveston to speak on this subject, Carter Wesley, whom White had chided for supporting Taft-Hartley, reported in the *Informer* that "the Galveston Branch had been taken over by Communists like the Houston Branch." White shrugged off this allegation, saying that these newspaper writers (including Wesley) and the FBI were present at the meeting at the urging of a "stool pigeon black woman who wanted to discredit [her]." In part due to statements by black critics such as Carter Wesley, most whites interpreted Lulu White's support for labor as the work of outside agitators, who surreptitiously were using White to change the economic order of this country. In the future, the Communist label would haunt White like a fire alarm in the night.

The Communist Threat

The accusation that Lulu White was a Communist arose primarily because of her affiliation with members of the CIO who were alleged to have Communist and/or socialist proclivities. When the CIO began its effort to organize unskilled workers in Texas in the mid-1930s, the Texas Communist Party became a formal and visible organization. In fact, a few of the grassroots CIO organizers were members of the Communist party. By the fall of 1935, the Texas Communist Party was firmly established in Houston, and literature bearing its logo was passed out everywhere along the Gulf Coast, especially where strikes occurred. Throughout the 1930s, the Communist party in Texas (Houston included) remained small and ineffectual, with no more than two hundred members at any given time. The CIO's move from left to center notwithstanding, throughout the 1940s the Communists maintained their influence in certain locals of the CIO. While traditional black leaders either joined in the "Red Scare" against the CIO at the end of World War II or remained neutral, awaiting proof of the organization's stand against Communism, Lulu White worked openly with the CIO before and after it made a public announcement to cleanse itself of such influence.[36] A review of her relationship with labor may shed some light on her position.

More than anything else, probably it was Lulu White's association with labor lawyers Arthur J. Mandell and Herman Wright that caused many individuals, white and black, to label her a Communist. Mandell and Wright were lawyers for the CIO during the 1930s and 1940s and were considered the "legal bulwark" behind the CIO's efforts to organize black workers along the Texas Gulf Coast. No doubt, Lulu White and these lawyers were in contact quite frequently, inasmuch as they took similar means to achieve a common goal—advancing the civil and economic rights of blacks. Though Mandell and Wright denied that they were Communists, their activities and the "left-of-center" approaches used to advance the cause of all workers gave the appearance that they were radicals and "anti-establishment."[37]

Arthur J. Mandell moved to Houston in 1930 and began practicing law shortly thereafter. It was not long before he apparently realized that his Jewish background, together with his political and economic views, placed him at odds with the Houston establishment. Consequently, he joined the CIO's struggle to organize labor unions and eventually became the organization's lawyer. Mandell was particularly active with the National Maritime Union (NMU) and with the maritime Communist and leftist factions.[38]

Herman Wright came to Houston from Australia in 1938. Almost immediately he became a follower of Mandell's radical politics and subsequently was Mandell's partner. Later the two would become known as labor agitators. In 1939, when a Galveston strike lasted from April through June and caused a great deal of disruption and violence, Mandell's firm became linked to Communism. The strike occurred when a dispute arose among the National Maritime Union (which represented many American seamen on the Gulf and Atlantic coasts), Standard Oil of New Jersey, and three other companies. The strikers' demands were familiar—higher wages, better working conditions, and unionization of more of the seamen operating tankers. Violence broke out when the workers prevented oil shipments from leaving Texas ports. This outbreak of violence played into the hands of the anti-union forces—newspapers, police, city leaders—who blamed the strike on foreign agents. From that time forward, the "Communist" label became associated with Mandell's firm, which represented the NMU.[39]

To make matters worse, in June 1947, Mandell and Wright added the civil rights struggle to their list of reforms needed in America and joined the local chapter of the NAACP. Herman Wright almost immediately became a member of the Legal Redress Committee. Needless to say, the membership of these radical, socialist labor lawyers was not greeted by jubilation in the black community. Many NAACP members, especially those who were caught up in the anti-Communist hysteria, were displeased.

At the time when Mandell and Wright joined the organization, Lulu White and Carter Wesley were engaged in a bitter dispute over whether to integrate the University of Texas or establish a separate black university in Houston. This disagreement, to be discussed in detail later, prompted Wesley to begin an unrelenting attack on Lulu White for what he called "Communist influence in the NAACP." In July 1947, he wrote in his *Informer* that "our NAACP [is] taken over by the infiltration of the Communists through the stupidity and nearsightedness of our leaders." In Wesley's opinion, these Communists were not merely allies of Lulu White but were dominating her thinking and influencing the formulation of branch policies. "They [helped] mimeograph sharp attacks against race prejudice and organized committees to go before City Council and protest discrimination. Our leaders think they are God," wrote Wesley.[40]

Wesley later would admit that he did not know if White was a Communist, but he knew the company she kept: "When a Communist is willing to go to Negro houses and drink liquor with them and call them by their first name, they know that as far as these white people are concerned, the race question is solved," wrote Wesley. It was common knowledge that Lulu White and Herman Wright had established a close friendship and that Wright was one among many whites who frequented her house and attended her twentieth wedding anniversary celebration. White's history and demeanor make it hard to accuse her of allowing anyone to do her thinking for her. Whatever White did, she did because she wanted to or because of her dedication to furthering racial integration.[41]

At the same time Wesley was making the above allegations, the Federal Bureau of Investigation (FBI) was launching a concerted effort to monitor all black organizations and individuals whom it deemed subversive. The surveillance of black Americans was established as part of the FBI's responsibilities during the administration of Franklin Roosevelt, but the monitoring intensified during the Cold War era. Thus, in 1938, in the area of domestic intelligence, Roosevelt expanded the FBI and encouraged it to gather information on the activities of individuals labeled "subversive." That same year, the FBI included a special "Negro Question" category as part of its regular Communist infiltration investigations. One year later, Roosevelt expanded the FBI's civil and criminal jurisdiction to include at least a cursory examination, if not a complete investigation, of almost every type of civil rights case from voter registration to police brutality and lynching. For more than twenty years after that, the FBI and its director, J. Edgar Hoover, pursued these dual mandates at their own discretion, investigating the political affairs of black activists and organizations thoroughly while treating civil rights investigations nonchalantly, if at all.[42]

In September 1947, the FBI sent out a circular letter to all its directors and field workers, asking them "to submit to the Bureau any information obtained from reliable and established sources indicating Communist infiltration, influence or connection of the local NAACP chapters." While admitting that the national office of the NAACP was not associated with Communist activities, the FBI insisted that some local chapters were "under the direct influence of the Communist elements." Because of this belief, whether accurate or not, the FBI began a "dead file" designed for local chapters but entitled "Communist Infiltration of the National Office." Information contained in this file was sent to the U.S. attorney general's Loyal Review Board, which had been established to analyze the information and determine if any of it suggested activities subversive to the government. Once such an analysis was completed, the attorney general published a list of individuals and organizations deemed to be anti-government. The list, published in December 1947, named the Civil Rights Congress and all of its affiliates as anti-government entities. One of the affiliates mentioned was located in Houston and had the same office and address as the Houston chapter of the NAACP—Room 288 of the Pilgrim Building, at 222 West Dallas.[43]

The Civil Rights Congress was formed in April 1946 as a merger between two organizations, the International Labor Defense and the National Federation of Constitutional Liberties. According to FBI records, this organization was not "dedicated to the broader issue of civil liberties, but to the defense of individual Communists and the Communist Party, and controlled by individuals who were either members of the Communist Party or openly loyal to it." In December 1947, the Civil Rights Congress put out a call for a legislative conference scheduled on January 17 and 18, 1948, in Washington, D.C. Members of the Civil Rights Congress asked Lulu White to sign the call for this conference, but she failed to respond. Nevertheless, when the flyer was sent out announcing the conference, White's name was listed as one of its sponsors. This undoubtedly was one of the reasons the local branch was viewed as an affiliate of the Civil Rights Congress.[44]

Upon hearing and reading about the Civil Rights Congress being linked to the Houston branch of the NAACP, Thurgood Marshall moved quickly to quash any speculations by the FBI. First he contacted Lulu White, then relayed her reply to J. Edgar Hoover, in order "to keep the record straight." "I have received the following report from our Houston Branch," wrote Marshall. "Neither at this time nor any other time has this office been affiliated with the Office of the Civil Rights Congress. It is true that they did hold about three meetings here about a year ago [but they are not part of the organization]." When Hoover replied, denying that the list had been sent from his office to the Dallas newspaper or that his office had anything to do with compiling the list, Marshall responded in kind, either facetiously or naïvely, saying, "I am happy to know that the listing does not appear in your file."[45]

Evidence reveals that Marshall, when he requested that Hoover clear this matter up, he probably was unaware that Hoover had instructed a field agent to make a "very discreet check on the Pilgrim Building #228" the day after the Dallas newspaper published the subversive list, telling the agent "to furnish the results [to Hoover] telephonically." The agent reported his findings the same day he received the communiqué. There was nothing in the office indicating that the Civil Rights Congress maintained an office in Houston. But "a check at the Post Office reflect[ed] that P.O. Box 1988 was rented on July 1, 1946. The application was signed by [deleted from FBI files] who gave as her business address: Civil Rights Congress, 228 Pilgrim Building, Houston, Texas . . . On the letterhead she is listed as the Temporary Executive Secretary." A further check showed that White had received two copies of the pamphlet, "The Southern People's Congress Program."[46]

Throughout this investigation, Lulu White maintained that she was not a Communist, and that the Civil Rights Congress was not a Communist organization. She insisted that her association with any labor organization reflected her concern for civil liberties. So strong did the attacks from both whites and blacks become, however, that Lulu White no longer could ignore them. Responding to Carter Wesley's charge that she was affiliated with Communists (Mandell and Wright), Lulu White wrote to Gloster Current: "I have talked to Maceo about this Communist business. He told me that the NAACP did not ask persons to declare their party affiliation before they join the organization." In this civil rights movement, White was of the opinion that "Negroes are supposed to take friends where they find them."[47]

To many, Lulu White seemed to move even farther to the left when she openly supported Henry A. Wallace's candidacy for president of the United States in 1948. Wallace, the Progressive party's presidential nominee, had served as secretary of agriculture in the 1930s and as vice president in FDR's third term. Between 1941 and 1945, few politicians were praised more highly by the NAACP than Wallace. He was lauded for his stance on racism, poll taxes, and Jim Crow. Even when President Harry S. Truman dropped him from the ticket, the NAACP still supported him. This situation changed, however, when it became apparent to the NAACP in 1948 that Wallace's candidacy would take black voters away from the Democratic party. Even so, a number of blacks continued to support Wallace. Among these were such notables as W. E. B. DuBois, Roscoe Dunjee, Gordon Hancock, Lena Horne, Paul Robeson, Lulu White, and Margaret Bush Wilson.[48]

On certain issues, Wallace appeared ambivalent; on others, he was either liberal or conservative. On civil rights he was considered a moderate and on foreign policy a Communist sympathizer. Arguing that he was neither Communist nor socialist and affirming that he wanted trade, not war, with the Soviet Union, Wallace was very sensitive to the interests and needs of the working class. Thus, for individuals who were dissatisfied with the Democratic party or disillusioned with the Republican party, and for members of the Communist party who had been unable to field a candidate of their own, the Progressive party, with Wallace as standard bearer, offered a suitable alternative.[49]

The three presidential candidates in 1948 were Republican Governor Thomas E. Dewey, Democratic incumbent Harry S. Truman, and Progressive party candidate Henry A. Wallace. Neither Dewey's personality nor his campaign aroused enthusiasm among his supporters. As far as Truman was concerned, there were signs as early as 1946 that he had lost control of the economic and political situation in this country. Labor resented his reaction to the railroad strikes. Farmers attempted to roll back Truman's meat prices. Conservatives denounced his civil rights proposals, and his "Doctrine of Containment" outraged Communist sympathizers in the North. Because of these views, the Progressives thought that their candidate, Henry Wallace, had a good chance of winning.

Supporters of the Communist Party USA had worked quietly since 1945 for the creation of a third party to field a presidential candidate in 1948. The existence of this voting bloc undoubtedly was a factor in convincing Wallace to run against Truman. Nevertheless, Wallace made his own decision to become a presidential candidate, and he did so at the request of many non-Communists. It should be noted, however, that Communists and pro-Wallace non-Communists had different interests in this campaign. For Lulu White, Wallace's campaign represented a radical, forward-looking approach to solving the race problem and bringing about economic parity in this country. Moreover, Wallace's platform included demands for a one-dollar-per-hour minimum wage, abolition of the poll tax, desegregation, repeal of the Taft-Hartley labor law, daycare centers for working mothers, and opposition to the military draft.[50]

The day after Wallace announced his candidacy, the pro-Wallace forces began working to establish a Texas Wallace campaign headquarters. This effort came to fruition on March 21, 1948, when the Wallace for President Committee held its first state meeting in Austin. The organizers included Elvierto Bela of Laredo, Harriet Leary of San Antonio, H. K. Deuchare of Galveston, Pat Lunford of Baytown, and Herman Wright of Houston. There were reports that Lulu White was part of this group, but she denied the rumors. When the news media heard of Lulu White's alleged involvement, pandemonium broke loose. Many newspapers carried headlines such as "An NAACP Official Endorses Wallace." The *Austin American-Statesman* reported that the "Director of the NAACP Was Elected Vice Chair of a Statewide Movement for Wallace." The NAACP leadership was very disturbed about this matter and called Lulu White's actions into question. White denied any involvement and asked these newspapers to print retractions. Never cast as a moderate, Lulu White made it clear in writing to the editors that she did not endorse Wallace in her official capacity, but that she personally "reserve[d] the right to support the candidate of her choice in any election."[51]

Having made her position clear to the public and the NAACP, Lulu White was active and visible in Wallace's two-day whistle-stop tour of Houston on September 28 and 29, 1948. The first of these hectic days included a Wallace press conference and speeches by the candidate at radio station KPRC, at the Black Businessmen Club's luncheon, and at a tea in the home of Lulu White. Present at White's reception was Paul Robeson, the black actor, singer, and professed socialist, whose passport had been revoked. Already a thorn in the side of many white conservatives, White now became a menace to be reckoned with, as a result of publicly supporting Wallace, embracing Paul Robeson, and holding a reception at her home for a racially mixed audience. White's position was underlined by Wallace the next day of his tour, when he spoke to approximately four hundred persons—black and white—at the Music Hall.[52]

While in Houston, Wallace encountered many hecklers who threw omelets and eggs at him and almost forced him out of town. The newspaper account of his two-day visit could give one the impression that Wallace was a viable candidate, although in fact he was only a third party candidate who stood no chance of winning. While Lulu White, along with a small number of other blacks throughout the country, supported Wallace, there is no evidence that she persuaded other blacks to do likewise. She took a fearless stand on Wallace's candidacy because she believed that Wallace shared some of her views on bettering the condition of "the common man and woman." In part because of Wallace's campaign, Carter Wesley's labeling of White as a Communist, and her affiliation with several socialists, Lulu White's name appeared on HUAC's list in 1948.[53]

The indomitable Lulu White was not one to walk away from a struggle and silently endure the pains of discrimination. She resolved to fight back, the Communist label notwithstanding. But her fortitude and courage were matched by the dogged cynicism of many of her critics, not least of whom was Carter Wesley. Wesley's constant bashing of her in his newspaper was enough to convince many blacks that, in the struggle for civil rights, Lulu White's behavior had moved from disorderly conduct to radicalism. Wesley, in an editorial dated June 11, 1949, cited what he saw as yet another case of her flirtation with socialists. He reported that Lulu White had joined forces with the CIO, the Civil Rights Congress, and the Texas Progressive party in signing a petition to protest Judge Harold Medina's jailing of the editor of the *Daily Worker*, along with three socialists, for contempt of court in a New York conspiracy trial. In Wesley's opinion, the actions of the petitioners were not spontaneous protests by aggrieved citizens but had been carefully orchestrated. Wesley was partially right in his assessment. Lulu White was an adept practitioner of coalition-building politics and would ally herself with almost any group if doing so meant bringing about political and economic parity for blacks. Her action in the above case, however, only fueled speculation that she was doing the bidding of the Communists. Because of this incident, Carter Wesley again called for White's resignation. This time she capitulated, stepping down almost immediately after publication of this editorial.[54]

Even after Lulu White left the helm of the local branch of the NAACP in 1949, she still was followed by the FBI. In 1951, an informant reported that, although she no longer worked in the office of the local chapter, Communist literature still was being sent to her at that address. In 1953, the same informant reported that Lulu White was not as active in the Communist party as she had been in the past and that she did not influence her successor, Christia Adair, who was described as anti-Communist. In 1956, when students at Texas Southern University (TSU) staged a protest against Governor Alan Shivers, who was guest speaker at the inauguration of Samuel M. Nabrit, TSU's second president, Lulu White was listed by the FBI as the instigator of that protest. The field agent bolstered this speculation by sending the FBI director a newspaper clipping under the headline, "New President Inaugurated: Shivers Ignores Pickets to Give TSU Speech."[55]

The TSU demonstration was a reaction to a speech made by Shivers condemning the Supreme Court's decision in *Brown v. Board of Education* (1954) and against his stance on integration of schools in particular. A poll taken by the informant revealed that most of the TSU student body favored the protest, because of the governor's segregationist stand. When Shivers arrived on campus on March 14, 1956, he met protesters carrying placards reading "We want integration, not Shivers"; "Not anti-TSU, just anti-Shivers"; "Alan Shivers, you sent your boy to an integrated school; why object to others?" This demonstration supposedly was staged by the local chapter of the NAACP, along with TSU students. But as Carter Wesley later would write, "Those on the inside knew that Lulu was the reason why the picketing came off. The people of the Local Chapter gave every indication of not wanting the picket to go forward . . . but Lulu consulted her lawyers and when told it would not be illegal to picket, she gathered her forces and went out to Texas Southern University." The demonstration proceeded without incident, but Lulu White was hounded by the FBI until her death.[56]

There is no hard data to support the claim that White was a Communist. But as happened with many whites, the combined forces of the Great Depression, the New Deal, and World War II pushed black political activities and thoughts leftward. Like their white counterparts, a number of African American reformers were affected by Marxist and non-Marxist class theories. Neither the NAACP nor the Urban League was immune to the economic and political impulses of the thirties and forties. Within the ranks of both organizations were individuals who advocated a more militant course of economic action. Young intellectuals such as E. Franklin Frazier and Ralph Bunch held that an expanded federal authority in the economy required new strategies and more radical demands by blacks for a comprehensive economic program. Somewhat impatient with what she felt was the unwillingness of the federal government to provide blacks with equal economic opportunities, Lulu White turned to building coalitions with other groups who suffered similar fates. What complicated her willingness to embrace an alternative economic perspective was her inclination to entertain an organized political struggle outside traditional legal, educational, and personal lobbying tactics associated with the NAACP. But if the means she employed were different, her objective always remained the same as that of the NAACP: to force the government to extend and expand the scope of its efforts to become more inclusive of African Americans. Lulu White's flirtation with alleged Communists in relation to her role in the NAACP was one of loyal opposition. There is no record to indicate that she tried to sway anyone to the leftist cause. In fact, her husband's business interests would have militated against that course. Her associations with individuals with socialist proclivities sometimes were useful in coalition building. At other times, they amounted to little more than a personal protest when government policies appeared antithetical to black needs.

Lulu White was no ordinary woman. Because she refused to accept the economic constraints created by the subordinate position of blacks in the workforce, many thought that she exhibited disorderly conduct, and still others felt that she was a radical inspired by Communism. To be sure, most times Lulu White's conduct was the antithesis of what "finer womanhood" dictated; but if she exhibited disorderly conduct, it was because wisdom born from experience had taught her that "power concedes nothing without a demand." White recognized that, in the Houston and Texas contexts, any progressive solution to the labor problem threatened the hierarchical division of race. She knew that, in a choice between political, social, and labor reform and the status quo, white Texans would choose to retain their superior position above blacks. Thus, she pushed for an integrated society, a society in which blacks would have the right to compete for jobs and would have an opportunity to accomplish at a level determined by their qualifications.

Lulu Belle Madison White as a student at Prairie View College, 1928. This photograph
hangs in Alumni Hall, Prairie View University. Courtesy Prairie View University

The home of Lulu B. White and Julius White, 2620 Tuam Street, Houston, in 1998.
Photograph © 1998 by Earlie Hudnall, Jr. All rights reserved. Used by permission.

Lulu White at a social gathering of the NAACP. (Other men and women are unidentified.) Courtesy Texas Southern University Archives

Julius White and Joe Louis in the home of Lulu and Julius White, Jan. 19, 1946. Courtesy Darrell Beck, photo by Sid

NAACP State Convention, Waco, Texas, 1954. *Front row, left to right:* Gloster Current, unidentified, C. V. Adair, two unidentified, H. Boyd Hall, Lulu White, unidentified, A. Maceo Smith. Item CN-09239, Juanita Jewel Shanks Craft Collection, Center for American History, Univ. of Texas at Austin. Used by permission.

NAACP mass meeting, Victoria, Texas, circa early 1940s. At far left are Julius and Lulu White. Item CN-09378, Juanita Jewel Shanks Craft Collection, Center for American History, University of Texas at Austin. Used by permission.

NAACP gathering to "Welcome Marshall, Sweatt, Durham, Burnett, Jones," March, 1950, Salem Baptist, Dallas, Texas. *Left to right:* U. S. Tate, two unidentified, A. M. Smith, Lulu White, Thurgood Marshall, J. J. Jones, J. E. Robinson, Juanita Craft, Donald Jones. Item CN-07645, Juanita Jewel Shanks Craft Collection, Center for American History, University of Texas at Austin

NAACP Louisiana-Texas Training Conference, Shreveport, Louisiana, Nov., 1946. *Front row, left to right:* Daniel Byrd, Leslie Perry, G. Current, J. H. Clouser, H. Boyd. *Second row, left to right:* Thurgood Marshall, unidentified, A. M. Smith, unidentified, Juanita Craft, Lulu White, C.V. Adair. Item CN-07646, Juanita Jewel Shanks Craft Collection, Center for American History, University of Texas at Austin

Celebration marking the twentieth wedding anniversary of Lulu B. White and Julius White, June 20, 1948. *Left to right:* Julius White, Lulu White, unidentified, Elizabeth James. Courtesy Texas Southern University Archives, Houston

Chat-an-Hour Coffee Club Christmas party in the late 1950s (after the death of Lulu B. White). Courtesy Texas Southern University Archives

CHAPTER 5

The Great Divide
Lulu White, the Black Community, and Equal Educational Opportunities

From Reconstruction through the twentieth century, Texans of African American descent engaged in a productive quest for educational opportunities. In fact, equality in education had been the chief objective of the Texas NAACP since the establishment of a statewide organization in 1937. Even so, it was only after proving itself in teachers' salary equalization cases throughout the state and achieving elimination of the white Democratic primary that the NAACP decided to attack Jim Crow in higher education. At the forefront of that struggle, Lulu White took a position in trying to solve the problems of segregated education that often placed her at odds with many in the black community.

Ironic as it may have appeared in the late 1940s and early 1950s, two of Houston's most popular personalities engaged in continuous warfare over the "separate but equal" doctrine in public education. Indeed, the feud between Lulu Belle White, executive secretary of the NAACP, and Carter Wesley, editor of the *Houston Informer*, lasted from 1945 to 1957. Oddly enough, White and Wesley had much in common. They had similar personalities, philosophies, and methods and drew their support from similar constituencies. Both were flamboyant, crowd-pleasing *prima donnas* who used their theatrical skills to hold center stage. Both stressed independence, sought coalitions, and challenged the white establishment. Both championed causes that would benefit the powerless and the racial and ethnic groups from which they themselves sprang. The feud occurred in part because of their personalities, philosophies, and methods, and in part because of the political context out of which each emerged. They clashed most pointedly on the issue of equalizing higher education in Texas—whether to integrate the University of Texas (UT) or establish Texas State University for Negroes (TSUN).

Carter W. Wesley's commitment to social justice was forged from personal experience. Born in Houston in 1892, he graduated from the public schools of the city, attended Fisk University in Nashville, and, during World War I, became one of the first black officers in the United States military. Upon his return, he pursued and earned a doctorate in jurisprudence from Northwestern University in Evanston, Illinois. After four years of legal practice in Oklahoma, Wesley returned to Houston in 1927. Finding his legal practice in Texas limited because of his race, he became a businessman and bought into a newly formed publishing company which owned the *Informer.* Thereafter, he used the *Informer* as a podium from which to battle racism and to speak on behalf of his people.[1]

Having gained control of the *Informer*'s parent company in 1934, Wesley used the paper to publicize the battle against the white Democratic primaries that effectively denied blacks the right to vote, until that battle was won in 1944. Thereafter he exhorted black men and women to pay their poll taxes, vote, and fight for equal rights. Not content to fight a private battle against discrimination, Wesley preferred to fight the battle for blacks everywhere—boycotting, criticizing, fundraising, publicizing or refusing to publicize an issue as his judgment dictated. So, when he fought to establish TSUN within the context of the "separate but equal" doctrine, he saw himself battling on behalf of all blacks. Undoubtedly his view was influenced by his own experiences as a black man struggling to achieve equality in American society.[2]

Lulu White, for her part, was a woman deeply dedicated to the cause of integration. In arriving at this position, she had encountered personal struggles and political constraints. However, once she reached a decision, she acted, despite the consequences. Sometimes a public injustice prompted a response. Other times, it was an appeal from individuals that spurred her to action. Simply put, she abhorred the Jim Crow system. Thus, she worked very hard at the forefront of the movement to integrate the University of Texas.

For more than seventy years, African Americans had expressed concern over Texas' failure to keep its promise to provide them with a colored "classical branch university" that would be equivalent to the whites-only University of Texas.[3] Two decades into the twentieth century, this still had not happened; and black Texans began to express concern not only about a branch university and about equal opportunities in general, but also about the lack of graduate and professional training for people of color. In the entire South, graduate and professional schools existed only at a few privately supported black institutions. The general feeling among African Americans was that each state should provide advanced training for blacks as well as whites.

A most significant step toward providing graduate and professional training for African Americans in the South was the decision of the Supreme Court in

Missouri ex rel. Gaines v. Canada (1938). This case involved twenty-four-year-old Lloyd Gaines, who had applied for admission to the University of Missouri Law School. But for his color, Gaines would have been admitted. He was asked to accept tuition to study in a nearby out-of-state institution offering legal training for blacks. Gaines refused and took his case all the way to the Supreme Court, which held (1) that it was the duty of each state to provide education for all of its citizens; (2) that this provision must be made within the state; and (3) that payment of tuition fees in another state does not remove discrimination.[4]

The Gaines case caused immediate consternation in Texas. For one thing, the State of Texas did not provide graduate and professional training or pay out-of-state tuition for African Americans. Further, the state conference of branches of the NAACP had made it clear in 1937 that one of its major goals was to eliminate discrimination in education in Texas. Thus, shortly after the Gaines decision, the NAACP arranged for George L. Allen, a black business executive, to register in a business course at the University of Texas, in the hope that a court action would force the legislature to provide out-of-state scholarships for blacks. "The only wrench in the whole machine," said Allen, "was that they admitted me."

When Allen arrived on the UT campus in October 1938, he presented for admission and was allowed to register and attend classes. Unintentionally, the university's tradition of segregation had been broken, but not for long. After attending classes for ten days, Allen was called in by university officials and asked to withdraw from the university. When he refused to do so, his classes were canceled. The NAACP's strategy of enrolling Allen had paid off, however. Within nine months after Allen's departure, the state legislature passed a law providing for out-of-state tuition for blacks seeking graduate-level education.[5]

By the mid-1940s, many Texans had begun to see the inadequacies of the scholarship program. Not only did it fail to compensate black students fully for attending out-of-state universities, but also funds were insufficient to provide aid to all qualified blacks who applied. As Lulu White put it, "The travel money was not enough to pay for the student's railroad fares,"[6] and the distances that separated them from their loved ones created hardships. These scholarships could not stand up under litigation and were rendered obsolete by the Court's ruling in the Gaines case. In Texas, however, these scholarships would stay in effect, the Gaines case notwithstanding, until Heman Marion Sweatt attempted to enter UT in 1946.

In June 1945, the NAACP, after waiting for many years, announced that it would challenge segregated public professional education in Texas. The state government's immediate response to this challenge was the passage of Senate Bill 228. This bill changed the name of Prairie View State Normal and Industrial College to Prairie View State University. Additionally, the measure authorized the Texas A&M Board of Regents to provide at Prairie View, upon demand, training in law, medicine, engineering, pharmacy, and journalism, as well as any other courses taught at UT.[7] The legislature's action initially baffled many blacks. Why would the legislature make Prairie View a university without according its white counterpart, Texas A&M, equal status? Soon, however, it became clear that the purpose was to prevent integration at UT.

About the same time that the NAACP decided to test the dual system of education in the state, another black group was organized. At its inception, the Southern Negro Conference for Equalization of Education (SNCEE), founded by Carter Wesley, denounced the South's dual school system but said nothing about integration. This stance implied that integration could not act as panacea for the problems blacks faced in education.

The SNCEE grew out of the Southern Regional Council. The Southern Regional Council had its beginning with a group of so-called moderate blacks who met in Durham, North Carolina, in October 1942 to discuss World War II and its effects on race relations. Mostly professionals (college presidents, school principals, publishers, business people, doctors, and social workers), the conference attenders affirmed their loyalty to the Allies' war policies. On the other hand, they maintained that such loyalty should not distract blacks from tackling the existing problems of poverty, educational inequity, and poll taxes. Although these blacks were fundamentally opposed to the principle and practice of compulsory segregation, they believed that it was more sensible and timely to attack other areas of racial discrimination.[8]

In June 1943, these black moderates came together in a second meeting and formally established the Southern Regional Council. While committed to improving race relations and the conditions of blacks in the South through education and improved government consideration of African Americans' social and economic concerns, the Southern Regional Council was vague and equivocal on segregation. The priorities established by the council did not include any direct attack on segregation. This position, shared by Wesley, would become his main bone of contention with Lulu White and the NAACP.[9]

When Wesley formed the Southern Negro Conference for Equalization of Education in 1945, he resolved to work for equalization of education at all levels. Still, he was opposed to making a frontal attack on segregation—the main obstacle to equal opportunity. Rather, his emphasis was on the manner of attaining civil rights. While he saw the need to pursue equality in the courts, he believed, idealistically or naïvely, that true equality could be accomplished under the "separate but equal" doctrine. He further postulated that a broad-based organization such as his own could help large numbers of blacks reach that goal.[10]

However wise his tactics may have been, Lulu White could not concur with

Wesley's views. She sharply rebuked his organization for its failure to confront the segregation question. She challenged the "separate but equal" alternative that proposed bringing black schools up to parity with white ones while keeping them separate. The fact that segregation was a violation of the Constitution made it awkward, in her mind, to pursue true equality in separate-but-equal schools. Wesley and White differed in that Wesley demanded equal opportunity under the current segregation law as stated in the Texas Constitution, while White could see no equality in segregation.[11]

To disarm critics who suspected that the SNCEE was unprogressive and compromising, Wesley in 1945 insisted that it would work hand in hand with the NAACP. Thurgood Marshall, the NAACP legal counsel, agreed.[12] Wesley proposed that the NAACP coordinate all court cases involving higher education and Marshall, in return, agreed to defend the SNCEE if the need should arise. In keeping with his promise to cooperate with the NAACP, Wesley provided substantial publicity in his newspaper about the anticipated lawsuit against UT, resulting in the collection of a huge sum of money to fund the suit. And when the NAACP had not found a plaintiff by September 1945, Thurgood Marshall asked Wesley for advice.[13] The two, along with A. Maceo Smith, the NAACP's executive secretary of branches, wrestled with the problem of finding the right person for the case, dismissing five prospective plaintiffs.

Then, in October, Lulu White wrote to Thurgood Marshall, "I think I have a plaintiff for the Education Case." The individual was Heman Marion Sweatt, a thirty-three-year-old Houstonian with a bachelor of science degree from Wiley College, who was employed full-time by the post office and part-time by the *Informer*.[14] Sweatt earlier had given some thought to attending UT, but he did not make this known until he heard Lulu White at a meeting appeal to the audience for a volunteer to serve as plaintiff in a lawsuit against the university. While he called it a "brash decision," Sweatt's willingness to become a plaintiff had a great deal to do with the discrimination that he had experienced at the Houston post office and his family's friendship with Lulu White. Before Sweat could have second thoughts, A. Maceo Smith and William J. Durham, resident counsel for the Texas NAACP, encouraged him to file application immediately for admission to the UT Law School. Sweatt told them that he could not do so until he had consulted his employer, Carter Wesley. Wesley approved the idea, assuring Sweatt that his job would be waiting for him after absences to appear in court.[15]

Urged on by the NAACP and accompanied by Lulu White and other supporters, Heman Sweatt attempted to register at UT in Austin on February 26, 1946. After a discussion with President Theophilus Painter and other university officials, Sweatt left his application at the campus and returned to Houston, hoping for a quick answer. During his stay on campus, Sweatt made no mention of his intention to file a lawsuit; but, given the wide publicity previously accorded the NAACP's plans, university officials realized that one was in the making. It is not surprising, then, that Painter wrote to Attorney General Grover Sellers, asking for an opinion on Sweatt's application: "This is to be a test case on the question of admission of Negro students in higher education of the state. . . . This applicant is duly qualified for admission to the Law School, save and except for the fact that he is a Negro. [Please advise.]"[16] Sellers's ruling did not come until March 16, at which time he upheld Texas law, which read, "No African or persons of African descent should be admitted to the University of Texas." Adding insult to injury, Sellers noted that Sweatt could apply for legal training at Prairie View, since in 1945, Senate Bill 228 had made it (on paper) a university.[17]

Sellers's opinion set things in motion, signaling the beginning of a concerted campaign to end segregated education in Texas. Conversely, it stimulated the thinking of some blacks who wanted a separate but equal university. Shortly after Sellers issued his opinion, A. Maceo Smith wrote to Wesley that the Sweatt case should be pursued, although "realism dictates that a special university is about all we are going to get . . . the Texas Council of Negro Organizations is the appropriate agency that should prepare for negotiation when the time arises."[18] Wesley countered that "mule" caution should guide blacks in accepting such an alternative. "The seeming advantage," he reasoned, "that we might have in putting them on the spot might trap us."[19] Wesley was very perceptive. Sweatt's registration attempt mobilized the political establishment to press for a black statutory university.

After Sweatt sued university officials on May 16, 1946, for denying him admission, Dudley K. Woodward, Jr., chair of the UT Board of Regents, began to talk about making provisions for a black university. He took the lead in advancing the cause of a black university not for humanitarian reasons, but to insure that a branch university for colored youth, required by the state constitution, would not threaten UT's Permanent University Fund. In Woodward's opinion, having a black university share the endowment would "entail consequences of [the] most destructive character"; creating another black university by statute would avoid this possibility since a state law mandated only UT and Texas A&M as benefactors of the Permanent University Fund. "It is of great importance," Woodward wrote, "that the [constitutional option] be effectually destroyed."[20]

On June 17, 1946, Judge Roy Archer made public his decision to postpone issuing a writ of mandamus to compel UT to admit Sweatt. This not only delayed Sweatt's action, but also allowed the Texas Legislature enough time to create a statutory black university that would be substantially "equal to whites."[21] Subsequent to Archer's ruling, which set December 17, 1946, as the date for final execution of the judgment, officials from UT and Texas A&M College, charged in 1945 with studying Negro education, held a joint meeting to address the issue. This Joint Committee on Negro Education recommended, in essence, that a black institution of higher education be established, and that Prairie View provide agricultural and mechanical training for blacks on the same order as Texas A&M did for whites. This group also recommended that the governor appoint a biracial committee to study its report and recommend to the governor proposals that could be presented to the legislature as soon as possible. When Lulu White heard about this group, she warned Thurgood Marshall that state officials were planning to establish a separate black university: "There is a possibility that the present Houston College for Negroes will be used as the nucleus around which the Negro University will be built."[22]

On July 25, 1946, the biracial committee met in Austin and approved the recommendations of the Joint Committee on Negro Education. The biracial committee also decided to hold a similar gathering with blacks on August 8, 1946, to discuss their concerns regarding an institution of higher learning. Realizing that such a meeting might be a fiasco unless blacks reached a consensus beforehand, A. Maceo Smith called a meeting of ninety-six black leaders from throughout the state, to take place on August 3, 1946. Eighty-three of the leaders there agreed that they should base any actions on article 7, section 14, of the Texas Constitution, which read, "The Legislature shall also, when deemed practical, establish and provide for the maintenance of a college branch university for the instruction of colored youths of the state." Blacks interpreted section 14 to mean that such a university would share in UT's endowment fund and would not exclude blacks from attending classes at the main UT campus. At the conclusion of this meeting, Carter Wesley and Joseph J. Rhoads, president of Bishop College in Dallas, were selected to present the views of the black leadership to the biracial committee.[23]

When Wesley and Rhoads made their presentation on August 8, 1946, their demands went a little farther than Gov. Coke Stevenson and his cohorts had expected. Blacks had agreed to support the NAACP in the Sweatt case but also demanded that a black university be established which would share equally with UT in an endowment fund. Further, they made it clear that they had no interest in a legislative arrangement by which a makeshift university would be established.[24]

Responding to this group, UT's President Theophilus Painter asserted that a black statutory university would be established. In an effort to head off integration of other professional areas, Painter told his audience that this university should be located in Houston, not only because the State of Texas would purchase Houston College for Negroes for this purpose, but also because the city's two black hospitals would enable the black university to establish its own medical school.[25] In a heated debate, Lulu White attacked Painter's statement as an insult to black people. She pointed out that the hospitals referred to were separate and unequal; one of them, Jefferson Davis, had refused to treat black patients. Painter's suggestion, she charged, was simply a ploy to prevent blacks from attending UT.[26]

Always skeptical of Wesley's Southern Negro Conference for Equalization of Education, Lulu White became incensed when, on September 3, 1946, she discovered that Wesley had written a letter to the Texas Council of Negro Organizations and other black groups in Texas, inviting them to form a new group to demand equality in segregation—that is, to accept Painter's position. Wesley called this group the Texas Negro Conference for Equalization of Education. White felt particularly bitten when she discovered that the names Wesley used to form his new organization came from the NAACP's membership list.[27]

White opposed this new group because, in her opinion, "when such an organization takes the members of the same organization that is fighting Jim Crow and [now asks them to maintain segregation], such an organization could only cloud the issue."[28] She argued that, if blacks wanted to establish a university under the present structure of segregation, they should join the Texas Council of Negro Organizations, a group already charged with pursuing that goal. She could not understand how A. Maceo Smith had allowed himself to be used to garner support for such a group.[29] Later White speculated that this new organization was racist in nature. Writing to Thurgood Marshall, she minced no words: Smith and Wesley "didn't want any white members. They said this was a Negro fight and we must have a Negro organization."[30]

The already heated debate got even hotter after A. Maceo Smith, executive secretary of the Texas Conference of Branches, selected Lulu White as director of state branches of the NAACP in March 1946. A. Maceo Smith called upon the state branches to endorse Wesley's organization, but White objected, saying there was no need for such an organization.[31] Her statement implied that the Texas branches should divorce themselves from Wesley's organization; she argued that the NAACP "needs to lead in all programs advancing the Negro in the state."[32] Wesley took this position to mean that Lulu White and the NAACP wanted the last word on all racial matters affecting blacks. At this point, the quarrel between White and Wesley seems to have reached an impasse. The feud was exacerbated as the NAACP's national office supported White.

Of special note is the fact that, when Wesley first introduced his organization to blacks of the Lone Star State, Thurgood Marshall warned both Wesley and Maceo Smith against allowing the Southern Negro Conference and the NAACP to duplicate efforts.[33] One year later, Wesley found himself increasingly under attack by Lulu White for his use of the NAACP's mailing list to establish the Texas Negro Conference for Equalization of Education, and for his favorable stance toward Judge Roy Archer's ruling of June 16, 1946. In language more forceful than he had employed previously, Marshall cautioned Wesley about the activities of his organization, telling him not to ask for something he found undesirable—segregation.[34] Disturbed by this letter, Wesley penned a scathing four-page reply, with carbon copies to all black leaders of Texas. Marshall responded in kind, and the battle was on between Marshall and Wesley, with Lulu White serving up the ammunition.[35]

Prior to 1946, Lulu White and Wesley were friends and collaborated on many issues. Similarly, Julius White, Lulu's husband, had a cordial relationship with Wesley. Once the educational struggle took center stage in Texas and the issue of integration versus separation became the focus of attention, however, all friendships came to a halt. After the fight became personal, neither Wesley nor Lulu White seemed able to hear what the other had to say. This became clear in many of Wesley's *Informer* editorials, beginning in 1946. In December 28, 1946, Wesley lambasted White for an alleged intransigence that ruled out any approach to eradicating inequity in education save for integration. Wesley maintained that the education fight in Texas should be fought by the Texas Negro Conference of Equalization of Education, the Texas Council of Negro Organizations, and the NAACP. He argued that the framework in which the state had to operate made it possible for blacks to have their cake and eat it, too—integration of UT *and* the establishment of a black university.[36]

In this article, Wesley made unwarranted allegations against White, causing her to resign as executive secretary of the local branch of the NAACP. Among the charges he levied were these: (1) White was a Communist; (2) the NAACP wanted a monopoly on racial issues; and (3) White was causing strife within the state's black leadership. Of the many allegations made by Wesley, the last carried the most weight. In her letter of resignation, White stated, "If something could be done to prove to Julius that I had not caused internal strife, I would stay on."[37]

Apparently something was done. The local branch refused to accept White's resignation and instead gave her a vote of confidence. She stayed on, with the blessings of Thurgood Marshall, who wrote, "I have been accused of giving comfort to you in your stand against segregation. I think you are absolutely right."[38] Subsequently, Wesley, by resigning, freed himself from all affiliation with the NAACP—the local branch, the state conference of branches, and the national organization.[39] Wesley's actions cleared the way for him to wage all-out war against Lulu White.

Meanwhile, during the interim between Judge Archer's initial ruling of June 16,

1946, and his final ruling on December 17, 1946, as White and Wesley continued to feud over a constitutional versus a statutory branch university, state officials embarked on a program to create a black-proof educational system. In November 1946, the Board of Regents of Texas A&M, under the authority of Senate Bill 228, passed in 1945, established a black law school in Houston, at 409-1/2 Milam Street.[40] Similarly, on December 17, 1946, when Judge Archer again denied Sweatt's petition for a writ of mandamus, the biracial committee recommended creation of a statutory university. The latter decision was made after officials from UT and Texas A&M predictably reported that their permanent university fund would be insufficient to support an additional university.[41]

Lulu White, along with many other black leaders, denounced the creation of a law school on Milam Street. Consequently, when its doors opened in February 1947, it closed shortly thereafter for lack of students. In something of a frenzy to counter Sweatt's challenge, UT's Board of Regents on February 28, 1947, established an interim black law school at 104 East 13th Street in Austin.

On March 3, 1947, the Texas Legislature passed Senate Bill 140, providing for the "establishment of a three-million-dollar Negro University, including a law school to be located in Houston." The passage of this bill was made easier by the fact that Houston College for Negroes, at the time under the supervision of the University of Houston, was experiencing financial problems. So, when the State of Texas made an offer to purchase the institution, those in charge responded affirmatively. With the passage of House Bill 780, the fifty-three-acre site was purchased from the University of Houston, and Texas State University for Negroes (TSUN; later called Texas Southern University, or TSU) came into being.[42]

To make sure that TSUN would continue to serve as a bulwark against desegregation, Attorney General Price Daniel served as temporary chairman of the university during the period when a nine-member Board of Regents was being formed. Among other things, he told the board that its duty was to sell the school to blacks—to convince them that the state, via the establishment of TSUN, had fulfilled its obligation to provide graduate and professional training. Seconding Daniel's remarks was future Chairman of the Board Craig Cullinan, who cautioned the group to be mindful of those blacks who were attempting to overthrow segregated education in Texas. When Lulu White got wind of Cullinan's remarks, she wrote Gloster Current and told him that the "Board of Regents of the Negro University was told that their first duty was to get the subversive element [the NAACP] that divided the Negroes out of the state." She also told him that "the Negro Regents took their oath of office with the understanding that they were to work for harmony among Negroes by keeping them in their place."[43]

While Wesley accepted the establishment of TSUN, Lulu White staged a protest, advocated a demonstration against Senate Bill 140, and insisted that the state had only raised the stakes in maintaining Jim Crow schools.[44] When Wesley pointed out that he embraced the black institution because he favored taking whatever the state had to "offer in the way of improved education,"[45] both Lulu White and Thurgood Marshall took this to mean that he no longer was willing to pursue integration in the courts. This was not the case at all. Wesley never wavered in his support of the Sweatt case, but he saw the case as a litmus test for the law that excluded blacks from tax-supported state professional schools in the absence of any semblance of separate but equal facilities.

From the editor's perspective, the NAACP's strategy was too narrowly focused on one area of discrimination. Because of the limitations of such a strategy, Wesley argued that an equalization case should accompany Sweatt's and that the NAACP should attack the makeshift law school in Austin, file suit for the Permanent University Fund monies at UT, and ask for reparations for the bricks given by blacks to Houston College for Negroes.[46] Similarly, his idealism led him to believe that his organization could force the State of Texas to live up to its responsibility to make separate equal.

Although Wesley devoted a great deal of attention to securing equality under segregation, his role in the civil rights movement should not be misrepresented. To be sure, Wesley's stance toward the doctrine of "separate but equal" reveals much about his approach. To focus on "separate but equal" outside the context of Wesley's other activities, however, is to distort his position. While never a separatist, Wesley did have doubts about whether the NAACP's efforts for integration, as manifested in the Sweatt case, would bring about the greatest good for the greatest number of blacks. But Wesley's quarrel was with the approach, not the intent, of the NAACP in seeking to make blacks first-class citizens. The record is replete with evidence of his efforts to achieve this goal.[47]

When Sweatt's hearing began on May 5, 1947, Wesley was there as a loyal supporter. At this hearing, the state's lawyers tried to prove that, since UT's basement law school provided individualized instruction for blacks, in many ways it was equal to or better than the white law school. That argument was destroyed by Thurgood Marshall before a packed courtroom. Using a quantitative analysis to show the inequalities in the two schools, Marshall pointed to differences in classroom space, library size, and number of books. As he continued to chip away at the state's case, one observer quipped that "Attorney General Price Daniel chewed two cigars." Despite what many considered Marshall's brilliant arguments, the judge unsurprisingly ruled in favor of the state. For the next three years, while the State of Texas paid lip service but gave scant attention to TSUN, the NAACP made plans to take this case to the Supreme Court. And, the Wesley-White feud continued.[48]

Meanwhile, A. Maceo Smith, trying to mediate between White and Wesley, on August 27, 1947, again asked White to embrace Wesley's new organization, noting, "The NAACP is part of the Texas State Conference for Equalization of Education."[49] White stubbornly refused and accused Smith of "trying to make the NAACP a puppet organization."[50] Writing in disgust to Thurgood Marshall, White said, "We should let Maceo go to hell with Carter. I may have been called dumb, but I simply cannot see equality in segregation. I hope I die just that dumb."[51]

Lulu White clearly held strong views about the inequities of segregation. Wisdom born of experience had taught her that "separate but equal" was a contradiction in terms. Thus, in responding to Wesley's argument, she enunciated the NAACP's position—the only thing blacks could gain from attacking the state on inequality was a rash of Jim Crow schools, and any attempt to sue for equality affirmed the legality of "separate but equal." More than anything else, White wanted to destroy the legal basis upon which Jim Crow rested.[52] So, while Wesley argued that "we put all whites against us when we attack segregation openly and practically,"[53] White took the opposite view. To her way of thinking, the vindication of constitutional rights in court cases such as Sweatt's demanded prompt relief. But any relief short of integrated schools and universities meant that blacks would continue to be deprived of these rights.

White worked very hard in Texas to implement the NAACP's frontal attack on segregation. In December 1947, to test the commitment of the State of Texas to equality in higher education, she encouraged W. Astor Kirk, a black professor from Tillotson College, to apply for admission to the graduate program in political science at TSUN. Kirk wanted to pursue a doctoral degree, but it was not long before he discovered that the black university had neither a professor to teach the courses nor a library staff. Kirk then applied to UT but was denied admission and encouraged to seek a graduate program out of state.[54] When he rejected this offer, the UT Board of Regents entered into a contractual agreement with the Board of Regents at TSUN. That is, Kirk was to register at the black university but be instructed elsewhere by white professors. The same arrangement had been made for Henry E. Doyle when he attended TSUN's basement law school in 1947. But, unlike Doyle, who had agreed to that arrangement, Kirk asked White and the NAACP for help and pursued his cause in the courts.[55]

White students aided and abetted the NAACP attack on Jim Crow. In 1948, two white students tried to enroll at TSUN. Whether the NAACP was responsible for these students' actions is uncertain. What is known is that, when the applications reached the campus, they went to three offices before a decision was made—the registrar's, the president's, and that of the chairman of the Board of Regents. When Chairman Craig Cullinan read these applications, he wasted no time before writing TSUN President Raphael O'Hara Lanier, voicing his opposition based on race. These students then sought out Lulu White, who gleefully wrote to Gloster Current, "We are raising hell down here on the educational front."[56]

In April 1949, Joseph J. Rhoads, president of Bishop College, organized a mass registration attempt, sending thirty-five black college seniors from across the state to apply to various professional programs at UT. Anticipating denial, these students were prepared to file suits in court. When they arrived at the registrar's office seeking admission, they were told that they could apply at TSUN. These students then decided to stage a demonstration, marching from the university to the State Capitol. They carried placards expressing their motives and intentions. One sign read, "Texas Can't Afford a Dual System of Graduate and Professional Education." Another proclaimed, "Separate and Equal Education Is a Mockery." A. Maceo Smith, straddling the fence in the Wesley-White feud, expressed to Thurgood Marshall his concern that this demonstration might greatly affect TSUN's appropriation and cause the legislature to pump more money into that Jim Crow school. Marshall partially agreed with Smith but thought that the demonstration should proceed cautiously, ensuring that placards and news releases only pointed to the students' opposition to segregated education.[57]

The *Houston Post* perceptively reported in 1948 that the NAACP was hitting the State of Texas where it was most vulnerable. Out of the 1949 demonstration would come two prospective plaintiffs—one an applicant for dental school and the other an applicant for medical school. Yet, when the legislature decided to create TSUN as a bulwark against integration, it paid little more than lip service to creating a medical school for African Americans. UT's President Theophilus Painter was given an estimated budget of $192,000 for the first two years of operation of the "colored" medical school. Prospective black students made inquiries immediately when they heard of the legislature's action, and two actually applied for medical school when TSUN opened in September 1947. Others sought the advice of black board member Willette R. Banks, principal (president) emeritus of Prairie View. Rather than work behind the scenes to help establish this medical school, Banks told Painter that these students did not want to embarrass the state, so he had suggested that they attend Meharry Medical College in Nashville, Tennessee.

Not only did blacks in Lulu White's camp vigorously protest Banks's stance, but they continued to remind the state of the need to train blacks in the medical profession. Under continued pressure to provide blacks with equal medical training, Painter announced in 1948 that he would support establishing a regional black medical school. The NAACP refused to accept this alternative. While intimating that the reason TSUN did not have a medical school was that its board did not push for it, Painter early in 1948 predicted that "[if the State of Texas] does not make adequate provisions for a medical school before September, we are going to have a hard time keeping Negroes out of Medical and Dental schools."[58]

Painter's prophecy came true when Herman Barnett applied for medical school in July 1949. The state legislature then belatedly appropriated $175,000 for a medical school at TSUN. The state's action was regarded as suspect, however. If the basement law school had proven unsuccessful, why should anyone expect a medical school, which was more expensive and required more expertise, to be different? Responding as it had when Sweatt applied to the UT Law School, the state asked UT to contract with TSUN to provide the necessary professional training in medicine for blacks. Under this plan, Barnett would take classes along with white students at UT, while registered at TSUN. Barnett was supposed to attend the University of Texas Medical Branch at Galveston (UTMB) only until the state had time to provide medical training at TSUN. As it turned out, the proposed medical school never materialized, and Barnett received his medical degree from UTMB in 1953.[59]

Throughout 1948 and 1949, Lulu White and Carter Wesley held fast to their respective philosophies and approaches to the doctrine of "separate but equal," while the black community frequently took sides. For example, in November 1949, White reported that the NAACP could expect very little from Prairie View alumni. White's statement followed a conversation with a graduate of that institution, who had chided her for her position on the doctrine of "separate but equal." Very forcefully this woman told Lulu White, "I wish all of you who want to be white would cross over, so we could stop all of this mess about segregation." Lulu White reportedly replied in "good, calm and collected English, [and told the lady] what she was, and all the so-and-so's like her." Despite the implicit humor, such exchanges illuminate a community caught up in the Wesley-White feud over equal educational opportunities for black Texans.[60]

The feud was intensified by Wesley's continued assertions that White was a Communist. Most whites simply refused to believe that local black demands for integrated education were exactly that. Given the racist premise that blacks were happy and content with the status quo, their failure to support Wesley's position could only be the result of some external force; thus, the NAACP must be linked to Communism. Lulu White did nothing to discourage this image; she openly associated with socialist sympathizers. Because of the allegations of Communist affiliation and continuing differences over the doctrine of "separate but equal," by 1949 Wesley was obsessed with having White removed as the executive secretary of the Houston chapter. He succeeded on June 13, 1949, when White tendered her resignation.[61]

Two years after the establishment of TSUN, Lulu White still pointed to the state's lack of interest in maintaining TSUN on the same level as UT. Because of inadequate funding from the state, TSUN had to put 119 students in an average-sized chemistry laboratory and had no space for its $30,000 worth of physics equipment. Similarly, the librarian had to stack magazines from floor to ceiling in her office.

Even as a rising tide of racial liberalism engulfed these Houstonians, Wesley and White continued to hammer away at each other. She argued that no group could be any good when its fundamental ideology was a repressive belief in segregation; she lamented that Wesley's group had been given so much publicity, since it was not committed to racial democracy. In short, White had a hard time discerning how one could believe in equality and segregation simultaneously. Wesley, on the other hand, saw a great tragedy in his opponent's liberal position: it would raise blacks' hopes momentarily but would not solve the problems of the masses of black students, who would continue to live in black neighborhoods and attend black institutions. Wesley's position was to prove prophetic, but the Supreme Court's ruling in the Sweatt case did not uphold his position.[62]

The Supreme Court announced its findings in *Sweatt v. Painter* on June 5, 1950. In a unanimous decision, the Court ordered Sweatt admitted to UT. Speaking for the majority of the Court, Chief Justice Fred Vinson asserted that there was no comparison between the two law schools. TSUN had 23 students, compared to 880 at UT. TSUN had less than one-third the number of full-time instructors, and the library was one-fourth the size of UT's. Moreover, unlike TSUN, UT published a law journal and had moot court facilities, scholarships, and many alumni.

Although Sweatt now could attend UT, just as Wesley had predicted, segregation still was not abolished. After the Supreme Court found the TSUN Law School inadequate in many areas, the legislature demonstrated its commitment to TSUN in a rather ironic way. In the following session (1951), it slashed TSUN's appropriation from $1,570,000 to $958,672. The Wesley-White feud, while dissipating somewhat after *Sweatt v. Painter*, continued throughout the years, with both parties saying, "I told you so."[63]

Indeed, the reactions of both Wesley and White to Jim Crow varied. Perhaps differences in the two leaders' personal styles explain a good deal of their conflict; in some respects, their styles seem to have been complementary. For example, Wesley valued the freedom to speak his mind fearlessly on any subject and to focus attention on wrongs that could be righted; White, though speaking her mind also, preferred being a team player with the NAACP. White above all sought governmentally mandated opportunities for blacks to enter white society on an equal footing; taking advantage of these opportunities, however, required a conformity that, some feared, could have the effect of diluting black culture. Wesley's tactics of gradual reform encouraged blacks to work for improvement but to accept often frustrating compromises; he asked them to accept the existing patterns of racial segregation while asking for favors within them.

In sum, both White and Wesley clung to the hope that their respective approaches to the doctrine of "separate but equal" ultimately would find vindication. However, the ambiguities in both approaches would continue to plague institutions of black higher education, such as Texas Southern University. The Wesley-White feud highlights questions which have made the long struggle for racial justice painful and perplexing, as blacks strive to attain equality in American society without losing their solidarity and their sense of identity.

CHAPTER 6

Workhorse or Team Player?

The NAACP Experience

I n any discussion of Lulu White, the centrality of the NAACP in her public life must be acknowledged. The social and economic reforms she advocated mirrored the philosophy of the NAACP. Collectively, they represented what she considered to be the strongest hope for the future of black people in this country. "We all agree," wrote Lulu White, "that the National Association for the Advancement of Colored People is the only weapon that the Negroes have to fight for their complete democratic rights as citizens in this great city, state, and country."[1] Within this framework of facts, assumptions, and beliefs, the NAACP became for White "the ship and all else the sea." Upon that premise she would base her arguments for, and her support of, the organization. This posture would serve as a guide for most of her activities as she functioned in the positions of executive secretary, state director of branches, national field worker, and private citizen. Energized by this philosophy, she found it rewarding and convenient to serve the organization as foot soldier, organizer, mobilizer, and fundraiser.

From its founding in 1909 until well past the mid-1930s, what highlighted the NAACP's activities and dramatized its work were its efforts to secure for African Americans their basic constitutional rights to life, liberty, and the pursuit of happiness. These rights often were threatened by mob violence and by gross mistreatment of African Americans in the criminal justice system. Not only did the NAACP devote nearly thirty years to a futile effort to achieve passage of a federal anti-lynching bill, but also the organization spent much of its energy on legal redress for individuals. Thus, the NAACP sought cases involving citizenship rights and racial discrimination. By the time Lulu White became an activist in the association in the 1940s, this kind of litigation had become too voluminous for the legal staff to handle; therefore, the organization decided to give preference to cases with potential to establish a new precedent of constitutional significance. Cases involving the white primaries and the fight against educational discrimination in the South fell into this category.[2]

In cases dealing with education, the NAACP employed a two-pronged strategy involving direct attack upon the exclusion of blacks from graduate and professional schools; and indirect assault on segregation in primary and secondary schools, based on such issues as equalization of salaries, length of school terms, and condition of physical facilities. This approach was designed to make segregated public schooling so expensive that the only available choices would be desegregation or economic ruin. These cases also served the NAACP as opportunities to raise funds and to increase its membership. Membership dues provided the basic revenue not only for local branches, but also for state and national operations. The salaries of all workers, cost of publications, travel expenses, and miscellaneous costs came from membership revenues. In a word, the organization's entire structure depended upon this source of income.[3]

Much credit for building local branches must go to countless black women whose roles have received scant attention from historians. Lulu Belle Madison White was one such individual. She was recognized and admired almost universally, as she traveled throughout the state organizing new branches and reviving old ones. Noted for her dynamic speaking, she had a singular capacity to impart courage and chase timidity. White moved people to action. She motivated crowds to fight for civil rights and worked with branch presidents and executive boards in developing strategies to achieve the desired results. She mobilized existing networks around the organizing goals of the NAACP, conveying information to various branches and coordinating their diverse activities. While she mediated conflicts, within the local branch she also created conflicts, causing some to wonder if she really were a team player. An examination of White's activities from 1943 to 1957 should shed some light on the extent to which she was a workhorse, a team player, or a *prima donna*.

Organizer and Mobilizer

When Lulu White assumed the post of executive secretary of the Houston chapter in 1943, her job description included managing the office, conducting branch activities, helping to organize other branches, and, most especially, directing membership and fundraising drives. On a salary of eighty-nine dollars per month and gasoline money for her automobile (the car was provided by her husband), White immediately set out to make the Houston branch one of the largest in the nation. Under her guidance, the Houston branch grew from 5,679 members in 1943 to 10,705 in 1944, and to 12,700 in 1945 (see table 1). Elated over Lulu White's performance, Daisy Lampkin wrote to her, "Each day, I marvel at the amount of work you are able to accomplish." A. Maceo Smith was equally pleased when White won first place in the organization's national membership drive in 1943. Partly because of White's efforts, between 1943 and 1945, 23,000 new members enrolled in the national association, and the number within the state of Texas branches increased from 36 to 104. This increase in membership enabled the Houston chapter to pay a subsidy to the national office for three consecutive years: 1945—$500, 1946—$700, and 1947—$500.[4]

The growth of the NAACP in Houston in the early 1940s represented tremendous progress. It reflected White's aggressive fieldwork recruiting of new members, the organization's enhanced appeal to black Texans and black Houstonians, and the charisma of many black leaders. The civil rights movement in Texas appears to have been dominated by charismatic "out front" leaders such as Lulu White, Carter Wesley, A. Maceo Smith, Richard R. Grovey, and Juanita J. S. Craft. The movement and White's role in it can be understood better by examining "layers of leadership," or "transcending leadership," by which leaders engage and create new "leader-followers."

The above model was especially applicable to Lulu White's relationship with Juanita Craft of Dallas. Craft joined the NAACP in 1935, after the Tubercular State Hospital refused to admit her terminally ill mother. Almost immediately she became involved in the Dallas chapter's membership drive. After several years of hearing and reading about Lulu White's work with the NAACP, Craft came to Houston to meet and consult with her on how to increase the membership of the Dallas branch. The two quickly became allies and set out on a mission to expand and strengthen the state organization of the NAACP. They often traveled together from town to town in White's car, recruiting new members. Be-

Table 1

Membership of the Houston NAACP

Year	Members	Subsidy
1943	5,679	N/A
1944	10,705	$500
1945	12,700	$700
1946	5,334	$500
1947	4,938	N/A
1948	3,333	N/A
1949	6,975	N/A

Source: Branch Department Files (Houston) in NAACP Files Scholarly Resource Inc. Microfilm Production (Wilmington, Del., 1996), Manuscript Division, Library of Congress, Washington, D.C.

cause of the quality of their efforts, in 1946 Lulu White was appointed state director of branches, and Juanita Craft was named state organizer.[5]

Due to her experience and contacts, White, as she went about establishing local chapters, was able to draw on the resources of the national organization and enlist help from other state and local offices. By engaging ministers and presidents of civic, political, professional, educational, and women's groups early in her career, she was able to establish a "leader-followership." It was mainly through association and work with individuals such as those mentioned above that White was able to keep the association healthy via membership and fundraising.

Lulu White's gallant efforts at recruitment and fundraising did not go unnoticed. As early as 1945, Rev. A. A. Lucas, president of the Houston chapter of the NAACP, publicly acknowledged her work. In his annual address to the local chapter's executive board, Lucas recommended a salary increase for White, arguing that "our executive secretary has done a grand job. We would not have been able to have gotten anyone for that price. She works almost twenty-four hours a day."[6] Lulu White received similar accolades from other groups for her role in the civil rights struggle. In 1945, the Zeta Phi Beta Sorority and the Baptist Ministerial Alliance selected her as Outstanding Lady of the Year—the "one who did most to make Houston a better place." At Prairie View College's 1946 spring commencement, President Edward B. Evans presented White the Alumnus of the Year Award for her service to both the NAACP and the national Prairie View alumni association.[7]

White performed her duties as executive secretary in an efficient manner despite a meager budget, lack of a support staff, and personal illness. As early as December 1945, Lulu White informed Walter White that, due to a heart ailment, she might have to "give up her place as executive director." The doctors indicated that she needed to rest for six months and had to lose sixty pounds. "Could you imagine me not working for the NAACP or having a close eye on it?" asked Lulu White. "In this atomic age, I may be able to keep the heart going through remote control." Walter White acknowledged her illness and cautioned her to safeguard her health, but this was to no avail.[8]

In part because of her illness but more because of her work with the NAACP, the 1906 Art, Literary and Charity Club gave Lulu White a testimonial dinner on January 25, 1946. Officials from the national, state, and local NAACP offices either read or sent tributes. Writing to Mrs. P. L. Lubin-Byars, president of the club, Walter White said of Lulu White: "She is one of the most valuable and capable officers of the association. She has brought fine quality of leadership to Houston . . . and has given many techniques and ideas to the other branches [in] various states." Thurgood Marshall, one of Lulu White's best friends, probably expressed the sentiments of the NAACP best when he said, "Mrs. White throughout her career of public service has given freely of her time and resources in the never-ending fight against racial discrimination." More importantly, Marshall was a living witness of the fact that Lulu White had been criticized by both blacks and whites "who did not believe as she [did] in the militant fight against discrimination." Acknowledging her role in recruitment for the organization, Marshall continued: "Her courage, wisdom and tremendous energy are considered by us in the national office as one of the greatest assets in our ever increasing membership." White was elated and encouraged by these accolades. They did much to boost her morale at a time when the local branch was experiencing its first decline in membership since she assumed the post of executive secretary. White also was embroiled in the bitter controversy with Carter Wesley over integration of the University of Texas and establishment of Texas State University for Negroes. These accolades did much to reinforce her resolve to endure and continue fighting for the cause.[9]

Given Lulu White's desire to remain with the NAACP, as well as her track record in membership drives, one could easily understand why A. Maceo Smith would ask her to become director of state branches for Texas on March 26, 1946. At the time of her appointment, White informed her good friend, national field worker Ella Baker, that she was disabled to a small degree by a heart ailment.[10] Six months later, she complained to Gloster Current of a "bad valve in the heart" and of the need for plenty of rest.[11] This ailment notwithstanding, White continued to perform her duties with efficiency—working sometimes out of her home and at other times out of her office. Working under incalculable odds, White operated her office on a budget of $275 per month. Out of this budget came her salary, now raised to $100 per month; $75 for a secretary; $32.50 for rental of a building; $30 for publicity; and $12 for telephones. White worked also as a file clerk and bookkeeper, without any of the latest stenographic equipment. Only after the diagnosis of her heart ailment did she purchase an A. B. Dick monograph duplicator and hire Christia V. Adair as administrative assistant. Thus, funds for telegrams, duplication, and administrative assistance depended upon Lulu White's fundraising ability. Upon hearing from White about the steps she had taken to keep the office running smoothly, Ella Baker replied, "For a gal who has a leaking heart, you are certainly going strong. Don't overdo it, but of course this advice is more easily given than followed."[12]

Ella Baker was very perceptive. Instead of the heart ailment slowing her down, White now would double her efforts, launching membership drives both as executive secretary and as director of state branches. On March 20, 1946, she told Lucille Black, national membership chair, "Texas will make you proud of her . . . We are not going to stop until we have one hundred thousand [members]. We are really trying to break a record with our Texas State Conference." Lulu

White subsequently established chapters at Rosenberg and New Waverly, with widespread interest from individuals in adjoining counties. Enjoying her work immensely, White told Ella Baker, "I get a big kick out of these people wanting branches, so I say get as many as fifty [members] and you may have a branch of your own and they start hustling for members."[13] Such infectious charisma and ability to sell her product—the NAACP—allowed White to develop the loyal following that was so necessary to the organization in the mid-1940s.

Setting her state membership goal at 100,000 in 1946, White urged Gloster Current to send her whatever supplies he had: "Any kind of stuff you have is needed. We have grouped the people into ten clusters of thirty members along with a captain and the minimum number we are expecting is 100,000." White assigned a captain of each group. These captains recruited members in all groups—churches, labor unions, postal workers, barbers, beauticians, professionals, and lay people, to name a few.[14]

The Texas civil rights movement is epitomized by the image of Lulu White up at the podium and black ministers and labor leaders down in the trenches organizing. It should not come as a surprise that Lulu White capitalized on the foundation laid by Rev. A. A. Lucas in soliciting membership from churches. As an organizational tool in the struggle for civil rights, the church stood second to none. As the oldest and most respected institution in the black community, it provided informational networks, furnished meeting places, and facilitated fundraising. The church—central to black culture, symbol of black historical experience, expression of African Americans' aspirations—gave blacks a sense of identity, solidarity, and self-respect. And when it came to arousing and manipulating an audience, the combination of black preachers and Lulu White had few rivals.

White's effectiveness in soliciting memberships and funds was closely connected to the "transcendent leadership" styles of black ministers. These local ministers had developed a "behind-the-scenes" leadership cadre whose style was the antithesis of Lulu White's "out front" style. The ministers were effective organizers because they knew their church members and knew how to motivate them, how to recognize local leaders, and how to put those leaders out front. They knew how to delegate responsibility, placing members of their congregation over an auxiliary and giving them a sense of "somebodiness," while exacting loyalty and work from them. It was through these church members that many ministers gained efficacy and through these ministers that Lulu White gained some of the tools needed for reaching the rest of the black community.

White applied the same model to her relationship with labor unions and fraternal organizations. With a cadre of leaders and members of labor unions, fraternal organizations, political parties, social clubs, and churches going from door to door, spreading the word about the NAACP, and seeking new recruits, the task of soliciting membership became easier for White. From the beginning, such organizing efforts were crucial to the success of the movement and to Lulu White's leadership. As a result, whenever the NAACP called a rally to discuss an issue, much of the work was already done. Ministers, union leaders, and fraternal and social organization presidents provided an audience, generated enthusiasm, and conferred legitimacy upon the goals that White so ably articulated.

More often than not, applying the above model in her membership and fundraising drives worked well. On occasions, however, Lulu White's success in these endeavors was overshadowed by distractions. For example, when White accepted the post of director of state branches, she not only was suffering from a heart ailment, but also was enduring internecine squabbles in her own local chapter. At times this infighting seemed too much to bear. Writing to national membership director Lucille Black in November 1946, she said: "I am not sure I will keep this position. I am not happy as I have been in my work [with the NAACP] . . . Happiness is about all I could call myself getting out of it and knowing that some good was actually done." White continued, "I love the NAACP . . . I would like to be part of it, but it is not necessary to keep on and not be happy."

Black responded with wisdom and encouragement: "Personally I can think of no one who could do a better job than you . . . I know there are times when most of us feel like throwing in the towel, but we don't because we know that the cause for which we are fighting is bigger than all the petty annoyances. We certainly cannot afford to lose your service."[15] With this kind of support from her superior, White remained and pressed forward with the NAACP's work. She went to Shreveport, Louisiana, for the NAACP Louisiana-Texas Leadership Training Conference for branch secretaries, where she made a presentation on "Making Branch Committees Work." When she returned from the conference, she successfully applied and put into practice what she had learned in Shreveport. She moved across the state, organizing branches in Bryan, Palacios, Taylor, and other locations. Additionally, she sought advice from Gloster Current, national director of branches, who gave her all the information that he could think of "to make the NAACP go forward in Texas." Elated, White responded in kind: "No program should do any better than a well-planned program for the NAACP."[16]

White did a good job as director of state branches, working with local leaders to mobilize communities, organizing new branches, and disseminating information from the national and state offices to the NAACP affiliates. Despite the service that Lulu White rendered as state director, her work in this post was affected greatly by her position as executive secretary of the Houston chapter. By November 1946, her quarrel with Carter Wesley had reached an impasse, and all indications were that things were going to get worse at the local level.

On December 31, 1946, White informed her superiors—Rev. Albert A. Lucas, president of the Houston chapter; Walter White, executive secretary of the NAACP's national office; and Thurgood Marshall, NAACP counsel—of her intention to resign as executive secretary. Complaining of Wesley's recent article, Lulu White told Roy Wilkins, "When Julius saw this article, he went to pieces." Her husband felt that it was unnecessary for her to continue to be subjected to Wesley's diatribes and asked her to resign.

Upon hearing of Lulu White's intention to step down, A. Maceo Smith and other NAACP leaders began to speculate that, if White left the local branch, she would resign as director of state branches as well. But Lulu's letter suggested that she was hesitant about making good on her promise to leave: "I would rather drop dead than give up at this stage of the game, [but Julius] cannot stay out of the mess when personalities enter."[17] It appeared that White was trying to find some way to justify staying on as executive secretary. "I would not quit for anything," White wrote, "but Julius demands it."

She got her wish when Thurgood Marshall wrote to her concerning her departure. "I have heard of your resignation, and I for one deeply appreciate your position, but we need people like you and Julius in the work of the NAACP," said Marshall. "I have been accused of giving aid and comfort to you in your stand against segregation, so I might as well repeat that I think you are absolutely correct in your stand opposing segregation of any kind in Texas." Toward the end of his letter, Marshall was more forceful in his plea: "The reason I think you are right is not only because I believe in you personally, but I don't believe the long fight of the NAACP against segregation is wrong."

This letter was effective in changing Julius's mind. On February 4, 1947, Lulu White replied to Marshall, "Julius has decided that even though I am still being attacked by Mr. Wesley in his *Informer,* I still can work. This is how much we both appreciate your letter."[18]

Partly because of Marshall's letter and partly because the Houston chapter refused to accept her resignation and instead gave her a vote of confidence, White continued as executive secretary and director of state branches. As such, she went forward with organizing and reorganizing branches, soliciting memberships, and raising money for the NAACP. Along with these activities, she continued to make frontal attacks on segregation, to organize cultural events, and to publicize black history. White performed all of the above tasks for two years without a paycheck—only to be reminded by her husband, when one did come in 1948, that it was not enough to pay for gas.[19]

Despite what often appeared to be a discouraging situation, White did find the time for social diversions. At national conventions, she and Julius always gave a party so that they could "hobnob with the bigwigs." Each summer she vacationed in California, Cuba, or Mexico. She continually held teas in her home, both as social gatherings and fundraisers. And the Whites' twentieth wedding anniversary, held on June 20, 1948, was the talk of the town. Attendees constituted a veritable *Who's Who* of the black community, and even prominent whites, including famed attorney Percy Foreman, were present.[20]

When weighing her pleasant moments against the bad publicity that she and the NAACP were receiving at Wesley's hands, the nagging question uppermost in Lulu White's mind from 1946 to 1948 was whether to remain and continue to fight as executive secretary. Although, as director of state branches, she had another major arena in which to fight, White was totally committed to the local chapter. Perhaps, as she indicated, she "had allowed herself to become too engrossed in its work." The local branch had become "bone of her bone, flesh of her flesh." Yet, over time, White began to weaken in her resolve to stay. On April 10, 1948, she wrote to the executive board (L. H. Simpson, president; James E. Robinson, treasurer; Sid Hilliard; and J. H. Jemison) of her intention to resign. These men turned a deaf ear to her request, but White persisted. When the board convened at its last meeting of the year, she insisted that it take action on her resignation. Again the board skirted the issue. On January 5, 1949, she told Roy Wilkins: "I hate to give up the work here [but] I am tired of fighting within and without. This Branch has not had confidence in itself since Mr. Wesley['s] tirades on me and Thurgood." After venting her frustration, White drafted still another letter of resignation to the executive board, again to no avail. At this point White was in a quandary. She was reluctant to step down, but at the same time was fearful that if she did not leave, Julius would hurt someone. It was said that Julius had broken the butt of his gun on Wesley's desk protesting his attack on Lulu. Julius had warned that if Wesley continued such attacks on his wife, he would break the butt of his gun on Wesley's head.[21]

Unmoved by Julius's threat, Wesley yet again attacked Lulu in print. In his editorial of June 11, 1949, he reiterated his charge that White was a Communist, citing her signature on a petition protesting the jailing of the editor of the *Daily Worker* in a New York conspiracy trial. Two days after this editorial appeared, White tendered her resignation and demanded that the board accept it. In this letter, she admonished her colleagues to keep the faith in their struggle for equality: "This effort of Mr. Wesley to kill my influence . . . is not without intention [but] my wound in not so great that it will not heal. Let us all rededicate ourselves to the full emancipation of our people." Somewhat relieved, White wrote to Roy Wilkins on June 22, 1949: "Home for sure this time, can't have trouble with Julius about it."

Despite her resolve, White had mixed feelings about abandoning the power base that she had labored so long to create. She suggested as much in her letter of resignation: "I will be standing by if there can be any reconciliation for the great cause by my husband," said White. After all, the local branch was familiar territory. White knew the people, the leaders and those in the trenches, and how together they could make things happen. In short, she knew the game plan.[22]

Field Agent

Lulu White stepped down but not out of the local branch. She remained active, influencing decisions from within as a member and from without as director of branches—decisions ranging from the branch's operation to selection of her successor. No sooner had White resigned than she started using her contacts at the national office to influence the latter choice. "Send me a copy of the criteria and an application blank for executive secretary," she wrote to Gloster Current. Current responded with two wishes: "that the person chosen would be as interested" as Lulu White in the organization and that White "would remain as director of state branches." Current's latter request was fulfilled, but Christia Adair was made executive secretary against both his and Lulu's wishes.[23]

Having first-hand knowledge of White's skill as an organizer and mobilizer, Roy Wilkins and A. Maceo Smith made White a special field worker for the NAACP's Southwest Regional Office. The idea of regional offices had been launched in the mid-1940s for several reasons: they offered support to distant branches, provided legal and organizational expertise when the national staff was unavailable, and transmitted information and directives to branches in the hope of simulating them to prepare lawsuits in high-priority areas.[24]

The Southwest Regional Office was established in 1946, at a time when membership was declining nationally. The association's ability to sustain this new administrative unit was based on the perceived health of local branches and their ability to increase membership and raise money. Considering the resources that the New York office had invested in this region—subsidizing a number of costly lawsuits and two full-time staffs—the national office looked to the Southwest Regional Office to help arrest the downward trend in membership. The national office also looked to Texas to take the lead in this venture. To this end, A. Maceo Smith told Roy Wilkins that Lulu White would be a strategic addition to the southwestern staff for a nationwide membership campaign in 1950. Wilkins acknowledged that, while White's service in Houston at that time was problematical, she possessed a variety of qualities that would be most helpful in other cities. Citing White's successful civil rights mobilization rally in Houston in 1950, her unquestioned loyalty to the NAACP, and her work as chair of the Regional Advisory Committee, Smith reminded Wilkins that White had "the respect of a great many leaders in the region." Wilkins concurred and, after securing approval from Smith and Lucille Black, director of membership, placed White on the national staff in the Branch Department at a salary of twenty-four dollars per week from February 15 to June 8, 1950.[25]

With her new assignment, White no longer directed the association's activities from within Texas but rather initiated action outside the state. One of her first assignments as special field agent was in Lake Charles, Louisiana. Encouraged by Lucille Black, White went about her work with fervor. Within one week of her arrival, White, together with Rev. A. Washington, the local branch president, had developed a "leader-follower" cadre that would prove effective in the future. White was an intelligent leader whose unfamiliarity with the people of Lake Charles led her to rely upon the leadership abilities of black ministers. Wisdom born of experience had taught her that this approach would yield results. In areas where a branch was dead or dying, of course, it was necessary first to arouse the ministers before they could stimulate their congregations. In such cases, that burden fell on White's shoulders. Always vocal in articulating blacks' concerns and bold and uncompromising in her attacks on Jim Crow, she did not find this task particularly difficult. Whatever she said or did in Lake Charles worked. In less than two weeks, her followers had enlisted over one hundred new recruits. Upon her departure, many board members expressed their gratitude to White for being so "neighborly in helping to revive a dying branch."[26]

From Lake Charles White went to St. Louis, Missouri, to help boost sagging membership in that city. St. Louis had been one of the largest branches in the country in the early 1940s, but in recent years its participation in the movement had begun to wane. What St. Louis needed was a motivator, an energizer—someone to articulate the history, enthusiasm, and vision of the organization. In Gloster Current's opinion, White was "just the right kind of person with the proper personality and knowledge of the NAACP to handle the St. Louis situation." When securing White's assistance, Current reaffirmed to Julius White his confidence in White's ability: "We want you to know how much we appreciate Lulu's help, how greatly she is needed in helping to conduct this membership campaign for the NAACP."[27]

After settling in St. Louis, White immediately took steps to deliver on her promise to rejuvenate an ailing branch. Relying on that "transcendent" leadership model which she had used so effectively in Houston and Lake Charles, White assured Gloster Current that everything would be all right: "I guarantee this will be a campaign. I am getting the organization of it completed this week and then we will hit the field with the campaign and the workers." White placed the workers into five groups, with a minister as captain of each. One could argue that White, by employing such a technique, trapped these ministers into leadership positions. If they dropped out of the campaign, they would be branded as cowards and traitors. If the membership increased, they would enjoy the role of coordinators. In stirring these ministers to action, she often pointed out that each repressive act by whites tightened the bonds of pride and trust binding preachers and people together. To reinforce this bond between leaders and followers, White secured the services of people across class lines. Additionally, she offered incentives, such as merit certificates, to anyone who brought in more than fifty members. In the end, White's efforts paid off. The membership increased, and the St. Louis branch returned to the respectable position it had occupied in previous years.[28]

After completing her work in St. Louis, Lulu White attended the NAACP's annual national convention—a convention at which she would have perfect attendance for twenty years. Since she did not have credentials, she wrote to Gloster Current and offered her services gratis, in exchange for a pass into the Boston meeting. Not only did Current accept this offer, but at the convention he convinced the Texas native that the national office needed her services in Arkansas. White was prepared to go to Arkansas in August 1950, but, due to the branch's financial problems, she did not leave until September 1950. Employed for four weeks, White's stay cost $340. This included living expenses, travel, postage, stationery, and the printing of leaflets. All expenditures were paid by the national office, because the treasury of Arkansas's state branch had a deficit. Part of White's assignment was to conduct a fundraising campaign, with the understanding that the funds raised in this drive would be used to reimburse the national office.[29]

Lulu White arrived in Little Rock, Arkansas, on September 21, 1950, to face what could only be described as a "grand mess." There was dissension within the branch, division along class lines, and alleged embezzlement of funds by some members. This situation prompted Lulu White to write to Gloster Current: "Boy-O-Boy, you guys can give me really tuft [sic] assignments. I thought St. Louis was tough enough, but it was as sweet as a lamb. That tells you what this is like." Unlike branches that she had established or revived in Texas, Louisiana, and Missouri, here White had little or no cooperation from native Arkansans. In fact, she began working under conditions that one Arkansan described as "so bad, words are unable to explain them." Still White set out to do the impossible and make something out of nothing—to mobilize troops that had defected.[30]

White's first task was to help the Arkansas branch become solvent. "The work of the NAACP in Arkansas is at its lowest ebb," wrote Lucille Black to Lulu White. "In order to continue, we must raise at least five thousand dollars ($5,000.00) at once." In keeping with this directive, White sent out two letters to members and friends soliciting funds. The first letter was an attempt at consciousness raising. Calling upon the members to "form a united front against Jim Crow," White said the lack of funds in the branch treasury prevented it from litigating court cases. The second letter was more to the point. It emphasized the urgency of the situation: "This letter to you is an emergency! . . . We must raise at least five thousand dollars at once. Time is of the essence. Act now . . . We need money now."[31]

Following this letter-writing campaign, White took to the field, making personal contacts with prospective members. Immediately she encountered friction within the black community. "Every black person is in a different class and he/she does not want to work with someone out of his/her class," she wrote to Current. "They even have what is called First Families of Arkansas," continued White. "But when I get through with them, they will at least know that there is one organization in Arkansas in which they all may take part. I hope to net about $2,000 bucks."

In hindsight, it is clear that, given the divisiveness that existed in Little Rock, it was wishful thinking for White to believe that she would raise two thousand dollars or that she would change blacks' attitudes about themselves or the NAACP. Acknowledging the difficulties and disappointments she had encountered, she wrote to Gloster midway through the campaign, "I have never worked so hard in all of my life. This is a tuft [sic] one. But by all the devils in torment, I am going to get the job done."[32]

Despite White's noble intentions, she was unable to achieve the fundraising goal of five thousand dollars during her four-week stay. In fact, she was able to muster only fifteen hundred dollars by the time of her departure. Yet she had set in motion the mechanism, energy, and drive for reaching the five-thousand-dollar goal set by the national office. Arkansas finally achieved its goal in November, one month after White's departure.[33] The fact that White did not accomplish her objective had a great deal to do with lack of cooperation by black ministers, who hindered her efforts to mobilize the foot soldiers of the movement. White was not as successful as she had hoped, too, because of the brevity of her stay. Without firm roots in the community and without a strong "leader-follower" cadre, four weeks simply was too short a time in which to accomplish very much.

Foot Soldier and Turf Fighter

Lulu White's travel, both as a special field agent and as director of state branches, took her away from Houston and out of local chapter politics for almost the entire year of 1950. Upon her return, however, she got back in "the thick of things." She soon discovered that the transition from her administration to Christia Adair's had taken a heavy toll on the organization. Sagging membership and internal fighting had become the order of the day. While White expressed particular interest in helping the Houston chapter regain its prior status as one of the nation's leading branches, at times she was at the forefront of fighting within the branch. For instance, White's fundraising campaign in the Sweatt case competed directly with that for the local NAACP's annual event. Also, as the branch debated which course of action to pursue in eradicating Jim Crow, White was uncompromising in advocating a frontal attack on segregation. Too, Christia Adair already had served several months as executive secretary when White returned to Houston, but still White became the leader of a group which asserted that the organization needed a more dynamic leader to pull the rank and file along.

Born in Victoria, Texas, in 1897, Christia V. Adair was a graduate of Prairie View College. Her involvement with the NAACP began in 1925, when she became recording secretary of the Houston branch. Adair left the branch in 1939, when an investigation by the national office resulted in charges of financial improprieties. In 1946, Lulu White hired Adair as her administrative assistant. According to oral sources, White started grooming Adair to become her successor, but the two parted company after a few years because of personality conflicts and political and philosophical differences. Adair, a shy, introverted widow, was quite the opposite of the bold, gregarious Lulu White. To many, it seemed that Christia Adair lacked the skills and personality needed to lead the Houston chapter in the early 1950s.[34] Yet she was elected because of influence that L. H. Simpson, branch president, had with the executive committee.

By 1950, the United States, and Houston with it, were entering the McCarthy era, a period of extreme fear and suspicion of Communism. While Houston never was considered a mecca of socialism, during the late 1930s and early 1940s the city did experience well-publicized activities by Communists, socialists, and labor radicals. Although in reality, by the fall of 1950, Communists sympathizers had lost whatever momentum they once possessed, Houston's leaders felt otherwise. Red-baiting had become the norm in Texas, and in Houston. Powerful anti-labor and anti-integrationist forces employed Red Scare tactics to defame civil rights activists or anyone deemed subversive. Red Scare leaders in Houston were members of local elites who had a high degree of community visibility and access to influential mass media. As such, they exacerbated the fear of Communism and enabled it to flourish, not because they believed the city was threatened by subversion but because they viewed any change in the social, political, and economic status quo as a threat to their power and status—a threat inspired by Communism, with the NAACP as its accomplice.[35]

The Red Scare was only one of many tactics used to discredit Adair's leadership. Many local members and most national NAACP officials thought she was not the right person for the job. Donald Jones, director of the Southwest Regional Office, expressed grave doubts about Adair's qualifications. Lulu White argued that Adair was too conservative and did not have the strong personality required to meet the challenges faced by the branch. The local board was divided on the issue, and its differences would only worsen as Lulu White became the leader of a dissident faction.[36]

Lulu White's roles as director of Texas state branches and member of the local chapter did not always sit well with Adair. Many times these dual positions overshadowed Adair's. White's "take-charge" personality often caused her to circumvent Adair's authority under the disguise of performing her duty as director of state branches. In some instances, White internalized the role of executive secretary and wanted the last word on any action taken by the local branch. Her personality often did not allow her to sit back and hold her tongue or defer to the executive secretary in the face of discrimination being meted out to blacks or to the local chapter. White's personality style, coupled with the fact that she was a favorite of the national office, soon caused a rift between her and Adair. For example, on June 15, 1950, Adair complained to Gloster Current that "the national office called Mrs. White to be responsible for [Heman] Sweatt getting to the conference and it seems, she was able to solicit a neat sum from the Branch constituency, but the Branch [office] did not know anything until most of the funds had been obtained. We are glad he got there and would have been very happy to participate in anything the National wants Houston to do."[37]

A. Maceo Smith intervened before Current could respond to Adair's complaint. He told Donald Jones that "the Houston branch is in a crisis which will take time to heal." On the issue of declining membership, Smith said, "The branch membership [drive] was launched at the same time as the Houston Committee for Sweatt Victory Fund." Additionally, Wesley's *Informer,* which had served as the official organ of the local chapter, no longer was operating in that capacity. According to Smith, "Carter still has disdain for the branch and he is now supporting a Sweatt Education Expense Fund." So, in an attempt to alleviate internal strife and breathe new life into the Houston chapter, Smith asked the national office to send a field representative to work with Adair for two or three weeks. "I find that many people are willing to work," said Smith to Donald Jones, "but there must be close understanding and cooperation between the local, state, regional and national offices." Jones concurred with Smith and gave his assurance of cooperation.[38]

Donald Jones subsequently went to Houston with a twofold purpose in mind—to bring harmony to the branch and to talk about a membership drive. Before making the trip, Jones's superior assured him that Christia Adair and branch president L. H. Simpson would welcome assistance from the national office. So, when Jones left for Houston, he was confident that Simpson would be eager to start a new membership campaign. It was not long, however, before he discovered that he was mistaken. When he first approached Simpson about the issue, Simpson assured him that his church would aid in boosting the membership of the Houston branch to ten thousand and would sponsor a membership drive in the near future. Having worked closely with membership and fundraising drives, and aware of the time and energy they require, Jones asked Simpson to postpone the membership and fundraising campaign until May 1950. Simpson refused and proceeded with the campaign, but instead of ten thousand members, he attracted only thirteen hundred new recruits. In reporting this episode to the national office, Jones said, "The entire Houston situation is extremely bad . . . the branch is saddled with a President who would neither cooperate nor permit cooperation." He went on to say that Adair was incompetent, citing incorrect grammar, misspelled words, and numerous typos in her communications as evidence of his charge.[39]

Fearful that the branch might fall into the hands of "unreliable leaders," Simpson and Adair worked closely together to maintain power. They associated with only a small group of people whom they trusted, even when this meant excluding board members from meetings. In part because of this, they showed a disinclination to mount large membership drives. Similarly, on most issues they had contempt for the opinions of national representatives, simply because they perceived them to be Lulu White's sympathizers.

A novice on the job who wanted to make a name for herself, Adair often exaggerated in her reports to the national office. In so doing, she opened herself to criticism by Lulu White. For example, in 1950 Adair, in an attempt to both gain the confidence of the national office and boost sagging membership, reported that, for the first time, black high school teachers and principals were 100 percent behind the NAACP. Concrete documentation is lacking, but it seems highly unlikely that even 50 percent of the teachers would have made public their support for the NAACP, lest they incur economic reprisals. This report did not go unquestioned by Lulu White.

White's ire was raised again in 1952, when a report showed that the branch then had 3,537 members, compared to the 200 that it had when Adair assumed office. This report prompted White to request a membership list from the national office, which revealed the following numbers: 1,315 in 1950; 2,520 in 1951; and 2,690 in 1952. Although the membership increased between 1951 and 1952, this advance was only temporary, and in no way did it compare to the totals in earlier years in the 1940s. Moreover, progress meant very little to the national office unless it received its share of membership receipts. The amount that it received from Houston was negligible. Declining membership reports from throughout the country were so troubling to the New York office in 1951 that Current asked Adair to devise a plan to boost her membership and send it to the national office. Adair did not reply until 1953.[40]

Disgusted with Adair's faulty and inaccurate reporting, but more upset about Houston's small membership, White in 1953 took on a special project—increasing the membership of the local chapter. In a very short time, her recruitment effort showed results. The executive committee not only applauded White activities but elected her to conduct the 1954 membership drive in Houston. Elated over her election, White wrote to Lucille Black, "As far as membership is concerned, the Houston Branch is going to take its place—right back where it belongs—among the top branches so help me God!"

Setting her goal for 1954 at ten thousand members, White told Black she "not only hoped it . . . but will be in there working like h——— to make it double." While White did not double it, she was largely responsible for increasing Houston's membership in the years of 1953, 1954, and 1955. Lucille Black was thrilled to hear of Lulu White's work and was confident that she could restore "the membership to the level it ought to be."

The national office was aware of the potentially large membership in Texas; therefore, it was thrilled to have an experienced professional like White undertake the above initiative in the largest city in the state. The local branch, too, was pleased to have her. Houston's membership had declined from 5,343 in 1946 to 1,312 in 1950, resulting in an annual loss of $3,700 to the national office. Although the membership increased in 1952 and 1953, the increase was not enough to offset the previously mentioned deficit. This revenue shortfall also affected efforts to organize chapters and raise money in small cities and rural areas.[41]

As White became more involved in the local membership drive, she also became more involved in the day-to-day operations of the branch. If the Houston branch were to return to its former prominence in terms of members, programs, and prestige, it would require cooperation among all officers, especially the executive secretary and the director of state branches. Instead of this membership drive bringing Adair and White closer together, however, it intensified the hostility between them. Adair saw a large membership as opening the door for Communists and other undesirables. White, for her part, viewed membership as a means of controlling the Houston branch.

Since early 1953, White and Adair had been on a collision course. Matters were made worse, however, in May of that year, when John Flamer, an NAACP assistant field worker touring several Texas cities, requested a membership list from Christia Adair. Upon informing Adair of his possible visit, he received a less-than-polite reply. The executive secretary told Flamer to bypass Houston because she already had conducted a membership drive that had yielded well over six thousand members and that she was not going to call the board together to greet him. As Adair made these comments, she did not know that, on his way to Beaumont, Flamer had stopped in Houston and met with members of the local branch, including Lulu White, who had painted a different picture. Flamer then decided to investigate this matter at the chapter's next board meeting.[42]

In May 1953, Flamer came to Houston without notice. Of course Adair was flabbergasted and perturbed. She made it clear to Flamer that she had not invited him, did not need his assistance, and would not contribute toward his travel expenses. When Flamer told her that he was there to help in the membership drive, Adair wasted no time in informing Simpson of the nature of Flamer's visit. Simpson, who had scheduled a membership meeting, then converted it into a church meeting. After this meeting, Simpson apologized to Flamer, saying that the reason for his action was to keep troublemakers from taking over the board. Flamer did not accept this apology, and he told the national office that the Houston branch "need[ed] a thorough going over."[43]

A few days before Simpson called the "church" meeting, Lulu White, as director of state branches, had launched an inquiry into the financial transactions and legal undertakings of the Houston branch. After a year and a half of responding to Flamer's criticisms and queries from the state and national offices, Adair sought to set the record straight. In the December 24, 1954, edition of the *Messenger*, the branch's weekly newsletter, Adair asserted that, in 1949, White had left the branch with a deficit: "Sometimes we hear a remark made so much that we get the feeling that this is true, but let us look at some facts," said Adair. "1949 left us with [the following debts]: former Executive Secretary—$700; Office Assistant—$374; past due office rent—$350; past due telephone—$127." White quickly responded to these allegations in a two-page letter to the board. Saying that Adair's entire report was untrue, White denied the following specific charges: a salary due an office assistant and delinquent bills for rent and telephone. Arguing that Adair's report did more harm than good because it pointed to inefficiency in the Houston branch, White copied her letter to the following: Houston branch members; A. Maceo Smith, executive secretary, Texas Conference of Branches; H. Boyd Hall, president, Texas Conference of Branches; J. J. Jones, chairman of the board, Texas Conference of Branches; Edwin Washington, assistant field secretary for Texas NAACP; Ora Lee Terry, secretary, Houston branch; Christia Adair, executive secretary, Houston branch; and Gloster Current, national director of branches.[44]

The strained relationship between White and Adair deteriorated even further when Simpson called a surprise meeting of the branch's board on December 5, 1954, although the board had been dormant for the entire year. Simpson, while admitting that the organization had been less than active, said the purpose of the meeting was to elect a nominating committee that would present a slate of officers to the branch for an election scheduled for December 16, 1954. Lulu White was dumbfounded when she heard of the first meeting, because she had plans to wrest control of the branch from Adair. She was betting on the enemies that Adair supposedly had acquired because of her inefficiency, and also on new recruits she had brought into the organization. Moreover, she felt assured of victory because L. H. Simpson had announced that he would not seek reelection. White was equally pleased that the constitution and bylaws of the local chapter had been revised to stipulate the procedures to be used in an election.[45]

Angry because Simpson was proceeding with the meeting and not following either the spirit or the letter of the new governing documents, Lulu White rushed to the local headquarters and put up a fight. She objected to the nominating committee's recommendation for an election scheduled for December 16, for the following reasons: (1) Simpson had not followed the constitution in establishing this committee; (2) the date would not allow enough time for other names to be placed in nomination; and (3) the date did not allow time for the board to interview prospective nominees. Unable to convince others to support her, White reported the same to the national office, which in turn instructed the local branch (via a telegram) to hold the election on December 23, 1954. These instructions were disregarded, with the local branch president, Simpson, expressing his determination to go forward with the election.

Before the balloting, White tried to stop the election by saying that all of Texas branches were part of the national organization and that she was not sure what would happen if a branch refused to obey the dictates of the national office. Simpson responded, "We run our business down here and I want to go ahead with this election." He then called for the nominating committee to report its slate of officers. After reading the report, James Robinson offered an amendment to the report to strike O. L. Bell's name for president and to substitute L. H. Simpson's. When some of Bell's supporters questioned to why his name was left off the ballot, Simpson took the floor and made a speech nominating himself. He said that, while he did not want to run, Robinson had a right to nominate him if he so desired. When White raised the constitutional issue of nominating a candidate, a minister friend of Simpson's came forward with a petition signed by three members. After a spirited debate and discussion, balloting was held at eleven o'clock that night. By that time, most people had left the meeting in protest over the manner in which the election was being carried out. Still, when the ballots were counted, there were more votes than voters. The excess ballots were discarded, with no criteria given for doing so.

Lulu White then called on A. Maceo Smith to do something about the leadership of the Houston branch. She made it clear that Simpson was there only to protect Adair. "The truth of the matter," said White, "is that they are all tired of Adair and none of them have the courage to fire her." Because of the suspicious circumstances surrounding this election and the misgivings about the officers-elect, White told Smith that the national office should investigate this situation. Meanwhile, Simpson went ahead and set the date for installation of officers for Sunday, February 13, 1955.[46]

Some members of the executive committee clearly were upset at Lulu White for trying to stop the election, while others felt that there was something personal between her and Adair. They were right on both points. White wanted the board to reflect her point of view, and she was willing to go to any lengths to prevent the nomination or confirmation of anyone who did not agree with her. On February 5, 1955, she wrote to Gloster Current: "It seems to me that as National Director, you could call this installation off until these unconstitutionally elected people were elected correctly." To the surprise of no one, the installation of officers went on over White's protest. But White would not let the issue die, and she continued to call and write to her superiors until Gloster Current decided to come to Houston in March 1955 to investigate the situation.[47]

Initially, neither the state conference of branches nor the national office wanted to intervene in the Houston branch controversy. Since the early part of 1954, the Houston branch had been receiving negative publicity about its management. A. Maceo Smith, more familiar with the situation than Current, urged extreme caution, although he, too, was dissatisfied with the manner in which Houston was conducting its business. Meanwhile, when Current arrived in Houston in March 1955, he proposed a meeting of members of the local executive committee, officials of the state conference, and himself. When informing Simpson of this meeting, Current described the purpose as a frank discussion to clarify the "supposed" misunderstanding between the board and the national office. Although the misunderstanding centered on White's complaints about the last election, Current did not want Adair and Simpson to know that he was acting at White's behest.

At the March 21, 1955, meeting, Current's motives soon became clear to everyone, as he focused on the performance of the executive secretary. As a leader, he found Adair to be inefficient and at times incompetent. Further, he cited a lack of cooperation with Texas Conference of Branches, poor quality of office work, and poor communication skills. He further called for an audit of all the branch's finances and legal transactions. His final and strongest point was that the branch never had submitted Adair's qualifications as executive secretary to the national office. As Current began to chip away at Adair's performance, Simpson promised full cooperation and quickly adjourned the meeting, basing his action on the death of Walter White in New York.[48]

In a letter to Gloster Current, James E. Robinson, treasurer of the local branch, enumerated a number of other charges against Adair. In Robinson's opinion, Adair was rude and discourteous to people seeking information: "There [have been] numerous times when she has insulted people to the extent that it has made it very embarrassing for the local branch. These were people of influence and wealth who could help the organization." According to Robinson, one of the main causes for the Houston branch's unrest was Adair's attitude toward Lulu White. She "seemed to be most bitterly opposed to Lulu White to the end that she is not willing to cooperate with her at all." Robinson argued that Adair's ineptitude and Simpson's ineffectiveness were stifling the board. He concluded his letter by saying that there was a consensus among the members that, if something was not done about the election of officers and declining membership, the branch eventually would die.[49]

Before Gloster Current could make a report of his investigation to the national office, Lulu White, acting in her capacity as director of state branches, held a meeting with the executive committee of the local branch on March 21, 1955, to discuss the present state of affairs. As a result of this meeting, Lulu White drafted a letter to the national office, requesting that it deny Adair's application on or before December 31, 1955. The reasons given for her proposed termination were: (1) the employee did not meet minimum qualifications; (2) the employee had a personality problem; (3) Houston branch had not cooperated with the national office nor the state conference of branches; and (4) desegregation had assumed major importance in the Southwest, and therefore Houston needed a well-run, efficient branch. In concluding this formal report, White was concise and to the point, saying, "We will not be able to develop a good branch as long as the present Executive Secretary is employed."[50]

By the end of March 1955, Current had decided to have Adair removed from office. Having taken a poll of the board members, he knew he could get the national office to support his endeavors. In a private conversation Current convinced Simpson to submit Adair's application. When the Committee of Branches met on June 16, 1955, it disapproved Adair's request, citing her failure to meet minimum qualifications for the position as executive secretary.

All was not lost for Adair, however, because Current had not done his homework before taking this action. The national office could remove a branch official only by two methods. The local chapter must agree to it, or the chapter's charter must be revoked. Current's action caused concern on national and local levels. Trying to exert a moderating influence, Roy Wilkins, who had just assumed the post as national executive secretary following Walter White's death, decided to take the issue under advisement. After reviewing the tactical error made by Current, Wilkins wrote to Simpson, requesting the local chapter's position on Adair. Wilkins made it clear in his letter that, "whatever the outcome of the decision between the Board and the Branch, the decision would not come until the end of the year."[51]

In an attempt to ease the tension in the Houston branch between pro- and anti-Adair factions, the national board met in October 1955 and decided to send a field representative to work with Adair and to ask Gloster Current to discuss the leadership crisis with the local executive committee. Meanwhile, the national office informed Adair of the arrival of these two individuals and asked her to call members of the executive committee to meet with them. But Adair did not follow through. "Mrs. Adair, as expected[,] did not get in touch with all of the members of the Executive Committee . . . Fearful the national office was going to do something to harm her, she took precaution to insure the presence only of those members favorable to her." In order to make sure that the Lulu White faction was informed of the national office decision, Gloster Current called White and asked her to inform others of the meeting.

At the meeting, after some discussion, a compromise was reached. Adair would remain as executive secretary under two conditions: she would give the field representative a "free hand" in trying to remedy the situation, and the national office would take responsibility for the conduct and direction of the membership and fundraising campaigns. Both sides agreed, and Adair and Simpson held onto their power.[52]

White's attack on Adair was not entirely personal. She had begun to complain about Simpson and the board's inactivity in 1948. In her opinion, the Houston branch no longer was in the vanguard of the civil rights struggle. As she put it, "If we do not lead in such cause, we will lose our identity as a branch." Troubled by what she perceived to be Simpson's lackadaisical attitude toward branch activities, it was natural that White would push for a successor who would be more aggressive than Simpson. This being the case, one can understand how she would employ the tactics described above to oust Adair from the organization.

For all Adair's inadequacies, she regained some respect by the NAACP's national staff in 1956, when Texas Attorney General John Ben Shepperd made a concerted effort to drive the NAACP out of Texas by suing the association, intimidating its leaders, and confiscating its records and membership lists. In the case known as *State of Texas v. NAACP,* Adair was grilled on the witness stand for seventeen days, but still she refused to divulge a single name.[53]

As for the conflict between Adair and White, from the beginning of her tenure as executive secretary, Adair was at a disadvantage. She had neither the blessing of the national office or a strong following among the members, much less the leader-follower cadres that White had developed among the city's ministers, union leaders, and presidents of fraternal orders and social and professional clubs. When Adair accomplished something positive, it tended to be eclipsed by the work or personality of Lulu White. Adair was at the helm of the NAACP when the Houston airport and Yellow Cab company were desegregated. Yet, when many blacks recount these events, they give credit to Lulu White.[54] A few days after desegregation at the airport became a *fait accompli,* a black observer wrote, "Lulu White and other civil rights activists were eating at a desegregated lunch counter at the airport."

Similarly, when Sen. Lyndon Baines Johnson came to Houston in October 1953, in what may be considered the beginning of his reelection campaign, Lulu White was the person from the black community with whom he conferred. Upon returning to Austin, he wrote to White, "It was wonderful to visit you recently. I get a great deal of strength just listening to fellow citizens like yourself, who make up the real backbone of our country. Glad I got to see you, and let me know when I can help in any way." In Houston and in Texas, Lulu White was a larger-than-life public personality. As one of her friends remarked, "When Lulu walked into a place, everyone knew that the NAACP was there." In sum, others saw Lulu as the NAACP and the NAACP as Lulu; and she came to feel that the two were one.[55]

Despite the hostility and opposition that she encountered during Adair's administration, White continued to work earnestly in her capacity as director of state branches. Constantly stressing "the need to strike a blow at Jim Crow," she held educational clinics, formulated plans of action, organized protest rallies, and raised money via freedom bonds. For example, on April 21, 1955, she launched the Texas Freedom Fund Campaign in honor of Walter White, executive director of the NAACP, who had died on March 21, 1955. The Texas Freedom Fund Campaign was part of a nationwide effort to secure a million dollars to aid the NAACP in its fight against Jim Crow—or, as Lulu White put it, "that we might be free by '63." In soliciting financial contributions, White often referred to the Supreme Court decision in *Brown v. Board of Education* (1954); and she admonished her followers that the back of segregation had been broken in this decision. Therefore, "we should now consolidate our efforts, and . . . give to the limit," because "victory is in sight but the cost will be heavy."[56]

Four months after Lulu White sent the above message to the state branches, the country witnessed the lynching of Emmett Till, a fourteen-year-old boy who allegedly had whistled at and said "bye baby" to a white Mississippi woman. On August 1, 1955, Till, a native of Chicago, who had been visiting his grandfather in Money, Mississippi, allegedly was taken by the husband of the complainant to some unknown destination and killed. Three days later, Till's body was found in the Tallahatchie River. A gouged-out eye, a crushed forehead, and bullets in his skull were evidence of the beating he had taken. Around his neck, attached by barbed wire, was a seventy-five-pound cotton-gin fan. At the request of his mother, the sheriff sent the decomposed body to Chicago for burial.[57]

Contrary to the wishes of Mississippi authorities, Mamie Bradley, Till's mother, held an open casket funeral. Thousands of black Chicagoans attended the viewing, and the black press followed the episode closely. *Jet* magazine published a picture of the mutilated corpse.[58] In the black community, Till's case became a *cause célèbre*. African Americans waited in disgust for what they knew would be the outcome of the trial. Although the accused were identified by Till's grandfather, in August 1955, an all-white male jury found the white defendants not guilty. In response to this verdict, a groundswell of black voices throughout the country demanded justice. Among the voices were those of Lulu White and the national office of the NAACP. White's letter to the members of the NAACP's State Conference of Branches, dated October 6, 1955, expressed her sentiments: "The hour of decision is here! We must meet the enemy face to face. . . . Emmett Till committed no crime. He is the victim of having been born a Negro."[59] Arguing that Till's death was part of a campaign that was being waged to instill fear in black Americans in order to stifle the civil rights movement, White told her constituents that, although Emmett Till had been murdered, "they cannot kill the indomitable spirit of Freedom in us." Urging those reading her letter "to send money to their local or state chapters to help fight against this lynching in Mississippi," she was straightforward and concise: "The life you save may be your own." As an organizer, mobilizer, and foot soldier of the NAACP, Lulu White would not let America, Texas, or Houston forget that "it was time for a change."[60]

In sum, it can be said that Lulu B. White was the quintessential workhorse and, to a certain extent, a team player for the NAACP. She dominated the affairs not only of the local chapter, but also, to some degree, of the state. Under her direction, the NAACP's Houston branch weathered some difficult times, but also during the war years, the organization's membership and prestige grew. As director of state branches, White was the national office's main source of information and advice concerning the welfare of blacks in Texas. Similarly, she promoted the cause of the NAACP with evangelical zeal when she served as national field worker.

As a leader, White was egocentric and at times vindictive when she believed her authority was being questioned or undermined. Conversely, she could be kind, gracious, and even self-deprecating when circumstances seemed to require it. Still, it was White's interpretation of the NAACP philosophy, and her link to persons of influence within that organization, that, in the 1940s and 1950s, determined the direction of her leadership and her response to African Americans' social, political, and economic conditions. At the same time, the NAACP's status was enhanced by White's willingness to associate its cause with federal government initiatives and by her close identification with liberal reform and reform liberalism.

CHAPTER 7

Lulu White and
the Issue of Gender

African American women have played significant roles in the ongoing struggle for freedom and equality. Beginning with the Abolitionist movement, black women have championed causes that promoted justice for all. Through all this, they have had to cope with issues and stereotypes related to their womanhood. This is especially true for black female activists such as Lulu Belle White, whose public career spans the years 1937 to 1957. As White daily confronted oppression based simultaneously upon race and sex, she engaged in a persistent struggle for change, embodying a protest tradition that she carried forward in both mixed-gender and gender-specific groups. Working with black men and women to redress their collective grievances, she saw herself as a critical link in the social movement designed to liberate the black community from second-class citizenship. Her participation in community liberation struggles during the era of Jim Crow served as a means to empower her as an individual, to define the "self," and to redefine her womanhood.

The activities and behavior of black female activists routinely have been associated with a negative evaluation of black womanhood. This negative assessment has been tied to black women's history in the United States, a history riddled with contradictions. Under slavery, there were times when black women were treated as gender neutral and other times when they were locked into an exclusively female role. For example, in the antebellum South, slave women had the major responsibility for rearing and nurturing the planter's children, but at the same time they were considered morally depraved. They were defeminized and treated as men when they were sold and exchanged for profit, but were feminized whenever the planter and other white males wished to ease their libidinous urges. To put it bluntly, black women were not viewed as equal to white women generally, much less those white "ladies" who were placed upon a metaphorical pedestal.[1]

By the nineteenth century, the political and economic changes in this country brought on by industrialization had had a profound impact on the definition of white womanhood. At that time, many middle-class white Americans became convinced that men and women were so different that their duties, obligations, and responsibilities should constitute separate spheres of influence. It is within this context that "proper female behavior" came to be defined as piety, purity, submissiveness, and domesticity. The general feeling was that a woman's duties should be limited to caring for children, meeting the needs of the husband, and overseeing the physical maintenance of the home. Black women of that time were considered guardians of the race but at the same time were subjected to both male and white authority. They were regarded as preservers of culture within the context of their own race but were seen as intellectually inferior to black men and to white men and women.[2]

Negative assessments of African American womanhood and restrictive notions of white womanhood persisted well into the twentieth century. Both black and white women were affected by these views but reacted differently to them. At the beginning of the twentieth century, many white women were intent upon questioning and testing old, established limits. They were eager to leave the house and become visible in the public sphere, as educational and job opportunities expanded and as reform work became more acceptable. Their restlessness to leave home contrasted sharply with black females' tradition of working and their history of racial discrimination. As black economic expectations rose after the two world wars, many African American women would have been delighted to remain at home and cultivate a separate female sphere of activity, but financial realities continued to push large numbers of them into the job market. For these women and other African Americans, race remained a dominant factor. The obstacles facing blacks were tremendous, as the majority were impoverished, landless, semiliterate, and voteless. During the first half of the twentieth century, it seemed to many that African Americans were suspended somewhere between slavery and citizenship.[3]

One of the dominant issues facing black female activists at that time was the extent to which they understood the relationship between their status as women and the growth and development of the African American race. Using as a frame of reference Jewel L. Prestage's study of the historical significance of traditional (polling people, voting, and participating in party politics) and nontraditional (participating in women's clubs, teacher organizations, and benevolent societies) political activism by the African American woman, one can argue that Lulu White understood the correlation between race and gender. Prestage maintains that (1) African American women always have engaged in political activities, the nature of which have been determined by prevailing legal and cultural customs of the time; (2) these political activities have been directed toward altering their disadvantaged status as both African Americans and women; and (3) historically, African American women have escalated their political activities progressively, moving from a predominance of nontraditional activities to a predominance of traditional activities and have emerged as the prime users of these traditional avenues.

Perhaps the most prevalent explanation of the actions of black female activists lies in political socialization theory. This theory attributes to men and women clearly defined roles and status, and explains sex differences in adult political behavior as products of sex differences in childhood socialization. For the black activist, however, socialization theory must be coupled with a consideration of marginality. The theory of marginality involves "some measure of unconventionality in thinking and the absence of a clear standard of conduct," characteristically associated with innovators and creative thinkers.[4]

"The absence of a clear standard of conduct" was central to Lulu White's activism. To be sure, she was not an exception in this regard. Women who seek to enter the world of political activism, whether they want to or not, reject some of the values and norms of majority female culture. White's posture as chief executive officer of the Houston NAACP illustrates this statement. For example, forty years after her death, friends and colleagues were able to recall Lulu White's demeanor, mannerisms, and actions with a great deal of clarity. One of her classmates at Prairie View remembered White "as a loud mouth and sassy, one who didn't take stuff off anyone." Most people of that era took this comment to mean that White was too assertive—too unladylike. Some associates described her as bold, others as fearless. Most, however, identified her as a "powerful" woman. More often than not, her friends contended that people in the NAACP did not view her as a man or a woman, but as a strength; gender was not an issue, since her personality was so strong.[5]

The prevalence of such a perception of Lulu White raises crucial questions. What influences in White's early life helped to determine the balance that she eventually would strike between her activism and her gender identity? How did she see the issue of gender in view of her growing power within the NAACP?

A review of Lulu's upbringing provides intriguing hints as to the influences that prompted her actions and shaped her views of a proper gender role. Lulu White was born in a house owned by her parents, a house that sat on thirty-five acres of land. Although the family did not have much money, Easter and Henry Madison managed to provide a fairly good living for their children. As important as the teaching and nurture that they provided were the examples that they set. Ownership of land meant that the Madisons did not have to depend on whites for a place to live, nor for a livelihood. Easter Madison's perseverance in acquiring rudimentary education after rearing several children speaks volumes about the importance that she attributed to hard work and education, and about the benefits that can accrue therefrom.[6]

As Lulu White and her siblings grew into adulthood, they had strong institutional support—their family, their own church, school, and social organizations. Within the values that governed their lives, the Madison children readily embraced the gender roles that were part of their value system. They knew that women were to be respected and that there were certain things within the domestic sphere—cooking, sewing, nurturing—that were exclusively female. These previously mentioned factors, along with a soft-spoken mother and the deference she paid to her husband, caused the Madison children to accept the notion of proper female behavior. Presumably the Madisons enjoyed a secure existence in their separate black world of Frog, Texas, during the first two decades of the twentieth century. No matter how insulated and comfortable they were, though, the realities of racism and segregation in East Texas managed to intrude into their lives from time to time. And the injurious effects of segregation were equally traumatic for males and females. Consequently, for the overwhelming majority of blacks, as for the Madisons, race counted much more than gender.

African Americans in the postwar years reacted in a variety of ways to the ugly realities of segregation. Some engaged in confrontations with the police; others joined labor unions and organized political, social, and self-help clubs. Still others staged campaigns to gain the right to vote. When White reached maturity and encountered segregation, she reacted to it quite strongly. When faced with working in an unpleasant Jim Crow situation after high school, she quit her job and went to college. White's college enrollment came at a time of heightened race consciousness, rising expectations, and growing interest in reassessing gender roles. During that time, the juxtaposition of race and gender issues served to focus particular attention on the African American female.[7]

When Lulu White came to Prairie View in 1924, amid a national revolution in manners and morals as well as a fledgling civil rights movement in Houston, the college tended to devote a great deal of attention to its female students. It broadened the definition of women's sphere of influence to include certain activities in the public sphere—public service, teaching, and nursing. Many blacks favored this kind of education because it took into consideration the realities of the black female experience, which always included work outside the home. Still, women's education at Prairie View, fostered by a goodly number of female instructors, was characterized by a strong adherence to the domestic ideology. White learned this lesson first hand living in the Home Economics Cottage, where emphasis was placed on making female students better housekeepers, though not necessarily domestic workers.[8]

At Prairie View, training for a profession, regardless of one's major, was more practical than classical education and was designed to transform female students into "true women." The college not only offered or required courses in orientation, home economics, and health education, where the tenets of true womanhood were taught; but also it reinforced this learning with extracurricular activities such as those of the Young Women's Christian Association. As both a student and an officer in the campus YWCA, White came to accept and exhibit the behavior considered proper for a middle-class female—at least as long as she was in the presence of her superiors. Most of her classmates who were interviewed for this study contended that she used foul language a great deal, but, as one of her friends put it, "Even when Lulu cursed, she cursed with refinement."[9]

As Lulu White pursued her degree, she became keenly aware of broader racial issues. She talked with other blacks who had suffered some of the same indignities that confronted her. She witnessed acts of discrimination and violence meted out to African Americans, and she also read books, articles, and magazines about the black struggle for equality. On the other hand, while a student she also saw signs of change. She observed aggression, assertiveness, and boldness on the part of black Houstonians and other Texans who were trying to overturn the white primary. The lawsuits filed by these individuals were powerful symbols of fearlessness; these people were determined to stand up for their civil rights.

While the Prairie View faculty worked hard to provide a nurturing and supportive atmosphere that encouraged students to think critically, like their counterparts at most historically black colleges and universities, they also provided training in etiquette. Throughout the first half of the twentieth century, many of Prairie View's faculty and administrators were committed to training "proper ladies" for their middle-class roles in society. On the one hand, they accepted the expanded limits of African American women's role in a segregated society; these females had an obligation to their race. In the process "of lifting as [they] climbed," however, Prairie View graduates were expected to exhibit traditionally female behavior—behavior reflecting high morals, spirituality, and self-sacrifice.[10]

Lulu White did not subscribe fully to the above tenets. When she left Prairie View, she was determined to become an agent for change. On her way to accomplishing this goal, she found it necessary to establish a home and a power base. Domesticity never was White's sole reason for creating a home. For her, home was not simply a physical structure, a dwelling place; it also was a psychological space in which she belonged and where she felt necessary and special. Her "marital" home was socially and emotionally satisfying, but it also was politically empowering. Very often it served as a meeting place for the fraternal orders or social clubs of which she was a member—the Grand Court of Calanthe; Eastern Star; the 1906 Art, Literary and Charity Club; the Married Ladies Social Club; the Ethel Ransom Art and Literary Club; and the Metropolitan Council of Negro Women. The activities of these federated clubs included embroidery, play writing, book reviews of African American authors, helping to finance a neighborhood playground, providing wood for heating for destitute families during the winter, sponsoring a fashion show for the Blue Triangle YWCA, visiting black residents and patients at convalescent homes, and celebrating National Club Women's Day. Like her experience in the dormitories at Prairie View, these clubs allowed White sustained interaction with women with whom she shared goals and hard work. Her intimacy with a community of women reinforced White's sense of belonging and, simultaneously, her desire for individuality.[11]

In 1943, Lulu White's long-held dream of becoming a public agent of change was realized when she was named executive secretary of the NAACP's Houston chapter. It was not long after assuming this post that White found it necessary to step outside the bounds of "proper middle-class behavior" to express some of the indignation that black Texans felt when treated as second-class citizens, especially in the area of public accommodations.

In a city noted during the first half of the twentieth century for its virility, lawlessness, and provincialism, blacks had to walk a tightrope over segregation. By and large, the hostility an African American might have felt toward Jim Crow was tempered by concern for her or his physical safety. Although resentful of Jim Crow laws, black Houstonians' behavior usually ranged from acceptance and avoidance to rationalization for maintaining self-respect. Overt expressions of hostility usually were reserved to boisterous, militant black males. In this regard, Lulu White was an anomaly. Unlike other female leaders, who, while resentful, were passive in their opposition to Jim Crow laws, she was equal to the most vocal black males in her opposition to segregation. A look at Lulu White's role in the struggle over public accommodations in the 1940s is, therefore, instructive.

In the 1940s, most white-owned establishments either refused to serve black patrons or made special arrangements for them. In many department stores, there was a certain section reserved for blacks, which was out of the sight of white customers. In other stores, black clerks were employed specifically to work with black customers. In still others, blacks were barred from trying on hats and undergarments. Starting in 1943, Lulu White made an earnest effort to change these practices. During that year, she walked into many stores and tried on hats, only to be told after the fact that she could not do so. White's response was, "I have," and then she walked out. The next day, she usually persuaded several other black women to follow her example. Reprisals were seldom made against Lulu White because many merchants were aware of her position with the NAACP and were afraid of a boycott.[12]

By and large, the attitudes of white owners of eateries were no different from those of department store owners. More often than not, they blatantly refused blacks service or made special arrangements for them. As Charles Johnson recorded in 1937, "Interracial contacts in eateries (restaurants) were sore spots in [Houston], although whites occasionally mingled with blacks in black-owned cafes and salons." It appears that, since many Africans Americans owned restaurants, they were less vocal in protesting exclusionary practices in such establishments than they were in other types of public businesses. This indignity did not escape Lulu White, however. She raised her voice against such discriminatory policies on the grounds that "separate but equal" was unconstitutional.

In 1948, she staged a protest to have signs reading "White" and "Colored" removed from the soda fountains at Kress's Department Store. She scored a big success, as the signs were removed and blacks were allowed to use the fountains. White's protest against separate soda fountains was not novel. The same thing occurred in Greensboro, North Carolina, in the 1940s. During that time, biracial teams quietly visited county offices, large department stores, and other downtown public facilities and bathrooms. Over a period of months and without any formal action, owners of these businesses painted over most of the discriminatory signs. The major difference between the Houston and Greensboro incidents was that Greensboro's was led by an Interracial Commission, which relied upon negotiation to achieve its goal. In Houston, White's use of direct confrontation caused many to criticize her for unladylike behavior.[13]

At least on one occasion when Lulu White used both negotiation and assistance from the Texas Commission on Interracial Cooperation, her actions nevertheless were perceived as going beyond the boundaries of "finer womanhood." At that time, White attempted to desegregate public performances held at the city auditorium, Music Hall, and Sam Houston Coliseum. More often than not, these public facilities prohibited blacks from attending the same performances as whites. Sometimes, however, they provided a section in the balcony for black patrons. At the time when White went before the Houston City Council to ask that measures be taken to remedy this situation, not many white women had appeared before this white-male-dominated governing body. With the help of the local NAACP chapter and the Interracial Committee, Lulu White was successful in getting the city to change its Jim Crow policies. Even so, the appearance of a forceful black woman at the council meeting was irritating, as White not only asked, but demanded, "that equal accommodations be granted rather than balcony only."[14]

Never one to "bite her tongue," Lulu White often told of a confrontation with the superintendent at Houston's Union Train Station in the "Colored" waiting room. As darkness approached, White asked the superintendent to turn on the lights, whereupon he replied, "I had no idea that it was dark."

White snapped back, "Somebody had an idea it was. I see the lights are on on the other side."

Becoming perturbed, the superintendent said, "What did you come here for, a fight?"

"Yes, I did," replied White. Exactly one hour earlier than was the custom, the lights came on on the "Colored" side.

Most of White's acquaintances can recount at least one similar story. Yet, the incident at Union Train Station stands out because it defies the mores of Southern society. For a black woman to question a white male authority figure and to admit openly that she was "picking a fight" with him not only struck white southerners as despicable behavior, but also defied the whole notion of a woman's place and "ladylike behavior."[15]

While White's actions and attitude were not unique, they fit within a context of boldness displayed by many African American women over time. Notably, Mary Church Terrell was at the forefront of the Women's Suffrage Movement. Recalling the 1898 meeting of the National American Women Suffrage Association (NAWSA), she took pride at having been among the few who stood when the presiding officer asked such behavior of those who believed that women should have the right to vote. "I forced myself to stand up, although it was hard for me to do so. In the early 1890s it required a great deal of courage for a woman to publicly acknowledge before an audience that she believed in suffrage for her sex when she knew the majority did not," said Terrell.

Similarly, Ida B. Wells-Barnett, a black journalist, led a campaign against lynching from 1890 to 1910 and proposed that bold actions be taken to stop violence. She urged readers of her newspaper to save their money and abandon any community that lynched innocent men. Wells dared to challenge the myth behind which lynch mobs had hidden. Asserting that white women willingly engaged in sexual acts with black men, Wells intended for her provocative words to be used as a defense for the men of her race; but these words also launched the anti-lynching movement in this country and ultimately forced Wells to leave the South.

Born in 1916 in the Mississippi Delta, Fannie Lou Hamer was the youngest of twenty children. When she was two years old, her family moved to Ruleville on a Sunflower plantation. After spending many years on that plantation and also as a sharecropper, Hamer came in contact with members of the Student Nonviolent Coordinating Committee (SNCC) in 1962 and her life was suddenly changed. These students were spending the summer in Mississippi in an effort to help blacks register to vote. Inspired by the action and speeches of SNCC members, Hamer led a group of nineteen blacks to the Ruleville Courthouse to register to vote. Despite the denial of the right to vote, the disorderly conduct that she exhibited and the subsequent violence and economic intimidation that followed, Hamer persevered until she became a registered voter in 1963. In 1964, she became one of the founders of the Mississippi Freedom Democratic Party (MFDP)—a party formed to challenge the seating of the regular all-white Mississippi delegation. In her capacity as vice chairperson of the MFDP, Hamer made a televised address to the convention. The results of which was that the national Democratic party pledged not to seat delegations that excluded black delegates at its future conventions.[16]

Although the behavior of the aforementioned activists did not always fit contemporary notions of proper female behavior, they still fit comfortably into the established tradition of African American female assertiveness that comes straight out of slavery. Consequently, black women, such as Lulu White, Mary C. Terrell, Ida B. Well-Barnett, and Fannie Lou Hamer, whose action was applauded by other African Americans, received a message from the larger American society that such action was unladylike. While the assertiveness, brashness, courage, and persistence were necessary for African American liberation, black women were treated differently from white women in a society that embraced white standards of conduct and beauty.

As membership in the Houston NAACP branch increased and changed over time, the branch became increasingly difficult to administer; Lulu White stayed the course, however, and in the process gained a reputation as an uncompromising administrator. She demanded hard work and dedication from all those around her. In fact, she enjoyed her work. She once told Lucille Black, "I get a kick out of these people telling me 'Mrs. White you work people harder than Daisy Lampkin.'" With the same intensity, she protested vehemently when NAACP members asked the government for a separate affiliate of the Office of Price Administration, and when Carter Wesley used the NAACP's mailing list to invite members of the Texas Council of Organizations to discuss integrating the University of Texas.

Such administrative fervor evoked a wide range of reactions from White's NAACP colleagues. Wesley opined that White thought the NAACP should have a monopoly on civil rights. Daisy Lampkin, however, was impressed by White's work habits. Gloster Current found her competent, while Christia Adair thought she was too demanding. In a word, one either liked or disliked Lulu White, agreed with her or did not. Surely, however, no one could accuse her of shirking her responsibilities.[17]

White's reputation as a tough administrator constituted an important challenge to the general notion of women's "place" in the 1940s. Even in an era when the role of women in the African American community expanded, White's position as a leader in a male-dominated organization rendered her an anomaly. Since men had an advantage in establishing themselves as leaders of the civil rights movement, by virtue of a near monopoly on political power within the black community, it seems remarkable that any woman achieved a position of such authority. To be sure, the NAACP was more democratic in this regard than most civil rights groups. The organization had many black female secretaries, project directors, and local leaders. At the time of White's appointment, however, it had no female executive secretary in the South. Established in the early 1940s, executive secretary posts usually went to black men of the Northeast. The fact that a black woman was appointed to such a post in the South suggests that Lulu White had leadership qualities that the organization deemed crucial.[18]

As a leader, Lulu White offered quite a contrast to those black women who challenged white authorities but deferred to black ministers, or who criticized male activities only in hindsight. White engaged in a long-drawn-out verbal war with Carter Wesley and C. W. Rice, and a tongue-lashing, letter-writing brawl with A. Maceo Smith and L. H. Simpson. When, unbeknownst to White, Smith wrote to the national headquarters complaining about the manner in which she followed procedures, she confronted him. "You know the Houston branch observed directions when almost none of the other branches did. Give directions to those branches who are not observing the rules," wrote White.

While some would question her boldness in taking on a man in public, it is likely that she did not consider herself "oppressed" by black men, whether inside or outside the movement. Consequently, she did not seek to alter her role as a female agent of change in a man's world. Rather, she fought for civil rights with her male peers, acting as an equal. Consequently, she was respected by her coworkers, male and female alike. Some suspected that, in an effort to maintain that respect, she intentionally projected the assertive, blunt, independent part of her nature.[19]

Looking beyond her leadership qualities, one can see another side of Lulu White. After all, the tough, uncompromising image White projected as a leader was incompatible with the qualities many Americans of the 1940s and 1950s thought a good wife should possess. Lulu White was no ordinary woman, but neither was she married to an ordinary man. Initially, Julius's involvement in the NAACP had a great impact on Lulu's thinking and work within the organization. As time passed and Lulu became more deeply involved, however, he had to cope with an uncommon situation. He was married to one of the most powerful leaders in the local branch of the NAACP. Although the two strong personalities often were complementary, strain was inevitable, given the nature of her job. One of the most important issues she had to resolve was the balance of power in their relationship. Obviously, Lulu White exercised a fair amount of power in the NAACP. But to what extent did such authority extend to her marriage? To some contemporaries, both Lulu and Julius seemed strong-willed individuals; others contended that Julius dominated the household, since he was the major breadwinner as well as the financial sponsor of many of Lulu's activities. While Lulu was sensitive to his likes and dislikes, it is safe to say that Julius White would not, could not, and did not dominate Lulu White.[20]

As has been mentioned, Lulu White's job took her outside the conventional mode of a married housewife. She often traveled for weeks, not only out of town, but out of state as well. Consumed by her work, White used her house and office interchangeably. Still, she made creative use of her leisure time. Despite her myriad responsibilities, she made extraordinary efforts to plan activities with NAACP friends whose company her husband enjoyed. For instance, before the 1946 national convention, she wrote to Ella Baker, "You and Bob and the 'Gang,' get ready for a good time in June. Believe it or not, we already have ringside seats to the Louis-Conn Fight and Julius White will be in one of them." When White did not hear from Baker, she wrote Lucille Black with the same message: "We really want to have a good time," said White. "Of course Julius does not drink, but will pay for plenty of drinks, ha, ha." A fun-loving person, White often invited members and friends of the NAACP to her house for tea, cocktails, and card games. Her closest friends and confidantes—Lucille Black, Daisy Lampkin, Gloster Current, and Thurgood Marshall—were frequent visitors. They were not only Lulu's friends, but also friends of her husband and their two adopted children. Julius welcomed them into their home and socialized with them at each national convention.[21]

Within their relationship, Lulu and Julius tested limits and tried to establish a balance of power. Their unique status in the NAACP as a wealthy husband–powerful wife team complicated the task of establishing that balance. For instance, in 1947, White asked the national headquarters about a paycheck that she had not received, "just to keep the record straight with the Big Boss at 2620 Tuam Street." No matter how hard White worked to keep their relationship in balance, stress became evident with the Carter Wesley controversy. On December 30, 1946, she called Thurgood Marshall collect to say that, at the insistence of her husband, she was resigning as executive secretary. Sometime afterward, she wrote to Lucille Black, "The Boss says I must go." A few weeks later, she reiterated the same theme: "I took a vow to obey." Writing to Walter White about the controversy with Wesley, Lulu White said, "If anyone can convince Julius that I was not the source of disruption in the NAACP, I'll stay on. . . .

I can not show him it is not my fight, but for the cause." In her letter of resignation to L. H. Simpson, she made the same argument: "I'm quitting because of Julius." Aware of the strain in their marriage and of the possibility of losing Lulu White's services, Gloster, Current, Thurgood Marshall, and A. Maceo Smith all wrote to Julius when seeking Lulu's assistance as a special field worker. She confirmed Roy Wilkins's suspicions concerning the strain in her marriage when, about a final letter of resignation, she wrote, "Home for good . . . No more trouble with Julius." In a sense, White had two marriages—one to Julius and one to the NAACP. Loving two was not always easy to manage.[22]

Lulu White's was a multifaceted personality. Although those characteristics most compatible with the popular notion of proper female behavior often were submerged in the intensity of her work, she did engage in gender-specific activities. Her memberships in women's clubs offer many examples. Like other black women's clubs at the turn of the century, hers were composed of women with shared traditions and outlooks, women trained early in social consciousness and community involvement. The members of the Married Ladies Social Club met once a month to discuss self-improvement, community development, and prevention of juvenile delinquency. Members of the Metropolitan Council of Negro Women, a unit of the De Pelchin Faith Home, were concerned with the care and adoption of black foster children. In contrast, the 1906 Art, Literary and Charity Club emphasized raising black consciousness via discussions of the latest works written by or about American and African American authors. In these clubs White enjoyed female bonding, through which she found lasting friendships.[23]

In addition to self-help and racial uplift, Lulu White had other interests in women's clubs. A case in point was the Chat-an-Hour Coffee Club, which White organized in 1949. Her underlying purposes in starting this club were to form a Political Action Committee (PAC) to get more blacks elected to public offices, to decide who was best suited to represent the black community in such positions, and to expand her own political power base in the community, since she had just been ousted as head of the local NAACP branch. The club, as conceived by White, had special responsibilities for its female members. Women of the Chat-an-Hour Coffee Club were responsible for community, educational, and cultural programs. They met weekly to discuss books or some other aspects of African American history. They also advocated improvements in the health care delivery system and called for an educational program predicated on African American values. Furthermore, the club gave women like Lulu White an opportunity to seek self-actualization and to expand their power outside, as well as within, the NAACP.[24]

The formation of the Chat-an-Hour Coffee Club represented no psychosocial shift in its members' personal identities or in their social or political agendas. Rather, it simply offered a new channel through which Lulu White and her followers could continue their struggle to improve their own lives as well as the general standard of living in the ever-broadening communities of which they were a part. The Chat-an-Hour Coffee Club gave White and her members an opportunity to design and implement reform programs within the context of their African American women's culture. And it afforded women means to utilize their informal networks to achieve the formal, structured, programmatic goals of the NAACP. Even so, the members' involvement did not preclude their playing meaningful roles in the NAACP itself. Indeed, White used her dual status as both outsider and insider not only to function effectively, but also to manipulate two worlds—one dominated by racism and the other dominated by sexism. Her clear understanding of her status as a woman and as a black person enabled her to play key roles in improving living conditions for African Americans in Houston. Her organized activities suggest a clearly articulated definition of black womanhood as both linked to the black community's interests and characterized by self-help, racial solidarity, and community uplift.[25]

It would be both unfair and erroneous to try to fit Lulu White's life into rigid categories. She was quite comfortable playing an assertive, commanding role and was equally comfortable playing a more conventionally feminine role. Even if other people saw a contradiction between those two stances, Lulu White did not. She was annoyed, though, by people who judged her solely on the basis of limited notions of "proper female behavior." Among these were groups and individuals who labeled her actions "Communist"—Carter Wesley, white newspapers, the superintendent of Houston's Union Train Station, and the Minute Women of Houston.

The Minute Women, formed in 1949 as a national organization, consisted mostly of white Republican women who wanted to prevent the spread of Communism in American institutions. They believed that conservative white women, if united and activated, could become a potent pressure group in the fight to preserve traditional political, economic, and moral values. In defending the traditional American way of life, they were dedicated to twelve principles: (1) belief in God and country, (2) principles embodied in the Constitution, (3) fairer taxes, (4) state's rights, (5) clean politics, (6) economy and efficiency in government, (7) a sound dollar, (8) free enterprise, (9) right to work, (10) a courageous and enlightened foreign policy, (11) free press and the truth, and (12) true patriotic teaching in schools and colleges. The terms used to designate the above principles had special meanings. For example, *state's rights* meant continued racial segregation. *Fairer taxes* alluded to repeal of the income tax law. *Right to work* referred to the Minute Women's opposition to labor unions and support of the open shop concept. Thus, White's positions on labor unions and segregation were diametrically opposed to those of the Minute Women.[26]

Between 1948 and 1950, many whites in Houston espoused the thinking and philosophy of the Minute Women, but the Houston chapter of the Minute Women, established by Eleanor Watt and Helen Darden Thomas, was not formalized until the spring of 1951. By 1952, the chapter had become the most militant Red Scare group in Houston. Most of this power and influence resulted from the dedicated work of about fifteen women. The one whose work stood out especially in this group was Helen Darden Thomas. She spent most of her time compiling a list of individuals whom she believed to be Communists or to have Communist proclivities. She gathered most of her information from the press, from letters that could not be substantiated, and from the discredited files of the House Un-American Activities Committee (HUAC). Although HUAC members refused to vouch for its accuracy, the list compiled by Thomas became the single most complete source used by these women to discredit people they deemed leftist sympathizers. Thomas relied heavily upon the information contained in HUAC publications to create a dossier of fellow Texans. She presented her findings in a report entitled "Individuals from Texas Reported as Having Been Affiliated with Communist or Communist Front Organizations."[27]

By the time that Thomas compiled this list, Lulu White had already been labeled a Communist by whites, as well as by some blacks. The FBI had her under surveillance, even though she had stepped down as executive secretary of the local chapter of the NAACP. Expectedly, the publication of Thomas's list served to reinforce the public's perception of White as a Communist. This list also reinforced the belief, widespread in southern society, that Communism was diametrically opposed to "proper female behavior." Unfortunately, a lack of evidence prevents one from knowing if there was any actual contact or communication between Lulu White and the Minute Women. One can infer, however, that, because White was associated with two organizations that the Minute Women viewed as Communist—the NAACP and organized labor—her behavior seemed to them the epitome of unladylike conduct.

Lulu White's unconventional actions sometimes reflected attitudes regarded as surprising and unpredictable. Yet, despite her strength, her vision, and the realities of her life, White evinced some very traditional attitudes regarding gender roles. Possessed by a burning desire to be a mother but unable to conceive, White adopted two children—a boy, Wilton Upsinger, and a girl, Dorothy Upsinger. When taking her nieces on summer vacations in California, White refused to discuss with them the Jim Crow encounters that they experienced at restaurants along the way. Not only did she provide lodging for Thurgood Marshall, Daisy

Lampkin, and Gloster Current whenever they came to Houston, but also she personally prepared lavish meals for them.[28]

In such activities, White was not alone. Historically, many black women have demonstrated similar attitudes. For example, in 1916, Mary Barnett Talbert told assembled delegates of the National Association of Colored Women that they should "take an active personal interest in everything that concerns the welfare of home, church, community, state . . . and [country]." Mary McLeod Bethune reminded black women of their roles in uplifting the race by stressing a three-fold commitment to family, career, and social betterment. Of the civil rights movement of the 1960s, Charles Lowery argued that "men led, but women organized . . . Of course they took civil rights workers into their homes, giving them a place to eat and sleep. They canvassed and showed up at more mass meetings and demonstrations than did men." So did Lulu White.[29]

Lulu White was an extremely complex individual, and any effort to assess her contribution to the civil rights movement in Texas during the 1940s and 1950s must recognize that part of her struggle was a continuing effort to hold onto her own sense of "self and womanhood" in the face of pervasive and pernicious stereotyped images—big, fat, black, wild, and female. Despite what anyone said or thought of her, Lulu White acted in ways she defined as necessary and appropriate and did things that she thought were important. If she experienced moments of doubt about achieving her goal of destroying the constitutional basis upon which Jim Crow rested, she did not let doubt stop her. Rather, she fulfilled the role or espoused the philosophy that mattered most to her. She functioned as a leader and a worker of the NAACP at local, state, and national levels. Doing these things was important to her. Moreover, she was a woman, a wife, a foster mother, and an aunt—and all those things were important to her, too!

She Was Not Afraid

ong a crusader for integration and civil rights, Lulu White lived to see the Unites States Supreme Court render the monumental decision in *Brown v. Board of Education* (1954). She did not live "to be free by '63," however; her untimely death came on July 7, 1957. White had suffered from a heart ailment since 1945. Most of the time she was able to lead a normal life; at other times, however, she was disabled by her infirmity.

On June 1, 1957, White was taken to the hospital in Houston, where she was described by Gloster Current as "seriously ill." Current, who had visited her in the hospital early in June, wrote to Roy Wilkins that "Lulu had one operation and is presently receiving treatment for possible malignancy." The available data are insufficient to determine if Lulu White died from a heart ailment, an ear infection, or a possible malignancy, but when Gloster Current departed from Saint Elizabeth's Hospital, he "left Lulu in good spirits and responding to treatment." According to Carter Wesley's *Informer,* White had been home for several days and was convalescing nicely before she died.[1]

The news of Lulu White's death shocked Houston's black community, as well as members of the state and the national NAACP. The *Informer* reported that people called all day Saturday and Sunday to confirm the rumor of her death. As many lamented the passing of a great leader, the most fitting tribute came from two observers on the street. They said, "She was not afraid. She was a courageous woman."[2]

Funeral services were held on July 13, 1957. On that Tuesday morning in July, a string of limousines quietly arrived at Antioch Baptist Church, a modest brick building in the heart of one of Houston's largest black neighborhoods—Fourth Ward—near downtown. Inside, the church was lined neatly with cushioned pews, and light streamed in through beautiful stained-glass windows. While there was nothing really extraordinary about Antioch Baptist Church, an extraordinary scene was about to unfold. The limousines were filled mostly with national and state officials of the NAACP, all of whom had come to Antioch to attend the funeral of the Texas director of state branches. They had come a long way at considerable expense and on very short notice. The power elite of the NAACP had come to Houston to pay homage to a woman who had devoted her entire life to fighting to eradicate the constitutional basis for Jim Crow. The mourners of Houston had come not only to celebrate Lulu White's life, but also to draw inspiration from the work of a fighter, a friend, a heroine.

As the memorial service began, the audience listened to the reading of tributes from Thurgood Marshall, general counsel for the NAACP; H. Boyd Hall, president of the Texas Conference of Branches; Francis Scott Key Whittaker, president of the Houston Branch of the NAACP; Edward B. Evans, president of Prairie View College; and Rev. A. A. Lucas, former president of the Houston branch of the NAACP. The eulogy was given by the pastor of Antioch, Rev. Earl R. Boone, who narrated Lulu White's life story. Specific details concerning her work with the NAACP and vague references to family combined to create the impression of a woman of multiple interests and varied achievements. Lulu White's obituary referred to her as "State Director of Branches, champion and defender of civil rights, church woman, fraternalist, Christian and trustee of Butler College." Her life story, however, was summed up best in two lines of that obituary: "She wrote her name in the hearts of men. She served humanity."

Lulu White's active and honorary pallbearers were those closest to her "In Struggle Against Jim Crow." The active pallbearers included Lonnie B. Smith, plaintiff in *Smith v. Allwright*; J. H. Jemison, owner of Franklin Beauty School; George Kemp, lawyer; Breedlove Smith, entrepreneur; and George Willis, attorney. Honorary pallbearers were A. Maceo Smith, executive secretary of the Texas Conference of Branches; John H. Jones, chairman of the board of the Texas Conference of Branches; H. Boyd Hall, president of the Texas Conference of Branches; L. H. Spivey, entrepreneur and printshop owner; Moses Leroy, labor organizer and Lulu White's close friend; W. J. Dunbar, president of the Council of State Organizations; C. A. Dudley, physician; and Booker Williams, attorney.[3]

Lulu White's service to humanity was summed up aptly in a eulogy printed in the July 13, 1957 edition of the *Informer*. As Carter Wesley put it: "The more one thinks and ponders the unusual career of Lulu White, the more one realizes that the words of Robert Browning apply to her especially." Lulu White was one who "never turned her back, but marched breast forward, never doubted clouds would break, never dreamed . . . wrong would triumph."[4] If Lulu White was courageous, it was because she was educated in the "school of hard knocks" in Frog, Elmo, and Terrell, Texas. The fighting spirit that she brought to her job with the NAACP was rooted in racially segregated East Texas. If she was an optimist who shunned defeat and had the will and faith to go forward despite the odds, it was because she believed that the civil rights experiment ultimately would triumph.

Lulu B. White was a rare personality, endowed with ample intelligence, great courage, rock-solid conviction, and an arresting presence. Her role as a black leader was the product of the pattern of race relations that prevailed in her lifetime and her own qualities of mind and spirit. To the task she set for herself as an NAACP official, White brought an array of leadership qualities. She never was daunted by thoughts of failure, never dismayed by the enormity of the odds against her. She was a woman of unshakable aplomb.

White's success owed something to her bearing and manner. No one ever accused her of being aloof. Rather, she was noted for her candor and her sometimes folksy, "down-home" style. She did not lead through person-to-person negotiations behind closed doors; rather, she insisted on taking her message straight to the people. As a public speaker, Lulu White appealed to the eye as well as the ear. Her image as a public figure was enhanced by her good looks and her large stature, which were displayed to best advantage with a carefully selected wardrobe.

To the surprise of no one, White quickly moved up the ranks in the NAACP at the local and state levels. Yet it can be argued that her leadership in Texas derived both from charisma and from forces external to her. This statement is best understood by looking at the Texas/Houston experiment as a locally based mass movement, rather than simply as a reform movement led by national civil rights leaders.

The success of the Texas experiment required the mobilization of the black community and leaders capable of speaking persuasively to articulate the community's concerns to the white power structure. Lulu White's attributes and wide range of skills prepared her to meet the internal and external demands of the movement. Her understanding of the black world came from her day-to-day involvement in the community, her access to its institutions, and her regional and national network within the NAACP. It may be that White's greatest strength as a leader was her ability to mobilize the black community—its people, financial resources, and leaders. White gained the respect of a number of self-reliant grassroots leaders (one was George Nelson). Many of these leaders possessed charisma equal to her own, but they were unconcerned about who got the credit for successes. Their triple devotion to civil rights, the NAACP, and Lulu White contributed mightily to eliminating the white primary, eradicating some forms of job discrimination, and desegregating the University of Texas.

The civil rights struggle in Texas, especially in Houston during the 1940s and 1950s, as led by Lulu White, established the foundation for the broader civil rights movement that took place in the Deep South during the 1960s. It shifted the focus of the black movement away from the goals of individual freedom and toward those associated with collective advancement. When Texas blacks participated in the electoral process as a result of *Smith v. Allwright,* they were exercising more than their individual constitutional rights. They were asking to have their collective political power recognized by a society that previously had defined them as illegitimate. It was in the context of this collective assertion that Lulu White used the vote to make African Americans' will felt. She helped organize blacks to use their political and economic clout as leverage to achieve reform. In so doing, she witnessed civil rights advances and withstood challenges to her position, prestige, and character at the local, state, and national levels.

The struggle to desegregate the University of Texas, led by White and the NAACP, not only resulted in a Supreme Court decision requiring admission of blacks to graduate and professional schools in the state, but also established a precedent for *Brown v. Board of Education.* In the Sweatt case, the Court implied that the doctrine of "separate but equal" was unconstitutional. In *Brown,* the doctrine was declared null and void. Striking a major blow at the "separate-but-equal doctrine," the Sweatt case had far-ranging implications for Lulu White, the NAACP, and the state of Texas. For the state of Texas, it meant that *de jure* Jim Crow was on the decline and that segregation not only was costly but would become increasingly so over the years. The case strengthened the NAACP's efforts to dissolve the color line on all fronts, especially in education. Similarly, *Sweatt v. Painter* affirmed Lulu White's belief of the impossibility of true equality with separation. It also strengthened her resolve to move the black community forward in the emerging civil rights movement and to seek changes that she was unsure either blacks or whites were ready to accept.

Lulu White's gains were symbolic victories for all blacks. Her influence among blacks derived from her role with the NAACP in filing class-action lawsuits to destroy the constitutional basis for Jim Crow, and from her ability to create crises that focused attention on segregation, as a means of helping achieve the desired results. On the other hand, her influence among whites, especially businessmen, derived from fear of NAACP-sponsored demonstrations and boycotts. Looking toward future economic development, business leaders were hesitant to use extreme measures to preserve segregation, because they knew that Lulu White could and would create, around such measures, a controversy that would generate a great deal of adverse publicity.

White's efforts to end segregation through methods advocated by the NAACP made her both loved and hated. Still, her active leadership was more than simply the test of one woman or one idea. It was the culmination of two forces that had been active in the country for almost a century—the effort to segregate blacks from the mainstream of American life, and the movement to resist segregation.

White's impact on the NAACP campaign was that she brought militancy and immediacy to issues affecting blacks in Texas. This does not mean that other blacks in other regions of the country did not bring these same elements to bear. It simply means that Lulu White is one example of the black leadership that emerged (with the assistance of the NAACP) as black communities mobilized for sustained struggle against Jim Crow amid African Americans' rising expectations during and after World War II.

In many ways, the civil rights movement in Texas, especially Houston, served as a dress rehearsal for the second Reconstruction of the 1960s. Many tactics and strategies utilized, rights sought and acquired by black Houstonians, and questions raised (including the difficulty of mounting both city and statewide campaigns to destroy Jim Crow) surfaced again in Albany, Birmingham, New Orleans, and many other cities in the South. For answers to questions and for techniques and strategies to solve their problems (mobilizing the black community and fundraising), more often than not, blacks in these cities would turn to the Houston experiment. Black Houstonians knew that the campaign to end discrimination was an experiment and a chance to learn, but they also knew that, if successful, it would mean a major breakthrough in civil rights and southern politics. In less than ten years, then, Lulu White and the NAACP had designed, organized, and executed a program that would change the state's political landscape forever—a program that, in the future, would give rise to more black elected officials, more opportunities in the work place, and more civil rights in general.

Lulu White's personal attitude toward Jim Crow and civil rights was refracted through her understanding of democracy and what it entailed. White believed firmly that the preservation of democracy was inextricably tied to the government's obligation to protect the rights all of its citizens in life, liberty, and the pursuit of happiness. Thus, in fighting for economic and political rights, Lulu White was unconcerned with what some southerners called a disruption of Houston's or Texas' economic and political order. Her course of action, though at times openly defiant, reflected her concern for blacks as citizens. She pursued her main objective relentlessly, undeterred by the harassment of whites or the protests of blacks who could not convince her by logical argument that the confrontational, coalitionist, integrationist course she had chosen was not the best one.

It can be argued that, by waging war to give blacks equal access to jobs, Lulu White pitted herself against a white male business establishment and at the same time challenged the entire traditional *modus operandi* of the Texas business world. Likewise, by pushing for the right to vote and by publicizing and trying to eradicate racial discrimination, White alerted the City of Houston and the State of Texas to what then was called the "Negro Problem." By doing so, she fostered political awareness among blacks. Furthermore, she provided a means of communication for the inarticulate, teaching them how to fight, work, and ask for what they wanted and needed.

If Lulu White had known what her fighting spirit and efforts portended for the future, even her symbolic victories would have been sweeter. Her last campaign for blacks to run for public office resulted in the November 1957 election of Hattie M. White to the Houston school board,[5] making her the first black Texan to be elected to public office since Reconstruction. And it is upon Lulu White's and Hattie White's shoulders that Barbara Jordan stood in 1966, when she became the first black female elected to the Texas Senate, and in 1972, when she became the first black from the twentieth-century South to sit in the U.S. Congress.

The civil rights movement created a social space in which women, including Lulu White, developed a renewed sense of their own potential. The movement's vision translated into daily realities of hard work and responsibility which admitted few sexual limitations. Too, Lulu White's sense of purpose was reinforced by the knowledge that her work and the responsibilities she assumed were central to the movement. It goes without saying that, through involvement in the movement, she developed too much self-confidence and self-respect to passively accept a subordinate role. Like black female activists of the nineteenth century, White confronted the struggle for equality with the tools that the movement had given her—a language to name and describe oppression; the courage to challenge any social institution that failed to meet human needs; the ability to organize, and the audacity to be openly defiant and to engage in radical politics. In short, Lulu White was a rebel with a cause.

Notes

Abbreviations

CGR   Center for Genealogical Research, Clayton Library, Houston

FBI   Federal Bureau of Investigation

FBI Files   Files of the Federal Bureau of Investigation, in NAACP Collection, Rice University Library, Houston

HMRC   Houston Metropolitan Resource Center, Houston Public Library

HUAC   United States Congress, House Un-American Activities Committee

LBJ   Lyndon Baines Johnson

LBW   Lulu Belle Madison White

MDLC   Manuscript Division, Library of Congress, Washington, D.C.

NAACP   National Association for the Advancement of Colored People

NAACP Files NAACP Files, Manuscript Division, Library of Congress, Washington, D.C.

UTPOR   Records, Office of the President of the University of Texas, in Center for American History, University of Texas at Austin

Note: Unless explicitly noted, all correspondence cited in the notes is housed in NAACP Files, Manuscript Division, Library of Congress, Washington, D.C.

Chapter 1. Coming of Age in Texas

1. U.S. Bureau of the Census, *13th Census of the U.S., 1910: Population, Kaufman County, Texas, Elmo Supervision, District 3* National Archives Microfilm Publications (Washington, D.C.: National Archives, 1965) in the Clayton Library, CGR; Mississippi Marriage Prior to 1926, M-325, Mississippi State Archives, Microfilm Publications (Mississippi, 1910) in Clayton Library, CGR. Johnnie Jordan, interview by author, Feb. 7, 1987, transcript in author's collection, Houston, Tex.; Jordan is the niece of LBW.

2. Neil McMillan, *Dark Journey: Black Mississippi in the Age of Jim Crow* (Urbana: Univ. of Illinois Press, 1993), 36–71, 110–53.

3. Jack Stolz, *Terrell, Texas, 1873–1973: From Open Country to Modern City* (Terrell, Tex.: Naylor Co., 1973), 18, 19, 26. See also Robert Richard Butler, "A History of Kaufman County" (M.A. thesis, Univ. of Texas, 1940); Thomas R. Duncan, "A History of Kaufman County in World War I" (M.A. thesis, Univ. of Texas, 1935).

4. Stolz, *Terrell, Texas*, 18, 19, 26; Jack Stolz, "Kaufman County in the Civil War," *East Texas Historical Journal* 28 (1990): 37–44.

5. See U.S. Bureau of the Census, *12th Census of the U.S., 1900: Occupations*, vol. 4: *Kaufman County, Texas* (Washington, D.C.: Government Printing Office, 1900).

6. Lawrence D. Rice, *The Negro in Texas, 1874–1900* (Baton Rouge: Louisiana State Univ. Press, 1971), 133–39. Alwyn Barr, *From Reconstruction to Reform: Texas Politics, 1870–1900* (Austin: Univ. of Texas Press, 1971), 203. Darlene Clark Hine, *Black Victory: The Rise and Fall of the White Primary in Texas* (Millwood, N.Y.: KTO Press, 1979), 37–40. See also Stolz, *Terrell, Texas*, 18–19, 26.

7. Edwin and Billie Hardin, interview by author, Frog, Tex., June 27, 1997, transcript in author's collection, Houston, Tex. The Hardins are natives of Frog, Texas. Willie Taylor, interview by author, Fairfield, Calif., July 21, 1997, transcript in author's collection, Houston, Tex. Taylor grew up in Marshall, Texas. See also William H. Wilson, "Growing Up Black in East Texas: Some Twentieth-Century Experiences," *East Texas Historical Journal* 22 (1994): 49–54.

8. Alwyn Barr, *Black Texans: A History of the Negro in Texas, 1528–1995* (Norman: Univ. of Oklahoma Press, 1995), 136–38.

9. Rice, *Negro in Texas*, 253; Ray Stannard Baker, "What Is a Lynching? A Study of Mob Justice, South and North," *McClure's Magazine* 24 (Feb. 1905): 429; Bruce Glasrud, "Child or Beast?: White Texas' View of Blacks, 1900–1910," *East Texas Historical Journal* 15 (1977): 38–44; Kenneth R. Durham, Jr., "Longview Race Riot of 1919," *East Texas Historical Journal* 18 (1980): 13–24; Walter White, *A Man Called White: The Autobiography of Walter White* (New York: Viking, 1948); Robert Zangrando, *The NAACP Crusade Against Lynching, 1905–1950* (Philadelphia: Temple Univ. Press, 1980). *NAACP: Thirty Years of Lynching in the United States, 1889–1918* (New York: Privately printed, 1918). For more on violence in Texas during Reconstruction, see Merline Pitre, *Through Many Dangers, Toils and Snares: The Black Leadership of Texas, 1968–1900* (Austin: Eakin Press, 1997), 130, 144–45. See also Allen Trelease, *White Terror: Ku Klux Klan Conspiracy and Southern Reconstruction* (New York: Harper and Row, 1971), 103.

10. Barr, *Black Texans*, 136; Glasrud, "Child or Beast," 40–41.

11. Barr, *Black Texans*, 136. See Texarkana Lynching Files, in General Files 4-14/131, in Coke Stevenson Collection, Texas State Archives, Austin.

12. Jordan, interview by author, Feb. 7, 1987.

13. Ibid.

14. Ibid. Thelma Bryant, interview by author, Houston, Tex., Mar. 10, 1990, transcript in author's collection, Houston, Tex.; Bryant was a contemporary of LBW. Jimmie R. Phillips, interview by author, Prairie View, Tex., June 3, 1997, transcript in author's collection, Houston, Tex.; Phillips was LBW's classmate at Prairie View College.

15. Jordan, interview by author, Feb. 7, 1987. Stolz, *Terrell, Texas*, 18–19, 26; Edwin and Billie Hardin, interview by author, June 27, 1997; Wilson, "Growing Up Black in East Texas," 49–54.

16. Jordan, interview by author, Feb. 7, 1987.

17. William R. Davis, *The Development and Present Status of Negro Education in East Texas* (New York: Columbia Teachers College Press, 1934), 38. See also David A. Williams, "The History of Higher Education for Black Texans, 1872–1917" (Ed.D. diss., Baylor Univ., 1978); *Bishop Herald (Marshall, Tex.)*, Summer, 1977.

18. J. M. McCullen to Registrar of Prairie View College, July 19, 1926, in Scrapbook of LBW, 1926–28, in collection of Johnnie Jordan, Houston, Tex. During her stay at Butler College, LBW earned the following scores in her freshman courses: History of Education, 90; Virgil, 86; Chemistry, 85; History, 95; and American Literature, 94. The grades were based on a scale of 100.

19. George R. Woolfolk, *Prairie View: A Study in Public Consciousness, 1876–1946* (New York: Pageant Press, 1962), 29–36, 358.

20. Ibid., 235–45; George R. Woolfolk, "W. R. Banks: Public College Educator," in *Black Leaders: Texans for Their Times,* ed. Alwyn Barr and Robert A. Calvert, 129–58 (Austin: Texas State Historical Association, 1981); *Prairie View Standard,* June 23, 1928. See also *Prairie View College Annual Yearbook,* 1924, 1925, 1926. Well into the 20th century, a number of land grant and normal colleges had principals as their chief administrative officers. Thus, Banks's official title was *principal,* although many used the terms *president* and *principal* interchangeably when referring to him. Prairie View got its first president in 1945.

21. Woolfolk, *Prairie View,* 135–37, 142–43, 247. Jimmie R. Phillips, interview by author, Prairie View, Tex., Apr. 21, 1997, transcript in author's collection, Houston, Tex.

22. Woolfolk, *Prairie View,* 135–37, 142–43. Frances Mosely, interview by author, Houston, Tex., Feb. 27, 1987, transcript in author's collection, Houston, Tex.

23. A. Wendell Burks to LBW, Mar. 30, 1928, in Scrapbook of LBW; *Prairie View Standard,* Oct. 25, 1927, and Mar. 24, 1928.

24. L. M. Tobin to LBW, May 5, 1928, in Scrapbook of LBW.

25. U.S. Bureau of the Census, *15th Census of the U.S., 1920–1930: Occupations,* vol. 4 (Washington, D.C., 1935), 24, 1593–97; Andrew Webber Jackson, *A Sure Foundation and A Sketch of Negro Life in Texas* (Houston: Privately printed, 1938), 62, 385, 417.

26. *Prairie View Standard,* June 23, 1928. See also Scrapbook of LBW. During LBW's time at Prairie View, Julius served as a college booster, and in 1928 he was marshal for the college's Homecoming parade. After her graduation, LBW and Julius remained staunch Prairie View supporters. *Houston Sentinel,* Apr. 7, 1928.

27. *Houston Informer,* Dec. 29, 1948.

28. Althene Watson, interview by author, Houston, Tex., May 28, 1997, transcript in author's collection, Houston, Tex.; Ernestine Moore, interview by author, Houston, Tex., June 10, 1997, transcript in author's collection, Houston, Tex. See also Thelma Scott Bryant, *Pioneer Families of Houston: Early 1900s* (Houston: Privately printed, 1990); Thelma Scott Bryant, *Our Journey Through Houston and U.S. History* (Houston: Privately printed, 1997).

29. Onita Cavit, interview by author, Houston, Tex., Feb. 25, 1996, transcript in author's collection, Houston, Tex.; Ercelle Pinson Hall, interview by author, Houston, Tex., Feb. 25, 1996, transcript in author's collection, Houston, Tex.; Barbara Johnson, interview by author, Houston, Tex., Feb. 25, 1996, transcript in author's collection; Lois Wood, interview by author, Houston, Tex., Feb. 25, 1996, transcript in author's collection, Houston, Tex.; Martha Whiting, interview by author, Feb. 27, 1997; transcript in author's collection, Houston, Tex.; Ernestine Moore, interview by author, June 10, 1995; Althene Watson, interview by author, Houston, Tex., Apr. 28, 1997, transcript in author's collection, Houston, Tex.

30. See Robert Haynes, *A Night of Violence: Houston Riot, 1917* (Baton Rouge: Louisiana State Univ. Press, 1976).

31. Ibid. Kelley Miller, "The Disgrace of Democracy: An Open Letter to President Woodrow Wilson" (Washington, D.C.: Howard University Press, 1917), 14; Mary Berry and John Blassingame, *Long Memory: The Black Experience in America* (New York: Oxford Univ. Press, 1982), 302.

32. Calvin Smith, "Houston Riot, 1917, Revisited," *Houston Review* 13 (1991): 85–95; Calvin Smith, "On The Edge: The Houston Riot of 1917," *The Griot* 10 (Winter 1991): 3–12.

33. Howard Beeth, "A Black Elite Agenda in the Urban South: The Call for Political Change and Racial Solidarity in Houston during the 1920s," in *Essays in Economic and Business History* 10 (1992): 40–48 (Edwin J. Perkins, vol. ed.); Casey Green, "Guardians Against Change: The Ku Klux Klan in Houston and Harris County, 1920–1925," *Houston Review* 10 (1988): 3–20.

34. Beeth, "Black Elite Agenda," 42–43. See also Howard Beeth and Cary Wintz, eds., *Black Dixie: Afro-Texans' History and Culture in Houston* (College Station: Texas A&M Univ. Press, 1992); Cary Wintz, "Black Business in Houston," *Essays in Economic and Business History* 10 (1992): 29–40 (Edwin J. Perkins, vol. ed.).

35. *General Laws of Texas*, 38th Leg., 2d Called Sess. (1923), 74; J. Alston Atkins, *The Texas Negro and His Political Rights: A History of the Fight for Negroes to Enter the Democratic Primaries of Texas* (Houston: Webster Publishing Co., 1932), 6–24.

36. Hine, *Black Victory*, 26, 235.

37. U.S. Bureau of the Census, *12th Census of the U.S.: Population* vol. 3 (Washington, D.C.: Government Printing Office, 1910), 815; Walter Lindsey, "Black Houstonians' Challenge to the White Democratic Primary, 1924–1944" (M.A. thesis, Univ. of Houston, 1969). In 1898, Texas had approximately 509 black lodges, including those for males and females. These lodges placed a great deal of emphasis on economic self-help and had as their motto "Business, Wealth and Race Unity." See also Melvin J. Banks, "The Pursuit of Equality: The Movement for First-Class Citizenship among Negroes in Texas, 1920–1950" (Ds.S. diss., Syracuse Univ., 1962); James M. SoRelle, "The Darker Side of Heaven: The Black Community in Houston, Texas, 1917–1945" (Ph.D. diss., Kent State Univ., 1980); Howard Beeth, "Houston and History, Past and Present: A Look at Houston in the 1920s," *Southern Studies* 25 (Summer 1986): 172–87; Robert Haynes, "Race Relations in Houston," paper delivered at Texas Southern Univ., Houston, Feb. 5, 1988; Robert Bullard, *Invisible Houston: The Black Experience in Boom and Bust* (College Station: Texas A&M Univ. Press, 1987).

38. *Love v. Griffin* 266 U.S. 32–45, Sup. Ct. 12 (1924). *Love v. Griffin*, 236, SW 239 (Texas Civ. App., 1922); Hine, *Black Victory*, 59–61.

39. Thelma Bryant, interviews by author, Houston, Tex., Feb. 5, 1996, and Apr. 11, 1997, transcript in author's collection, Houston, Tex.; Jordan, interview by author, Feb. 7, 1987.

40. W. E. B. DuBois, "The National Association for the Advancement of Colored People," *Crisis* 29 (Feb. 1925): 156; Hine, *Black Victory*, 61. See also Robert Brisbane, *Black Vanguard: The Origin of Negro Social Revolution, 1900–1960* (Valley Forge, Pa.: Judson Press, 1970), 128–32; *Houston Chronicle*, Mar. 8, 1927.

41. *Nixon v. Herndon*, 273 U.S. 538; 47 Sup. Ct. 446 (1927); *Nixon v. Condon*, 286 U.S. 73–106 (1932). See also *Chandler v. Neff*, 298, Fed. 515, Western District of Texas (1924); *Newberry v. United States*, 256 U.S. 232 (1921). Texas Legislature, *House Journal*, 40th Leg., 1st Called Sess. (1927), 207. See also Conrey Bryson, *Dr. Lawrence D. Nixon and the White Primary* (El Paso: Texas Western Press, 1947).

42. O. P. DeWalt to Robert Bagnall, Sept. 8, 1928; Bagnall to DeWalt, Sept. 13 and Oct. 31, 1928; DeWalt to Bagnall, Nov. 30, 1928.

43. Hine, *Black Victory,* 129–32; *Houston Informer,* Jan. 17, Nov. 22, and Nov. 30, 1930; see copy of *C. N. Love v. the Democratic Executive Committee of the City of Houston, Texas,* LBJ Library, University of Texas at Austin, Nixon Papers. Carter Wesley to Fred Knollenberg, Jan. 14, 1941.

44. Hine, *Black Victory,* 132–33; *Houston Informer,* Jan. 31, 1931, and Jan. 9, 1932; *Houston Post,* July 1, 1934. See also *White v. Lubbock,* 30 S.W. 724 (Texas, 1930); Harris County Negro Democratic Club to O. E. Smith, Jan. 27, 1932, in NAACP Files, MDLC.

45. *Nixon v. Condon,* 73–106. See *amicus curiae* brief in *Nixon v. Condon,* in A. B. Spingarn Papers, in NAACP Files, MDLC.

46. *White v. County Democratic Committee,* 60 F. 2d 973 (S.D. Texas, 1932); *Houston Informer,* July 22, 1932; Atkins, *Texas Negro,* 9.

47. Lindsey, "Black Houstonians' Challenge," 26–27; *Grovey v. Townsend,* 295 U.S. 45 (1935); Hine, *Black Victory,* 167–83.

48. Hine, *Black Victory,* 130; Robert Hayes, "Black Houstonians and the White Democratic Primary, 1920–1945," in *Black Dixie: Afro-Texans' History and Culture in Houston,* ed. Howard Beeth and Cary Wintz (College Station: Texas A&M Univ. Press, 1992), 198; *Houston Informer,* Feb. 2, 1935.

49. Hine, *Black Victory,* 168–69; *Houston Informer,* Jan. 16, Mar. 2 and 30, and Aug. 24, 1935; Jan. 18, 1941. *Dallas Express,* Jan. 18, 1941.

50. *Houston Informer,* Apr. 6, 1935; William J. Thompkins to Marvin Hunter McIntyre, assistant secretary to President Franklin D. Roosevelt, Apr. 23, 1935, in Roosevelt Papers, FDR Library, Hyde Park, N.Y.; Walter White, *A Man Called White,* 87–89. See also Thurgood Marshall, "The Rise and Collapse of the White Democratic Party," *Columbia Law Review* 42 (Nov.–Dec. 1943): 1022–77; *C. F. Richardson et al. v. Executive Committee of the Democratic Party of Houston,* 200 U.S. Dist. Ct., 20 (1938).

Chapter 2. Carving a Niche in the NAACP

1. Martha Gruening to James Weldon Johnson, n.d.; Henry L. Mims to John R. Shillady, July 12, 1918; Mary Child Norn to Mims, Feb. 5, 1918, and May 11, 1919; M. B. Patten to Walter White, June 26, 1918; C. F. Richardson to Board of Directors, Jan. 26, 1919; O. E. Smith to Walter White, May 22, 1919; Walter White to O. E. Smith, June 3, 1919. Martha Gruening, "Houston: NAACP Investigation," *Crisis* 15 (Nov. 1917): 14–19.

2. James M. SoRelle, "The Emergence of Black Business in Houston, Texas: A Study in Race and Ideology, 1915–45," in Beeth and Wintz, *Black Dixie,* 110; Hine, *Black Victory,* 58–59, 193–94.

3. John M. Adkins to Bagnall, Mar. 24 and Nov. 24, 1922; Apr. 4, 1923. SoRelle, "Darker Side of Heaven," 360–67.

4. "Houston Texas NAACP Saves Luther Collins from Death Penalty," NAACP Press Release, Nov. 7, 1924, in NAACP Files, MDLC. Walter White to DeWalt, Nov. 24, 1926; DeWalt to Walter White, Dec. 1, 1926. SoRelle, "Darker Side of Heaven," 370–72.

5. Adkins to Bagnall, [Mar. 1922], in NAACP Files, MDLC.

6. William Pickens to G. Duke Crawford, July 5, 1933.

7. Roy Leeland Hopkins to Juanita E. Jackson, Jan. 13, 1937; Sanders Mason to Walter

White, Jan. 22, 1937; Juanita E. Jackson to Hopkins, Feb. 17, 1937; Juanita E. Jackson to Mason, Feb. 23, 1937. *Houston Informer,* Mar. 25, 1937, and Dec. 16, 1939; SoRelle, "Darker Side of Heaven," 374.

8. LBW to Roy Wilkins, Oct. 25, 1946. *Houston Informer* Mar. 25, 1937, Dec. 16, 1939. Thelma Bryant, interview with author, Houston, Tex., Mar. 5, 1988, transcript in author's collection, Houston, Tex. See 1906 Arts, Literary and Charity Club [Houston], Minutes, 1906–53, in HMRC.

9. NAACP, Houston Branch, *Annual Reports,* 1940–44, in NAACP Files, MDLC.

10. Charles Shaw to Walter White, May 1937. Hine, *Black Victory,* 196–97; SoRelle, "Darker Side of Heaven," 372–75.

11. NAACP, Minutes of the State Conference of Branches, June 18 and 19, 1937; "State Conference Constitution and By-Laws," 1940; "Resolution of the State Conference of Branches," Dallas, June 19, 1937, all in NAACP Files, MDLC. Michael Gillette, "The Rise of the NAACP in Texas," *Southwestern Historical Quarterly* 81 (Apr. 1978): 393–95; Michael Gillette, "The NAACP in Texas, 1937–1957" (Ph.D. diss., Univ. of Texas at Austin, 1984).

12. C. F. Richardson to Charles Houston, June 25, 1938. *C. F. Richardson et al. v. Executive Committee of the Democratic Party of Houston,* Civil Action no. 20, U.S. Dist. Ct. (S. Dist. Texas, 1938).

13. *Houston Informer,* Aug. 12, 1939; Sidney Hasgett et al. to Walter White, Aug. 15, 1939; *Houston Informer,* Aug. 19, 1939; Secretary's Report, Meeting of the Board of Directors, Sept. 1939, in NAACP Files, MDLC; Gillette, "Rise of the NAACP," 396–97.

14. LBW to Walter White, Sept. 15, 1939. Gillette, "Rise of the NAACP," 396; SoRelle, "Darker Side of Heaven," 376–80.

15. Edna Chappell McKenzie, "Elizabeth Daisy Lampkin," in *Black Women in America An Historical Encyclopedia,* ed. Darlene Clark Hine, vol. 1, (Brooklyn, N.Y.: Carlson Publishers, 1993), 690–93.

16. Ibid.

17. Ibid.

18. Daisy Lampkin to Richetta Randolph, Oct. 31, 1939; Lampkin to Walter White, Oct. 30, 1939.

19. Lampkin to Walter White, Nov. 6, 1939; Walter White to Lampkin, Nov. 15, 1939; Lampkin to Walter White, Nov. 16, 1939; Hine, *Black Victory,* 196; SoRelle, "Darker Side of Heaven," 378–80.

20. Walter White to Lampkin, Nov. 6, 1939. *Houston Informer,* Aug. 28, 1939; Lampkin to Walter White, Oct. 30, 1939.

21. Andrew Webber Jackson, *Sure Foundation,* 45–47; Hine, *Black Victory,* 198.

22. Hine, *Black Victory,* 198–99; Lindsey, "Black Houstonian Challenge," 55–56; *Houston Informer,* Mar. 23 and Nov. 18, 1940.

23. A. Maceo Smith to Walter White, Mar. 23, 1940; Marshall to Walter White, May 14, 1940. Gillette, "Rise of the NAACP," 404. See Official Program of 4th Annual Session of the Texas Conference of Branches of the NAACP, Corpus Christi, Tex., May 10–12, 1940; in NAACP Files, MDLC.

24. Gillette, "Rise of the NAACP," 404–406.

25. *Hasgett v. Werner,* 449 U.S. Dist. Ct. (S. Dist. of Texas, 1941); *United States v. Classic,* 313 U.S. 299 (1941); Hine, *Black Victory,* 201–207.

25. Gillette, "Rise of the NAACP," 408–409.
26. *Smith v. Allwright*, 321 U.S. 657, 64 Sup. Ct. 757 (1944); Gillette, "Rise of the NAACP," 408–409.
27. Hine, *Black Victory*, 207.
28. Lampkin to Lucille Black, Mar. 31, 1943; LBW to Lampkin, Feb. 2, 1944; Donald Jones to LBW, n.d.; Donald Jones to Rev. A. A. Lucus, Apr. 18, 1943.
29. LBW to Walter White, Apr. 13, 1943. See also Memorandum [on] Financing Regional Offices, Dec. 17, 1944, in NAACP Files, MDLC.

Chapter 3. Raising Her Voice: Gadfly or Crusader?

1. Gunnar Myrdal, *An American Dilemma: The Negro Problem and Modern Democracy* (New York: Harper and Bros., 1944), 1:997. See also David R. Goldfield, *Black, White and Southern: Race Relations and Southern Culture, 1940 to the Present* (Baton Rouge: Louisiana State Univ. Press, 1990).
2. U.S. Bureau of the Census, *16th Census of the U.S., 1940: Population*, vol. 3 (Washington, D.C.: Government Printing Office, 1943); U.S. Bureau of the Census, *17th Census of the U.S., 1950* (Washington, D.C.: Government Printing Office, 1953), 595–96; Don E. Carleton, *Red Scare! Right-Wing Hysteria: The Fifties and Their Legacy in Texas* (Austin: Texas Monthly Press, 1985).
3. David R. Goldfield, *Promised Land: The South Since 1945* (Wheeling, Ill.: Harlan-Davidson, 1987), 5–6; Richard M. Dalfiume, "The Forgotten Years of the Negro Revolution," *Journal of American History* 55 (June 1968): 90–106.
4. NAACP, Houston Branch, *Annual Report*, 1943, in NAACP Files, MDLC. Alan Nimer and George Nelson, interview by author, Houston, Tex., Feb. 25, 1989, transcript in author's collection, Houston, Tex.; George Nelson, civil rights veteran, died in May 1997 at age 90. Quentin Mease, interview by Antrece Baggett, Houston, Tex., Mar. 27, 1998, transcript in Antrece Baggett's possession, Houston, Tex.
5. NAACP, Houston Branch, *Annual Report*, 1943, in NAACP Files, MDLC.
6. Harvard Sitkoff, "Racial Militancy and Interracial Violence in the Second World War," *Journal of American History* 58 (Dec. 1971): 672. See affidavit of L. P. Riddeaux, Aug. 11, 1943, in NAACP Files, MDLC. See also James A. Burran, "Violence in an Arsenal of Democracy: The Beaumont Race Riot, 1943," *East Texas Historical Journal* 15 (1976): 39–52.
7. David J. Butler to LBW, Sept. 4, 1943. See also *Houston Post*, June 18, 1943; *Beaumont Enterprise*, June 17, 1943.
8. R. T. Tatum to LBW, Sept. 2, 1943. See affidavit of Beulah Johnson, Sept. 3, 1943, in NAACP Files, MDLC.
9. David Manual to LBW, Sept. 4, 1943.
10. LBW to Walter White, Sept. 16, 1943. See affidavit of Frank Hadnott, Sept. 3, 1943, in NAACP Files, MDLC. See also LBW to Marshall, Oct. 12, 1943; Marshall to LBW, Oct. 18, 1943. The Beaumont branch of the NAACP was organized in July 3, 1918. Between 1918 and the mid-1920s, the Beaumont branch did little besides recruit new members and raise money for the national office. In 1924, the secretary of the branch reported to the national office that the local group was disbanding temporarily "on account of the high race feelings in this part of the state." In 1930, the new leadership

rechartered the branch. From 1930 to 1935, the branch experienced internal problems, resulting in the ouster of its president. Then, from 1935 to 1950, the branch lay dormant. It was revived in February 1950, with LBW's assistance. Nancy Daily, "History of Beaumont Chapter of the National Association for the Advancement of Colored People, 1918–1970" (M.A. thesis, Lamar Univ., Beaumont, Tex., 1971), 98–100.

11. Brisbane, *Black Vanguard*, 144–45; Charles Flint Kellogg, *NAACP: A History of the National Association for the Advancement of Colored People* (Baltimore, Md.: John Hopkins Univ. Press, 1967). See "A History of the Houston Branch," in NAACP, Houston Branch, *Annual Report*, 1943 and 1944, both in NAACP Files, MDLC; *Houston Informer*, Feb. 5, 1944.

12. *Houston Informer*, Feb. 5 and Apr. 10, 1944; *Smith v. Allwright*, 321 U.S. 657, 64 Sup. Ct. 757 (1944). See also Marshall, "Rise and Collapse of the White Democratic Primary"; Thomas R. Brooks, *Walls Come Tumbling: A History of the Civil Rights Movement, 1940–1970* (Englewood Cliffs, N.J.: Prentice-Hall, 1989).

13. Lampkin to LBW, May 8, 1944. See also NAACP, Houston Branch, *Annual Report*, 1944, and also the membership list.

14. Hunter Brooks, *Historical Highlights of Antioch Baptist Church* (Houston: Privately printed, 1976); *Houston Informer*, June 12, 1946.

15. Neil G. Sapper, "Survey of the History of Black People of Texas, 1930–1954" (Ph.D. diss., Texas Tech Univ., 1972), 160–63.

16. *Houston Informer*, Jan. 24, Sept. 14, and Nov. 2 and 30, 1946.

17. Chandler Davidson, "Negro Politics and the Rise of the Civil Rights Movement in Houston, Texas" (Ph.D. diss., Princeton Univ., 1965), 35–41; Chandler Davidson, *Biracial Politics: Conflict and Coalition in Metropolitan South* (Baton Rouge: Louisiana State Univ. Press, 1972), 84. The latter is a revision of Davidson's dissertation. The material referred to in the dissertation is not found in the published version. See also Rev. L. H. Simpson Collection, HMRC; and Steven E. Lawson, *Running for Freedom: Civil Rights and Black Politics in America Since 1941* (New York: McGraw-Hill, 1991).

18. *Houston Post*, Oct. 6, 1946; *Houston Informer*, Nov. 2, 1946.

19. LBW to Walter White, Oct. 16 and 18, 1946; LBW to Wilkins, Oct. 30, 1946.

20. Wilkins to LBW, Oct. 28, 1946; LBW to Wilkins, Oct. 30, 1946.

21. LBW to Lee Shirar, Oct. 23, 1946; Memo, LBW to Citizens' Charter Committee, Oct. 30, 1946; see also *Houston Post*, Oct. 14, 1946.

22. *Houston Informer*, Nov. 2, 1946; LBW to Walter White, Oct. 16, 1946.

23. *Houston Informer*, Oct. 8, 1946.

24. *Houston Informer*, Nov. 30, 1946.

25. LBW to Wilkins, Oct. 30, 1946.

26. LBW to Walter White, Oct. 18, 1946; *Houston Informer*, Nov. 30, 1946.

27. *Houston Informer*, July 27, Aug. 24, Sept. 14, and Oct. 5, 1946; *Houston Post*, Oct. 8 and Nov. 2, 1946.

28. *Houston Informer*, July 27, Aug. 24, Sept. 14, and Oct. 5, 1946.

29. *Houston Informer*, July 27, Sept. 14, 1946.

30. *Houston Informer*, Apr. 10 and July 16, 1948.

31. "NAACP Resolution on Police Brutality," July 16, 1948, in NAACP Files, MDLC; *Houston Informer*, July 12, 1948.

32. W. Marvin Dulaney, "The Texas Negro Peace Officer Association: The Origin of Black Police Unionism," *Houston Review* 12 (1990): 60–71. See also W. Marvin Dulaney, *Black Police in America* (Bloomington: Indiana Univ. Press, 1996); Howard N. Rabinowitz, "The Conflict Between Blacks and the New Police in the Urban South, 1865–1900," *Historian* 39 (Nov. 1976): 62–76; *Houston Telegraph*, Dec. 1870; Louis A. Marchifava, "The Houston Police, 1878–1948," *Rice Univ. Studies* 63 (Spring 1977).

33. LBW to Gloster Current, Dec. 1, 1948; LBW to Wilkins, Nov. 1, 1946; LBW to Walter White, Aug. 5, 1946.

34. Sapper, "Survey of the History of Black People," 166–70; Barr, *Black Texans*, 173–76.

35. See "Complete House Voting Record by Subject, Public Activities" May 13, 1947, Dec. 31, 1948, 1947–48, LBJ Archives, Box 75, in LBJ Library, Univ. of Texas, Austin.

36. Frank Cox, "'Nearly a Statesman': LBJ and Texas Blacks in the 1948 Election," *Social Science Quarterly* 74 (June 1993): 242–45. See also Christie L. Bourgeois, "Stepping Over Lines: Lyndon B. Johnson, Black Texans and the National Youth Administration, 1935–1937," *Southwestern Historical Quarterly* 91 (Oct. 1987): 149–72; Monroe Billington, "Lyndon B. Johnson and Blacks: The Early Years," *Journal of Negro History* 62 (Jan. 1977): 26–42.

37. Cox, " Nearly a Statesman," 245, 254–56; *Houston Informer*, July 24, 1948.

38. Cox, "Nearly a Statesman," 257–59. See also *Houston Post*, Aug. 30, 1948; Bourgeois, "Stepping Over Lines," 258.

39. Gov. Coke Stevenson to U.S. Atty. Gen. Francis Biddle, July 27, 1942, General Files 4-14/131, Coke Stevenson Collection, Texas State Archives, Austin; *Houston Informer*, July 24, 1948.

40. LBW to LBJ, Mar. 10, 1949, in Speeches—Filibustering, Senate 1946–1961, Civil Rights, LBJ Library, Univ. of Texas, Austin; LBJ to LBW, Oct. 24, 1953.

41. Mrs. L. Pearl to LBW, Sept. 24, 1944, in *Houston Informer*, Oct. 1, 1944; *Houston Informer*, June 9, 1944; NAACP, Houston Branch, *Annual Report*, 1943. LBW remained active in politics throughout her life, serving as secretary to the judge of Houston's Precinct 153 until her death.

Chapter 4. Taking a Fearless Stand: The Fight for Economic Parity

1. L. M. Tobin to Supervisors of Houston Industries, May 5, 1928; Tobin to LBW, May 5, 1928, in Scrapbook of LBW.

2. Ira B. Bryant, Jr., *The Development of Houston Negro Schools* (Houston: D. Armstrong, 1934), 6–8; *Houston Informer*, Jan. 23, 1932. See also William H. Kellar, "Make Haste Slowly: A History of School Desegregation in Houston, Texas" (Ph.D. diss., Univ. of Houston, 1995).

3. Vernon McDaniel, *History of the Teachers State Association of Texas* (Washington D.C.: National Education Association Publishers, 1977), 44–45; A. Maceo Smith to Marshall, Oct. 2, 1942; *Houston Informer*, Mar. 6, 1943; Donald Jones to Wilkins, Apr. 9, 1943. See SoRelle, "Darker Side of Heaven," 87–92.

4. *Houston Informer*, Jan. 30, 1943. On average, black teachers' salaries were only 61% of white teachers' at the beginning of 1940. See William Joseph Brophy, "The Black Texan, 1900–1950" (Ph.D. diss., Vanderbilt Univ., 1974), 35.

5. *Houston Informer,* Mar. 6, 1943. See Ruth Winegarten, *Black Texan Women: 150 Years of Trials and Triumph* (Austin: Univ. of Texas Press, 1995), 255. Thelma Paige served as plaintiff in the Dallas case.

6. *Houston Informer,* Mar. 6, 1943.

7. *Houston Informer,* Mar. 13, Apr. 3 and 17, and Oct. 13, 1943; *Houston Post,* Apr. 13, 1943.

8. U.S. Bureau of the Census, *16th Census of the U.S.: Occupation,* vol. 4 (Washington, D.C.: Government Printing Office, 1943), 595–96. See also SoRelle, "Darker Side of Heaven," 87–89, 91–92; James M. SoRelle, "'An De Po Cullud Man Is in De Wuss Fix Uv Awl': Black Occupational Status in Houston, Texas, 1920–1940," *Houston Review* 1 (Spring 1979): 15–26.

9. Carleton, *Red Scare,* 12–18.

10. NAACP, Houston Branch, *Annual Report,* 1943, in NAACP Files, MDLC.

11. LBW to A. Maceo Smith, July 22, 1948.

12. Ibid. See also Elizabeth Jacoway and David R. Colburn, eds., *Southern Businessmen and Desegregation* (Baton Rouge: Louisiana State Univ. Press, 1982).

13. James M. SoRelle, "The Emergence of Black Business in Houston, Texas," in Beeth and Wintz, *Black Dixie,* 110.

14. LBW to Marshall, Aug. 17, 1945; Marshall to White, Aug. 21, 1945.

15. Philip Foner, *Organized Labor and the Black Worker, 1916–1973* (New York: International Publishers, 1974), 241–49; Dalfiume, "Forgotten Years," 90–106; Brisbane, *Black Vanguard,* 171–83. See also Herbert Garfinkel, *When Negroes March: The March on Washington Movement in the Organizational Politics of FEPC* (Glencoe, Ill.: Free Press, 1969); Earnest Obadele Stark, "The Road to Jericho: Black Workers, the FEPC and the Struggle for Racial Equality in the Upper Texas Gulf Coast, 1941–1947" (Ph.D. diss., Univ. of Houston, 1996).

16. Willie Lee O'Daniel to LBW, June 29, 1945; Tom Connally to A. A. Lucas, July 19, 1945; Current to LBW, Jan. 27, 1944; Marshall to LBW, Sept. 1945.

17. *Houston Informer,* Jan. 27, 1946. *To Secure These Rights: Report of the Presidential Committee on Civil Rights* (Washington, D.C., 1949) 166. See William C. Berman, *The Politics of Civil Rights in the Truman Administration* (Columbus: Ohio State Univ. Press, 1970).

18. LBW to A. Maceo Smith, July 27, 1947; Robert Korstad and Nelson Lichtenstein, "Opportunities Found and Lost: Labor Radicals and the Early Civil Rights Movement," *Journal of American History* 75 (Dec. 1988): 780–811. See also Peter J. Kellogg, "Civil Rights Consciousness in the 1940s," *Historian* 42 (Nov. 1979): 18–41.

19. Harvard Sitkoff, *A New Deal for Blacks: The Emergence of Civil Rights as a National Issue* (New York: Oxford Univ. Press, 1978), 32–33. See also Harvard Sitkoff, *The Struggle for Black Equality, 1954–1980* (New York: Hill and Wang, 1981).

20. Patricia Sullivan, *Days of Hope: Race and Democracy in the New Deal Era* (Chapel Hill: Univ. of North Carolina Press, 1996), 149.

21. Ibid. *Houston Informer,* Apr. 6, 1943, and Sept. 14, 1946. NAACP, Houston Branch, *Annual Report,* 1943 and 1946, both in NAACP Files, MDLC. See also Dennis K. McDaniel, "The CIO Political Action Committee and Congressman Martin Dies' Departure from Congress: Labor's Inflated Claim," *East Texas Historical Journal* 32 (1993): 48–56.

22. *Houston Informer,* Jan. 29 and Feb. 5 and 12, 1946; *Houston Post,* Feb. 12, 1946; *Houston Chronicle,* Feb. 12, 1946.

23. *Houston Informer,* Jan. 29 and Feb. 5 and 12, 1946. See Michael Botson, "Jim Crow Wearing Steel-Toed Shoes and Safety Glass: Dual Unionism at the Hughes Tool Company, 1918–1942," *East Texas Historical Journal* 16 (1994): 101–16.

24. *Houston Informer,* Jan. 29 and Feb. 5 and 12, 1946.

25. *Houston Informer,* Jan. 29 and Feb. 5, 1946.

26. *Houston Informer,* June 26 and Oct. 9, 1932; May 15, 1937; Apr. 23, 1938; June 3 and Aug. 12, 1939. *Negro Labor News,* June 10, Sept. 2, and Nov. 25, 1939. SoRelle, "Darker Side of Heaven," 159–69. *Negro Labor News,* Apr. 13, May 18, and Oct. 19, 1940; *Houston Informer,* July 5 and Oct. 4, 1941.

27. LBW to Walter White, Aug. 12, 1946.

28. Marilyn D. Rhinehart, "Lesson in Unity: The Houston Municipal Workers Strike, 1946," *Houston Review* 4 (Fall 1982): 139–53; *Houston Chronicle,* Feb. 20, 1946. See also Daniel Nelson, *Managers and Workers: Origin of the New Factory System in the United States, 1880–1920* (Madison: Univ. of Wisconsin Press, 1975); Herbert Gutman, *Work, Culture, and Society in Industrializing America* (New York: Vintage Books, 1976); Joe Feagin, *Free Enterprise City: Houston in Political Economic Perspective* (New Brunswick, N.J.: Rutgers Univ. Press, 1988).

29. Rhinehart, "Lesson in Unity," 139–53.

30. LBW to Current, May 9, 1948. In this letter LBW acknowledges the role of Moses Leroy as a "Labor" man. She tells Current that Leroy and his team, "members of the labor division," already have brought more than a thousand members into the NAACP; therefore, words of encouragement from Current "[would] mean a lots" to Leroy. See Moses Leroy Collection, HMRC.

31. Rhinehart, "Lesson in Unity," 148–51. See Robert Eli Teel, "Discrimination Against Negro Workers in Texas: Extent and Effects" (M.A. thesis, Univ. of Texas, 1947).

32. *Proceedings and Resolutions of Houston Labor Conference,* in NAACP Files, MDLC; Current to LBW, Jan. 27, 1945. In 1946, the local chapter investigated discrimination in CIO and AFL auxiliaries in Houston. See NAACP, Houston Branch, *Annual Report,* 1946.

33. LBW to Wilkins, Oct. 30, 1946.

34. LBW to Walter White, Oct. 16, 1946; Roy Wilkins, "What Are Our Branches Doing," *Crisis* 12 (Dec. 1946): 377.

35. Texas Legislature, *Senate Journal,* 15th Leg., Reg. Sess., p. 406; Texas Legislature, *House Journal,* 15th Leg., Reg. Sess., p. 1666; Texas Legislature, *General and Specific Laws of the Senate the State of Texas Passed by the Regular Session of the Fifteenth Legislature* (Austin: 1947) 107–108; Rhinehart, "Lesson in Unity," 151; *Houston Informer,* July 19, 1947; *Houston Post,* Feb. 25 and 26, 1946; *Houston Chronicle,* Feb. 26 and 27, 1946.

36. Carleton, *Red Scare,* 19–20.

37. Ibid.

38. Ibid.

39. Ibid., 20–24.

40. LBW to A. Maceo Smith, July 27, 147; LBW to Black, Dec. 11, 1946; LBW to Current, Jan. 20, 1947; *Houston Informer,* July 19, 1947; June 5 and 28, 1948.

41. *Houston Informer,* July 19 and Aug. 16, 1947, and June 11, 1949.

42. Kenneth O'Reilly, "Roosevelt Administration and Black Americans: Federal Surveillance Policy and Civil Rights During the New Deal and World War II," *Phylon* 48

(1987): 1–10; Kenneth O'Reilly, "The FBI Secret Files on Black Americans," *Journal of American History* 69 (Dec. 1987): 638; Kenneth O'Reilly, *Black Americans: FBI Files* (New York: Carroll and Graf Publishers, 1994).

43. "Communist Infiltration of the NAACP Internal Search," memo, FBI Files, in NAACP FBI Files, 1941–57, Scholarly Resource Inc. Microfilm Publications (Wilmington, Dela., 1996) in Rice University Library. Unless otherwise indicated all other FBI material comes out of this file. See FBI Circular Letters Regarding Surveillance of NAACP Offices, Oct. 1947; and Marshall to J. Edgar Hoover, Dec. 11, 1947; both in FBI Files. See also D. M. Ladd, "Memo on Subject of Civil Rights Congress Largess," Dec. 16, 1947, in FBI Files; *Dallas Morning News,* Dec. 4, 1947.

44. Ladd, "Memo on Civil Rights Congress."

45. Marshall to Hoover, Dec. 11, 1947, and Hoover to Marshall, Dec. 17, 1947, both in FBI Files. Walter White to LBW, Dec. 24, 1947; LBW to Walter White, Dec. 24, 1947; Memo, Current to Henry Lee Moon, Jan. 13, 1948. See also Memo, Current to Henry Lee Moon, Jan. 12, 1949, denying that LBW was a sponsor of the scheduled event. The other African American listed as a sponsor was W. E. B. DuBois.

46. Marshall to Hoover, Jan. 17, 1948, in FBI Files. See FBI File 100-764—Administrative Page Confidential; FBI File 100-9032—Confidential SAC Houston, Oct. 1947; FBI File 100-7677 (Houston)—Security Matter C; and Memo, Ladd to Mr. Tamm regarding the Civil Rights Congress, Dec. 16, 1947, all in FBI Files. Memo, Current to Moon, Jan. 13, 1949; LBW to Walter White, Jan. 13, 1953. Henry Doyle and Matthew Plummer are listed in these files for their roles as attorneys for the NAACP.

47. LBW to Current, Jan. 20, 1947. See memo, Current to Moon, Jan. 12, 1949.

48. Curtis D. MacDougall, *Gideon's Army* (New York: Marzani and Munsell, 1965), 357–88, 393–95, 400, 406–407, 662–65, 686, 741–45; Gerald Horne, *Black and Red: W. E. B. DuBois and Afro-American Response to the Cold War, 1944–1963* (New York: State Univ. of New York Press, 1986).

49. Graham White and John Maze, *Henry A. Wallace: His Search for a New World Order* (Chapel Hill: Univ. of North Carolina Press, 1995), 147–79; see also Edward Schapsmeier and Frederick Schapsmeier, *Prophet in Politics: Henry A. Wallace and the War Years, 1940–1965* (Ames: Iowa State Univ. Press, 1971) ; Norman A. Markowitz, *The Rise and Fall of the People's Century: Henry A. Wallace and American Liberalism, 1941–1948* (New York: Free Press, 1973).

50. Carleton, *Red Scare,* 41–48, 52–55.

51. LBW to Weldon Hart, in NAACP Files, MDLC; *Austin American-Statesman,* Mar. 24, 1948; LBW to Ed Killen, in NAACP Files, MDLC; *Houston Post,* Mar. 24, 1948; LBW to Walter White, Dec. 24, 1948. See Minutes of the Committee to Get Wallace on the Ballot in Texas, in NAACP Files, MDLC. See also Minutes of the National Alliance of Postal Employees, 1948, in NAACP Files, MDLC; *Houston Labor News,* Mar. 13, 1948.

52. Carleton, *Red Scare,* 46–47; 50–52; *Houston Informer,* Sept. 19, 1948. See also Martin Duberman, *Paul Robeson: A Biography* (New York: Knopf, 1988), 316–35; Paul Robeson, *Here I Stand* (New York: Athello Associates, 1958).

53. U.S. Congress, HUAC, *The Negro in the Communist Party* (Washington, D.C.: Goverment Printing Office, 1953), 24. See Helen D. Thomas, "Individuals from Texas Reported as Having Been Affiliated with Communist Front Organizations, as Compiled from Official Government Reports, 1934–1954" (Houston, 1956), in Texas

NAACP Files, Center for American History, Univ. of Texas at Austin; *Houston Informer*, Sept. 19, 1948.

54. *Houston Informer*, June 11, 1949; *Houston Post*, June 6, 1949.

55. FBI File 100-9032; FBI Confidential Files on Director of the NAACP Branch for the State of Texas; both in FBI Files. Christia Adair, interview by author, Houston, Tex., Mar. 5, 1986, transcript in author's collection, Houston, Tex. See Sam Kinch and Stuart Long, *Alan Shivers: The Pied Piper of Texas Politics* (Austin: Shoal Creek Publishers, 1973).

56. *Houston Chronicle*, Mar. 19, 1956. This clipping is also found in the FBI Files; *Houston Informer*, Mar. 19 and Apr. 13, 1956; Richard Kluger, *Simple Justice: The History of Brown v. Board of Education and Black America's Struggle for Equality* (New York: Knopf, 1975); Mark V. Tushnet, *The NAACP's Legal Strategy Against Segregated Education, 1925–1950* (Chapel Hill: Univ. of North Carolina Press, 1957).

Chapter 5. The Great Divide: Lulu White, the Black Community, and Equal Educational Opportunities

1. Nancy Ruth Bessent, "Carter Wesley as a Journalist" (Ph.D. diss., Univ. of Texas, 1981), 27. Portions of this chapter appeared in an earlier form in Merline Pitre, "Black Houstonians and the 'Separate and Equal' Doctrine: Carter W. Wesley Versus LBW," *Houston Review* 12 (1990): 23–36.

2. Bessent, "Carter Wesley as a Journalist," 238–43.

3. *Texas Constitution* (1876), Art. 7, Sec. 14. See Alton Hornsby, Jr., "The Colored Branch University Issue in Texas—Prelude to *Sweatt v. Painter*," *Journal of Negro History* 41 (Jan. 1976): 51–60; Pitre, *Through Many Dangers*, 75–76; Merline Pitre, "The Evolution of a Black University in Texas," *Western Journal of Black Studies* 3 (Fall 1979): 216–17. See also Amilcar Shabazz, "The Opening of the Southern Mind: Desegregation of Higher Education in Texas, 1865–1965" (Ph.D. diss., Univ. of Houston, 1997).

4. *Missouri ex rel. Gaines v. Canada*, 305 U.S. 33 (1938).

5. *Dallas Express*, Oct. 15, 22, and 29, 1938. See Texas Legislature, *Special Laws of the State of Texas Passed by the Regular Session of the 46th Legislature* (Austin: N.d.), H.B. 255, p. 359; Michael Gillette, "Blacks Challenge the White University," *Southwestern Historical Quarterly* 86 (Oct. 1982): 321–22.

6. LBW to Current, Dec. 5, 1947. *Dallas Morning News*, Feb. 4, Mar. 20, Apr. 25, May 2, and June 6, 1945. See also Gillette, "Blacks Challenge the White University," 322.

7. Texas Legislature, *Texas General Laws of the State of Texas* Passed by the Regular Session of the 49th Legislature (Austin: 1945), 506.

8. Thomas A. Krueger, *And Promises to Keep: The Southern Conference for Human Welfare, 1938–1948* (Nashville, Tenn.: Vanderbilt Univ. Press, 1967), 119–21; Morton Sosna, *In Search of the Silent South: Southern Liberals and the Race Issue* (New York: Columbia Univ. Press, 1977), 114–20, 152–67.

9. Krueger, *Promises to Keep*, 119–21; Sosna, *In Search of the Silent South*, 114–20, 152–67. R. L. Carter to A. Maceo Smith, Mar. 30, 1947.

10. *Houston Informer*, Feb. 8, June 7, and Aug. 16, 1947.

11. LBW to Walter White, Jan. 2, 1947; LBW to Marshall, Jan. 14, 1947; LBW to Current, Jan. 20, 1947.

12. Wesley to Marshall, Aug. 1, 1945; Marshall to Wesley, Aug. 21, 1945; Marshall to Wesley, Oct. 10, 1947.

13. Marshall to Wesley, Sept. 26, 1945; LBW to Marshall, Oct. 10, 1945. Michael Gillette, "Heman Marion Sweatt: Civil Rights Plaintiff," in *Black Leaders: Texans for Their Times*, ed. Alwyn Barr and Robert A. Calvert (Austin: Texas State Historical Association, 1981), 161.

14. LBW to Marshall, Oct. 10, 1945.

15. A. Maceo Smith to LBW, Nov. 19, 1945; W. J. Durham to Marshall, Jan. 28, 1946.

16. Theophilus A. Painter to Grover Sellers, Feb. 26, 1946. This letter was leaked to the press and later published in its entirety in the *Houston Informer*, Mar. 2, 1946.

17. *Texas Attorney General Opinion*, Texas, no. 0-7126, Mar. 16, 1946. See also *Senate Bill #288*, Texas Legislature, *General and Special Laws of the State of Texas Passed by the Regular Session of the 49th Legislature* (Austin, 1945).

18. A. Maceo Smith to Wesley, Mar. 21, 1946. A small group of blacks supported Smith's position, in the hope that Prairie View would be transformed from a normal school into a "classical" university. See also LBW to Marshall, Nov. 26, 1949.

19. Wesley to A. Maceo Smith, Mar. 30, 1946; Wesley to W. J. Durham, Mar. 22, 1946. Wesley was in favor of a "classical" black university but was undecided as to whether Prairie View should be converted into such. For the time being, he wanted to have a black board of regents and a black president for Prairie View. According to oral sources, when Houston College for Negroes was first established, black families, friends, and individuals donated bricks for the construction of the first classroom building. It is this action to which Wesley refers when he speaks of reparation.

20. Dudley K. Woodward to Gibb Gilchrist, June 20, 1946, in General Files—Negroes in College, 1939–1954, UTPOR. See also Gillette, "Blacks Challenge the White University," 344–84.

21. *Houston Chronicle*, May 17, 1946.

22. A. Maceo Smith to R. L. Carter, Aug. 9, 1946. Also Mark Magee to Coke Stevenson, Dec. 6, 1946, and Bi-Racial Commission Report, Dec. 17, 1946; both in General Files—Negroes in College, 1939–1954, UTPOR. The two black members of the committee were Willette R. Banks, principal of Prairie View College, and Everett H. Givens, dentist from Austin. See also LBW to Marshall, July 30, 1946.

23. A. Maceo Smith to R. L. Carter, Aug. 9, 1946; *Houston Post*, Aug. 9, 1946.

24. A. Maceo Smith to R. L. Carter, Aug. 9, 1946; "Resolution of the Texas Council of Negro Organizations to the Governor's Bi-Racial Commission," Aug. 8, 1946, in NAACP Files, MDLC.

25. *Houston Post*, Aug. 9, 1946.

26. Ibid.

27. LBW to Walter White, Jan. 2, 1947; LBW to Lucas, Dec. 31, 1946; A. Maceo Smith to Wesley, Sept. 3, 1946.

28. LBW to Walter White, Jan. 2, 1947.

29. LBW to Current, Jan. 20, 1947; LBW to Walter White, Jan. 2, 1947; A. Maceo Smith to R. L. Carter, Oct. 16, 1946.

30. LBW to Walter White, n.d.

31. LBW to Black, Nov. 22, 1946; LBW to Walter White, Jan. 2, 1947.

32. LBW to Walter White, Jan. 2, 1947; LBW to Marshall, Dec. 11, 1946.

33. Marshall to Wesley, Aug. 21, 1945; Wesley to A. Maceo Smith, Mar. 26, 1946.

34. Marshall to Wesley, Oct. 25, 1946.

35. Wesley to Marshall, Dec. 23, 1946; Marshall to Wesley, Dec. 27, 1946.

36. *Houston Informer,* Dec. 28, 1946.

37. LBW to Lucas, Dec. 31, 1946

38. Marshall to LBW, Jan. 14, 1947; LBW to Lucas, Dec. 30, 1946.

39. Wesley to Marshall, Dec. 27, 1946.

40. *Houston Informer,* Dec. 7, 1946.

41. Mark Magee to Coke Stevenson, Dec. 17, 1946, and Bi-Racial Commission Report, Dec. 6, 1946; both in General Files—Negroes in College, 1939–1954, UTPOR. *Houston Post,* Feb. 25, 1947.

42. Neil G. Sapper, "The Fall of the NAACP in Texas," *Houston Review* 7 (Nov. 2, 1985): 63–68. Texas Legislature, House and Senate, *General and Specific Laws Passed in the Regular Session of the 50th Legislature* (Austin, 1947), S.B. 140 and H.B. 780, pp. 36–40.

43. LBW to Current, May 9, 1947.

44. A. Maceo Smith to Leslie Perry, Feb. 21, 1947; LBW to Marshall, Dec. 11, 1946.

45. Wesley to A. Maceo Smith, Mar. 1946; *Houston Informer,* June 7 and Aug. 16, 1947; LBW to Lucas, Dec. 31, 1946.

46. *Houston Informer,* June 7 and Aug. 6, 1947.

47. *Houston Informer,* June 7, 1947.

48. Curtis McDonald, interview by author, Houston, Tex., June 5, 1996, transcript in author's collection, Houston, Tex.

49. LBW to Marshall, Aug. 27, 1947. LBW's close relationship with Marshall is suggested by her handwritten note in the margin of this letter: "This is a long letter, but put your big feet on your desk and read all of it, please!"

50. Ibid.

51. Ibid.

52. LBW to Wilkins, June 14, 1948.

53. *Houston Informer,* June 7 and Aug. 16, 1947.

54. *Daily Texan,* Dec. 5 and 10, 1947; LBW to W. Astor Kirk.

55. LBW to Current, Dec. 5, 1947; LBW to Marshall, Sept. 23, 1947; Painter to Woodward, Jan. 3, 1948, in General Files—Negroes in College, 1939–1954, UTPOR; Gillette, "Blacks Challenge the White University," 331. See also, all in UTPOR: Painter to Kirk, Jan. 21, 1948, and May 4, 1949; Raphael O'Hara Lanier to Craig Cullinan, Nov. 11, 1949; and Lanier to Painter, June 18, 1948, and June 4, 1950.

56. Cullinan to Lanier, Dec. 17, 1948; Lanier to Harold Schachter, Dec. 2, 1948, in NAACP Files, MDLC and UTPOR; LBW to Current, Dec. 5, 1947.

57. *Daily Texan* (Austin), Apr. 28, 1948; *Austin American-Statesman,* Apr. 28, 1949. Marshall to Mercer Tate, May 10 and 18, 1949. Painter to Ben Davis, Mar. 22, 1947, in General Subject Files—Texas State University for Negroes, 1946–1952, UTPOR.

58. *Houston Post,* Apr. 28, 1948. Painter to I. H. Maddox, Sept. 1, 1949, in General Files—Negroes in College, 1939–1945, UTPOR. Cullinan to Painter, July 13, 1949, in General Subject Files, Texas State Univ. for Negroes, 1946–1952, UTPOR. See Alwyn Barr, "African Americans in Texas: From Stereotypes to Diverse Roles," in *Texas Through Time: Evolving Interpretations,* ed. Walter L. Buenger and Robert A. Calvert (College Station: Texas A&M Univ. Press, 1991), 78. See also Martin Kuhlman, "The Civil

Rights Movement in Texas: Desegregation of Public Accommodation" (Ph.D. diss., Texas Tech Univ., 1994).

59. Gillette, " Blacks Challenge the White University," 336; Sapper, "Fall of the NAACP," 61–62. Herman Barnett, a native from Lockett, Texas, attended Tillotson College. After graduating with honors in 1946, he applied for medical school at both the University of Texas and Meharry College in Nashville, Tenn. Subsequently he was accepted at Meharry, but, instead of going there, he became a plaintiff in a test case involving the University of Texas. *Houston Informer*, Aug. 27, 1946.

60. LBW to Marshall, Nov. 26, 1949.

61. LBW to L. H. Simpson, June 13, 1949. *Houston Informer*, June 11, 1949.

62. Sapper, "Fall of the NAACP," 59.

63. Ibid. *Sweatt v. Painter* 339 U.S. 629, 70 Sup. Ct. 848–51 (1950). See Sapper, "Fall of the NAACP," 63–68; *Houston Informer*, June 10, 1950; *Daily Texan*, June 7, 1950. Gillette, "Heman Marion Sweatt," 178.

Chapter 6. Workhorse or Team Player? The NAACP Experience

1. Minutes of the National Labor Convention of Colored Men, held in Houston, 1946; in NAACP Files, MDLC.

2. August Meier and John Bracey, Jr., "The NAACP as a Reform Movement, 1909–1965: To Reach the Conscience of America," *Journal of Southern History* 59 (Feb. 1993): 3–30. See also Charles Flint Kellogg, *NAACP*; Kenneth W. Goings, *The NAACP Comes of Age: The Defeat of Judge John Parker* (Bloomington: Indiana Univ. Press, 1990); Elliot Rudwick and August Meier, "The Rise of the Black Secretariat in the NAACP, 1909–1935," in *Along the Color Line: Explorations in the Black Experience*, ed. August Meier and Elliot Rudwick, 94–127 (Urbana: Univ. of Illinois Press, 1976); John Bracey, Jr., and August Meier, "Allies or Adversaries? The NAACP, A. Philip Randolph and the 1941 March on Washington," *Georgia Historical Quarterly* 74 (Spring 1991): 1–17; Tushnet, *NAACP's Legal Strategy.*

3. Meier and Bracey, "NAACP as a Reform Movement," 15. See also Genna Rae McNeil, *Groundwork: Charles Hamilton Houston and the Struggle for Civil Rights* (Philadelphia: Univ. of Pennsylvania Press, 1983); John Hope Franklin and Genna Rae McNeil, eds., *African Americans and the Living Constitution* (Washington, D.C.: Smithsonian Institution Press, 1996).

4. Walter White to Ora Lee Terry, Apr. 13, 1943. See duties of executive secretary, in NAACP, Houston Branch, *Constitution and By-Laws*, 5–6, in NAACP Files, MDLC. Black to LBW, Oct. 26, 1945; A. Maceo Smith to LBW, Oct. 26, 1945.

5. In 1948, LBW and Juanita Craft had a conference with the mayor of Bay City, Matagorda County, Texas, regarding the existence of a white Man's Union Primary. After the meeting, the mayor assured these women that he was 100% behind the NAACP and requested that an attorney and photographer be on the scene on election day, Apr. 10, 1948. That same year, LBW worked closely with Craft on Dallas's November 1948 NAACP membership drive. See also LBW to Wilkins, Mar. 9, 1948.

Craft was the first black woman deputized to sell poll taxes in Texas and was a pioneer in helping to break down racial barriers in Dallas's public facilities. At age 73, she won a seat on the Dallas City Council and serve for two consecutive terms, 1975 to

1979. She died in 1985 at age 83, after receiving the Eleanor Roosevelt Pioneer Award from the University of Texas. Juanita J. S. Craft Collection, Dallas Public Library. Dorothy Robinson, "Interview with Juanita Craft," Jan. 20, 1977, in the Black Woman Oral History Project (Schlesinger Library at Radcliffe College, Cambridge, Mass. and K. C. Saur Verlag), pp. 3:12, 3:14. Juanita Jewel Shanks Craft Collection, Center for American History, Univ. of Texas at Austin. *Fort Worth Star Telegram,* Oct. 10, 1984; *Dallas Morning News,* Oct. 12, 1984. W. Marvin Dulaney, "Whatever Happened to the Civil Rights Movement in Dallas, Texas?" in *Essays on the Civil Rights Movement,* ed. W. Marvin Dulaney and Kathleen Underwood (College Station: Texas A&M Univ. Press, 1993), 26–27. *Dallas Morning News,* Oct. 12, 1984; Winegarten, *Black Texan Women,* 178, 222–23, 242–44, 256–57, 275, 298; Patricia Prather and Bob Lee, "Juanita Craft," *Texas Trailblazer Series* 16 (Houston: The Texas Trailblazer Preservation Association and the Summerlee Foundation, 1996), 1; Gillette, "Rise of the NAACP," 411–13; LBW to Wilkins, Mar. 9, 1948.

6. Lucas to Wilkins, Jan. 1, 1945; Lucas to Wilkins, Feb. 19, 1945; A. Maceo Smith to Lucas, Oct. 25, 1945.
7. LBW to Ella Baker, Aug. 15, 1945; LBW to Marshall, Feb. 4, 1947. LBW served as recording secretary and president of Prairie View's National Alumni Association during the 1940s. Today, in recognition of her service in these positions, her picture adorns the university's Alumni Hall.
8. LBW to Walter White, Dec. 4, 1945; Walter White to LBW, Dec. 12, 1945; LBW to Marshall, Feb. 4, 1947.
9. Walter White to L. P. Lubin-Byars, Jan. 11, 1946; Marshall to Lubin-Byars, Jan. 24, 1946. LBW's father lived to see her receive these accolades; he died shortly thereafter. LBW to Wilkins, Jan. 5, 1946.
10. LBW to Ella Baker, Mar. 1 and 20, 1946; LBW to Black, May 17, 1946.
11. LBW to Current, Nov. 27, 1946.
12. Ella Baker to LBW, Mar. 20, 1946.
13. LBW to Ella Baker, Mar. 1 and Apr. 24, 1946.
14. LBW to Current, Dec. 7, 1946. See also LBW to Current, May 9, 1948; LBW to Ella Baker, Mar. 18, 1946.
15. LBW to Black, Nov. 22, 1946; Black to LBW, Feb. 7, 1947.
16. LBW to Current, Mar. 1 and Dec. 7, 1946.
17. LBW to Lucas, Dec. 31, 1946; LBW to Walter White, Jan. 2, 1947; Memo, Marshall to Walter White, Dec. 30, 1946; *Houston Informer,* Dec. 23 and 31, 1946; LBW to Wilkins, Jan. 14, 1947.
18. LBW to Marshall, Jan. 14, 1947; Marshall to LBW, Feb. 4, 1947. See also LBW to Current, Dec. 7. 1946.
19. LBW to Wilkins, Dec. 8, 1947.
20. LBW to Baker, Apr. 24, 1946; LBW to Black, May 17, 1946, *Houston Informer,* June 5 and 20, 1948.
21. LBW to Simpson, Executive Board et al., Apr. 10, 1948, and Jan. 5, 1949. George McElroy, interview by author, Houston, Tex., Feb. 10, 1987, transcript in author's collection, Houston, Tex.
22. LBW to Wilkins, June 22, 1949; LBW to Simpson, June 13, 1949.
23. LBW to Current, June 12 and 22, 1947; LBW to Simpson, June 13, 1949.

24. A. Maceo Smith to Wilkins, Jan. 30, 1950; Donald Jones to Wilkins, Feb. 5, 1950; Donald Jones to Current, Jan. 3, 1950.

25. A. Maceo Smith to Wilkins, Jan. 30, 1950. See also Donald Jones to Current, Jan. 3, 1950; Current to Donald Jones, Sept. 27, 1950. The NAACP's Southwest Regional Office consisted of Texas, Louisiana, and Oklahoma. Gillette, "Rise of the NAACP," 149.

26. Black to LBW, Mar. 8, 1950; LBW to Black, Mar. 20, 1950. See also memo, Mrs. Williams to LBW, May 8, 1950; A. G. Washington to Wilkins, Apr. 14, 1950.

27. Current to Julius White, Apr. 12, 1960; Current to LBW, Apr. 13, 1950; LBW to Current, Apr. 19, 1950.

28. LBW to Current, Apr. 19, 1950; Donald Jones to Current, Aug. 13, 1950; Memo, Current to Wilkins, Aug. 21, 1950; Memo, Wilkins to Current, Aug. 28, 1950; LBW to Current, Sept. 13, 1950; Current to LBW, Sept. 20, 1950.

29. Current to Wilkins, June 18, 1957.

30. LBW to Current, Sept. 16, 1950.

31. LBW, "$5,000 Fund Drive for Freedom," Circular Letter, Sept. 15, 1950, in NAACP Files, MDLC. Black to LBW, Sept. 16, 1950; Thaddeus D. Williams to Current, Nov. 7, 1950.

32. LBW to Black, Oct. 3, 1950; LBW to Current, Sept. 16, 1950; Current to LBW, Sept. 20, 1950.

33. LBW to Current, Sept. 16, 1950; Current to LBW, Sept. 20, 1950. Thaddeus D. Williams to Current, Nov. 7, 1950.

34. Dorothy Robinson, "Interview with Christia Adair," Apr. 25, 1977, in the Black Woman Oral History Project (Schlesinger Library at Radcliffe College, Cambridge, Mass. and K. C. Saur Verlag), 1:62–67, 1:89, 1:96. See also Christia V. Adair Collection, HMRC. *Houston Informer*, Feb. 9, 1946; Winegarten, *Black Texas Women*, 244–45; Gillette, "Rise of the NAACP," 178. Adair died in 1992, at age 96.

35. Carleton, *Red Scare*, xii, 65–100.

36. Donald Jones to Current, July 15, 1950; Donald Jones to LBW, Jan. 3, 1950; A. Maceo Smith to Current, Nov. 1, 1950. See [LBW], draft of "Houston Branch Request to National Headquarters," n.d., in NAACP Files, MDLC.

37. Adair to Current, June 15, 1950.

38. A. Maceo Smith to Donald Jones, Nov. 14, 1940.

39. Donald Jones to Current, July 15, 1950; A. Maceo Smith to Donald Jones, Nov. 14, 1950. See also Simpson to LBW, June 12, 1948.

40. Current to Adair, Nov. 1951; Current to John Flamer, Jan. 29, 1953. See also NAACP, Houston Branch, *Annual Report*, 1953, in NAACP Files, MDLC; and Memo, Flamer to Current, May 14–27, 1953.

41. LBW to Black, Sept. 18, 1954; James E. Robinson to Current, Apr. 5, 1955; LBW to Black, Sept. 18, 1954; Black to LBW, Sept. 29, 1954; LBW to Black, Dec. 15, 1954.

42. Flamer to Current, Apr. 1, 1953; Current to Flamer, Jan. 29, 1953; Current to Adair, Nov. 14, 1951. See also Gillette, "NAACP in Texas."

43. Memos, Flamer to Current, May 14–27 and Aug. 3, 1953.

44. *Weekly Messenger*, Dec. 24, 1954, in NAACP Files, MDLC; Adair to Current, Apr. 7, 1954; NAACP, Houston Branch, *Annual Report*, 1954, in NAACP Files, MDLC; Current to A. Maceo Smith, Apr. 1, 1954.

45. *Weekly Messenger,* Dec. 24, 1954. NAACP, Houston Branch, *Annual Report,* 1954, in NAACP Files, MDLC. LBW to A. Maceo Smith, Dec. 2 and 17, 1954; LBW to Current, Dec. 6, 1954.

46. LBW to A. Maceo Smith, Dec. 2 and 17, 1954; LBW to Current, Feb. 5, 1955.

47. Current to A. Maceo Smith, Apr. 1, 1955; LBW to Current, Feb. 5, 1955;

48. Current to A. Maceo Smith, Mar. 30, 1955; Current to Simpson, June 16, 1955.

49. James E. Robinson to Current, Apr. 5, 1955.

50. Minutes of Executive Board Meeting of Houston Branch of NAACP, Mar. 21 and Oct. 16, 1955, in NAACP Files, MDLC, Current to A. Maceo Smith, Mar. 30, 1955. See "Branch Request to National Headquarters for Approval of Christia Adair," n.d, in NAACP Files, MDLC.

51. Current to Simpson, June 16, 1955; Wilkins to Simpson, June 18, 1955.

52. Current to Mercer Tate, Oct. 11, 1955, Simpson to Current, Sept. 8, 1955; A. Maceo Smith to Current, Oct. 13, 1955. See also A. Maceo Smith to Wilkins, July 27, 1955; Current to A. Maceo Smith, Aug. 31, 1955.

53. *The State of Texas v. the National Association for the Advancement of Colored People, a Corporation, et al.,* 56 U.S. Dist. Ct., 649 (1957) no. 56-649. John Ben Shepperd to NAACP Officers, Sept. 18, 1956, in Attorney General's Records Folder, Texas State Archives, Austin. See *Austin American-Statesman,* Sept. 15, 22, and 24, 1956; *Texas Observer,* Sept. 26 and Oct. 3, 1956. See also Robyn Duff Ladino, *Desegregating Texas Schools: Eisenhower, Shivers and the Crisis at Mansfield High* (Austin: Univ. of Texas Press, 1996), 134. As the State of Texas pressed the Houston branch for its membership list, LBW watched from the sidelines. As the NAACP's director of state branches, she stayed in close contact with the national headquarters, informing the office of the chapters and state organizations that had submitted their membership lists in compliance with the attorney general's request. LBW to Wilkins, Sept. 22, 1956. The trial was held in the vicinity of LBW's birthplace, Tyler, Texas. See also Dorothy Robinson, "Interview with Christia Adair," 1:62–67, 1:72, 1:92.

54. LBW to Simpson, June 6, 1948; LBW to Wilkins, Jan. 5, 1949; Daniel Byrd to Simpson, May 20, 1955.

55. LBJ to LBW, Oct. 24, 1953; *Houston Informer,* May 20, 1955; Lois Woods, interview by author, Houston, Tex., Feb. 7, 1995, transcript in author's collection, Houston, Tex.

56. LBW, Circular Letters to Members of the NAACP, Apr. 21 and May 9, 1955.

57. Stephen J. Whitfield, *A Death in the Delta: The Story of Emmett Till* (New York: Free Press, 1980), 15–45. See also Juan Williams, *Eye on the Prize: America's Civil Rights Years* (New York: Viking Press, 1987), 52.

58. Whitfield, *A Death in the Delta,* 15–45.

59. LBW, Circular Letter to Members of the NAACP, Oct. 6, 1955.

60. Ibid.

Chapter 7. Lulu White and the Issue of Gender

1. Deborah Gray White, *Ar'n't I a Woman? Female Slaves in the Plantation South* (New York: W. W. Norton, 1989), 68–80, 161–67; John Blassingame, *The Slave Community: Plantation Life in the Antebellum South* (New York: Oxford Univ. Press, 1978), 77–103; Angela Davis, *Women, Race and Class* (New York: Vintage Books, 1983), 6; Elizabeth

Fox-Genovese, *Within the Plantation Household: Black and White Women of the Old South* (Chapel Hill: Univ. of North Carolina, 1988), 372–96.

2. Glenda Riley, *Inventing the American Woman* (Wheeling, Ill.: Harlan-Davidson, 1995), 65–69; Barbara Welter, "The Cult of True Womanhood, 1820–1860," *American Quarterly* 18 (Summer 1966): 5; Carl Degler, *At Odds: Women and the Family in America: From Revolution to the Present* (New York: Oxford Univ. Press, 1980), 20. See also Mary Ryan, *Womanhood in America: From Colonial Times to the Present* (New York: New Viewpoints, 1995).

3. Jewel L. Prestage, "In Quest of African-American Political Woman," *Annals of the American Academy of Political and Social Sciences* 515 (May 1991): 88–103; Marianne Githens and Jewel L. Prestage, eds., *A Portrait of Marginality: The Political Behavior of American Woman* (New York: David McKay, 1977), 6–8; Laurily Keir Epstein, ed., *Women in the Profession* (Lexington, Mass.: D. C. Heath, 1978), 6–7; Jewel L. Prestage, "Political Behavior of Black American Women: An Overview," in *The Black Woman*, ed. LaFrances Rodgers-Rose (Beverly Hills, Calif.: Sage Publications, 1980), 233; Jewel L. Prestage, "Black Women Judges: An Examination of Their Socio-Economic, Educational and Political Backgrounds and Judicial Placement," in *Readings in American Political Issues*, ed. Franklin Jones, Sanders Anderson, et al., 324–44 (Dubuque, Iowa: Kendall-Hunt, 1987). See also Gloria J. Baxton, "African American Women and Politics: Research Trends and Directions," *National Political Science Review* 4 (1994): 281–96.

4. William H. Chafe, *The Paradox of Change: American Women in the Twentieth Century* (New York: Oxford Univ. Press, 1991), 176; Beverly Guy-Sheftall, *Daughters of Sorrow: Attitudes Toward Black Women, 1880–1920* (Brooklyn, N.Y.: Carlson Publishers, 1990), 159–76.

5. Lois Woods, interview by author, Houston, Tex., Feb. 12, 1995, transcript in author's collection, Houston, Tex.; Pearl Suel, interview by author, Houston, Tex., Feb. 26, 1997, transcript in author's collection, Houston, Tex.; Grace G. Wetlaw, interview by author, Houston, Tex., June 6, 1996, transcript in author's collection, Houston, Tex.; Mosely, interview by author, Feb. 27, 1987; Mease, interview by Baggett, Mar. 27, 1998.

6. Jordan, interview by author, Feb. 7, 1987; Johnnie Jordan, interview by author, Houston, Tex., Feb. 12, 1987, transcript in author's collection, Houston, Tex.

7. Hine, *Black Victory,* 54–55; Melvin J. Banks, "Pursuit of Equality," 295–97; Davidson, *Biracial Politics,* 18; Guy-Sheftall, *Daughters of Sorrow,* 140–50.

8. *Prairie View College Bulletin,* 1928; Woolfolk, *Prairie View,* 230, 236, 240–41, 246–48, 250. Jordan, interview by author, Feb. 5, 1997; Jimmie R. Phillips, interview by author, Houston, Tex., Apr. 13, 1997, transcript in author's collection, Houston, Tex.

9. Woolfolk, *Prairie View,* 250–52. On LBW's affiliation with the YWCA, see Scrapbook of LBW. Lois Woods, interview by author, Feb. 12, 1995. *Prairie View Standard,* Oct. 25, 1927, and Mar. 24, 1928.

10. Woolfolk, *Prairie View,* 142–43, 246–52; Pearl Suel, interview by author, Houston, Tex., Feb. 27, 1995, transcript in author's collection, Houston, Tex.

11. *Houston Informer,* Nov. 4, 1944, and Jan. 12, 1946. Known as the "fraternal capital" of the U.S., Texas had over 500 African American lodges at the turn of the century. The most noted of these were the Masons, Eastern Stars, Invincible Sons and Daughters of Commerce, and the Grand Court of Calanthe. LBW belonged to the True Heart

Chapter 193, Order of Eastern Star; and the Pride of Houston Chapter 244, Grand Court of Calanthe. The Grand Court of Calanthe was the richest of the women's fraternal orders. Founded in 1897 in Texas, the Grand Court of Calanthe served as a benevolent burial insurance association. In 1933, when most insurance companies went bankrupt, the Grand Court had an assests of $611,540 and loaned thousands of dollars to members to pay their taxes.

The by-laws of the Married Ladies Social Club required that members be "respectable married women living with their husbands." See also By-Laws of the 1906 Art, Literary and Charity Club, rm 1970, in HMRC; Winegarten, *Black Texan Women*, 186.

Spearheaded by Jennie Bell Covington, the Blue Triangle Branch of Houston YWCA was established Jan. 1918 and became a member of the central association in 1920. In the early 1930s, a permanent residence was purchased for the Blue Triangle and was furnished with gifts from churches, clubs, and friends. According to oral sources, LBW gave huge amounts to the "Y." On Jan. 25, 1947, LBW was the main speaker of the Sunday Forum at the Blue Triangle; her topic was "How May the Program of the NAACP Serve the Community?" Lois Woods, interview by author, Houston, Tex., Mar. 22, 1996, transcript in author's collection, Houston, Tex. NAACP, Houston Branch, *Annual Report,* 1947, in NAACP Files, MDLC. See also Howard Jones, *Red Diary: A Chronological History of Black Americans in Houston and Some Neighboring Harris County Communities—122 Years* (Austin, Tex.: Eakin Press, 1991).

12. Pearl Suel, interview by author, Houston, Tex., Oct. 13, 1996, transcript in author's collection, Houston, Tex.; Nimer and George Nelson, interview by Pitre, Feb. 25, 1989. See also Jacoway and Colburn, *Southern Businessmen and Desegregation.*

13. LBW to Walter White, July 26, 1943. William H. Chafe, *Civilities and Civil Rights: Greensboro, North Carolina, and the Black Struggle for Freedom* (New York: Oxford Univ. Press, 1980), 29; Charles S. Johnson, *Patterns of Negro Segregation* (New York: Harper and Bros., 1943); James SoRelle, "Race Relations in Heavenly Houston, 1919–45" in Beeth and Wintz, *Black Dixie,* 186–87. See also Vicki Crawford, Jacqueline A. Rouse, and Barbara Woods, eds., *Women in the Civil Rights Movement: Trailblazers and Torchbearers, 1941–1945* (Bloomington: Indiana Univ. Press, 1993), esp. Barbara Woods, "Modjeska Simkins and the South Carolina Conference of the NAACP, 1939–1957," 99–120.

14. *Houston Informer,* Feb. 5, 1944

15. *Houston Informer,* Oct. 3, 1945.

16. Alfreda M. Duster, ed., *Crusader for Justice: The Autobiography of Ida B. Wells* (Chicago: Univ. of Chicago Press, 1970), 117; David M. Tucker, "Miss Ida B. Wells and the Memphis Lynching," *Phylon* 32 (Summer 1971): 112–12; Gail Bedeman, "Civilization: The Decline of Middle-Class Manliness and Ida B. Wells-Barnett's Anti-Lynching Campaign, 1892–1894," in *We Specialize in the Wholly Impossible,* ed. Darlene C. Hine, Linda Reed, and William King (Brooklyn, N.Y.: Carlson Publishers, 1994), II:407–32; Rosalyn Terborg-Penn, "Discontented Black Feminists: Prelude and Postscripts to the Passage of the Nineteenth Amendment," in *We Specialize in the Wholly Impossible,* ed. Darlene C. Hine, Linda Reed, and William King (Brooklyn, N.Y.: Carlson Publishers, 1994), II:487–504; Linda Reed, "Fannie Lou Hamer, 1917–1977," in *Black Women in America: An Historical Encyclopedia,* ed. Darlene Clark Hine (Brooklyn, N.Y.: Carlson Publishers, 1993), 518–20; Mamie E. Lock, "Is This America? Fannie Lou Hamer and

the Mississippi Freedom Democratic Party," in *Women in the Civil Rights Movement*, ed. Vicki Crawford, Jacqueline A. Rouse, and Barbara Woods, 27–38 (Bloomington: Indiana Univ. Press, 1993).

17. LBW to Marshall, Aug. 21, 1945; LBW to Walter White, Jan. 2, 1947; *Houston Informer*, Dec. 28, 1946; Current to LBW, Apr. 13, 1950; Current to Julius White, Apr. 12, 1950; A. Maceo Smith to LBW Oct. 26, 1945; Lampkin to LBW, May 8, 1944; Adair to Current, June 15, 1950; A. Maceo Smith to LBW, Oct. 26, 1948; LBW to Black, Nov. 30, 1948.

18. Meier and Bracey, "NAACP as a Reform Movement," 321.

19. LBW to Walter White, Jan. 2, 1947; LBW to Current, Jan. 20, 1947; Marshall to Wesley, Aug. 21, Oct. 25, 1946; Wesley to A. Maceo Smith, Mar. 26, 1946; LBW to Simpson, Jan. 18, 1955; LBW to A. Maceo Smith, Sept., 27, 1944.

20. Luelelia Harrison, interview by author, Houston, Tex., Feb. 10, 1997, transcript in author's collection, Houston, Tex.

21. LBW to Ella Baker, Apr. 24, 1946; LBW to Black, May 17, 1946; LBW to Current, Dec. 7, 1946.

22. LBW to Walter White, Jan. 2, 1949; LBW to Marshall, Feb. 4, 1967; Marshall to LBW, Feb. 4, 1947; Current to Julius White, Sept. 13, 1950; Marshall to Julius White, Feb. 4, 1947; LBW to Black, Nov. 22, 1946; Memo, Marshall to LBW, Dec. 30, 1946; LBW to Marshall, Jan. 16, 1947; LBW to Wilkins, June 22, 1949.

23. *Houston Informer*, Apr. 12, 1947; Winegarten, *Black Texas Women*, 185–205; Andrew Webber Jackson, *Sure Foundation*, 290–99; see also Minutes of the 1906 Arts, Literary and Charity Club and its "By-Laws and Constitution," both in HMRC.

24. Minutes of the Chat-an-Hour Coffee Club, Mar. 3 and Dec. 8, 1949; Feb. 9, 1950; and Apr. 24, 1958; all in HMRC.

25. Minutes of the Chat-an-Hour Coffee Club, Mar. 3 and Dec. 8, 1949.

26. Carleton, *Red Scare*, 110–38.

27. U.S. Congress HUAC, *The Negroes in the Communist Party* (Washington, D.C.: Government Printing Office, 1953), 24. See Helen D. Thomas, "Individuals from Texas Reported as Having Been Affiliated with Communist Front Organizations, as Compiled from the 70th Official Government Reports 1934–1954" (Houston, 1956) in Texas NAACP Files in Center for American History, Univ. of Texas at Austin.

28. Thelma Bryant, interview by author, Houston, Tex., Mar. 5, 1997, transcript in author's collection, Houston, Tex.; LBW to Wilkins, Oct. 25, 1946.

29. Karen Sach, "Gender and Grassroots Leadership" (unpub. paper, Univ. of California at Los Angeles, n.d.), 5–16.

Epilogue

1. Current to A. Maceo Smith, June 7, 1957; Adair to Black, June 20, 1957; *Houston Informer*, July 6 and 13, 1957.

2. *Houston Informer*, July 6, 1957.

3. *Houston Informer*, July 13, 1957. Funeral program of LBW, in collection of Johnnie Jordan, Houston, Tex. This obituary was taken from LBW funeral program.

4. *Houston Informer*, July 13, 1957.

5. Hattie White, interview by author, Hosuton, Tex., Feb. 10, 1978, transcript in author's collection, Houston, Tex.

Index

New Waverly, Tex., 109
Nickerson, Williams, Jr., 20
1906 Art, Literary and Charity, 108,
    134, 140
Nixon, L. A., 20
Nixon v. Condon, 21–22
Nixon v. Herndon, 20, 27
Northwestern University, 90

O'Daniel, Willie Lee, 62
Odd Fellows Temple, 13
Office of Price Administration (OPA),
    60–61
Oklahoma, 90
Okinawa, 63
Old Terrell Colored High School, 8
Old Washington Colored High
    School, 14

Painter, Theolophius, 95–96, 101
Palacios, Tex., 111
Party: Communist, 76, 71, 78;
    Democratic, 22–26; Lily White, 26;
    People's, 46; Progressive, 78;
    Republican, 26
Pascagoula, Miss., 39
Patten, M. B., 26
Pensacola, Fla., 39
People's Party, 46
Permanent University Fund, 94, 99
Phelps, R. L., 66
Phi Beta Sigma, 34
Pilgrim Building, 74–75
Pittsburgh, Pa., 31–32
Pittsburgh Courier, 31–32
Pleasant Hill Baptist Church, 48
police: brutality, 51; officers, 51–52
Political Action Committee (PAC), 65,
    140–41
Polk, Neal, 50–51
Porgy and Bess production, 42
Prairie View State College, 9–14, 53,
    108, 131–33, 145
Prestage, Jewel L., 130
Price, Albert L., 40
Progressive Party, 78

Progressive Voters League, 26, 34, 54

race relations: in East Texas, 4–8, 132;
    in Houston, 16–19; in Lufkin, 15;
    in Terrell, 5–6
race riot: Beaumont, 40–41: Houston,
    1917, 17, 25, 131; Longview, 1919, 6
Rainey, Homer, 52
Randolph, A. Philip, 39
Randolph, Richetta, 32
Reading, Pa., 31
Recorder of Deeds, 24
Red Scare, 71, 118, 142
Reed Roller Bit, 66–67
Reheem Manufacturing, 66–67
Republican Party, 26
Reserve Officer Training Corps Unit,
    42
Rhoads, Joseph J., 95, 101
Rice, C. W., 67, 68
Richardson, Clifton (Clif) F. Sr., 26–
    32, 35
Richardson, Clifton F. Jr., 35
Richmond, Va., 31
Riddeaux, L. P. 40
Right to Work Act, 71
Riverside Hospital, 47
Rob, J. H., 66
Robeson, Paul, 75
Robinson, James E., 113, 123–25, 138
Robinson, Nellie, 13
Roger, Wesley, 51
Roosevelt, Eleanor, 31
Roosevelt, Franklin, (FDR), 52–53,
    60–61, 73, 75
Rosenberg, Tex., 109
Ruleville, Miss., 136–37

Sabine River, 4
Saint Elizabeth Hospital, 144
Sam Houston Coliseum, 135
San Antonio, 18
Scott Bakery, 80
Sellers, Grover, 94
Senate bill: #140, 98; #288, 98
Shady Grove Elementary School, 8

Twenty-Fourth Infantry, 17
Tyler, Tex., 4, 6, 9, 10